The Gold Thread

Essays on George MacDonald

The Gold Thread

Essays on George MacDonald

edited by
William Raeper

EDINBURGH UNIVERSITY PRESS

© EDINBURGH UNIVERSITY PRESS 1990
22 George Square, Edinburgh

Set in Digitek Goudy by
Waverley Graphics Ltd, Edinburgh and
printed in Great Britain by
Page Bros, Norwich

British Library Cataloguing
  in Publication Data
The Gold Thread: essays on George MacDonald
1. Fiction in English. MacDonald, George, 1824-1905
I. Raeper, William 1959-
823.8
ISBN   0 7486 0166 X

The publisher acknowledges subsidy from
the Scottish Arts Council towards
the publication of this volume

Contents

Notes on Contributors

Gillian Avery is the author of children's books and a historian of children's literature. Her books include *Nineteenth Century Children* and *Childhood's Pattern*. She is completing a history of American children's books.

F. Hal Broome graduated from the University of Edinburgh's School of Scottish Studies in 1986 with a PhD. on George MacDonald. A native of Mississippi, he now lives in California where he is a free-lance writer and computer engineer.

Edmund Cusick studied English Literature at the University of Aberdeen. He has recently completed his doctoral thesis, entitled 'George MacDonald and Victorian Fantasy', at St Cross College, Oxford. He is now lecturer in English at St David's University College, Lampeter.

Catherine Durie used to teach at the University of Aberdeen and now teaches part-time for the Open University. She has worked on the Victorian Religious Novels (including the novel of George MacDonald) and has taught on C.S. Lewis in the United States. She is now writing a critical book about C.S. Lewis's work.

Roderick F. McGillis lectures at the University of Calgary, Canada, in English Literature. He is editor of the *Children's Literature Association Quarterly* and has written extensively on MacDonald.

Colin Manlove is Reader in English Literature at the University of Edinburgh, and author of *Modern Fantasy: Five Studies, Literature and Reality, 1600-1800 The Gap in Shakespeare: the Motif of Division from Richard II to The Tempest, The Impulse of Fantasy Literature, Science Fiction: Ten Explorations, C.S. Lewis: his Literary Achievement* and *Critical Thinking: a Guide to Interpreting Literary Texts*.

Stephen Prickett is Regius Professor of English Language and Literature at the University of Glasgow. He is the author of, among other books, *Romanticism and Religion, Victorian Fantasy* and *Words and the Word*, and is a member of the advisory boards of *Seven, Literature and Theology* and *Christianity and Literature*. He has taught at universities in the United Kingdom, the United States, and Australia.

William Raeper is the author of *George MacDonald*, a biography of the writer. He lives in Oxford where he teaches and writes.

David S. Robb is a lecturer in English at the University of Dundee. He is the author of a book and several essays on George MacDonald, and has also published essays on various aspects of twentieth-century Scottish Literature. He has co-edited a forthcoming volume of essays on Edwin Muir, and is at present preparing an edition of Hugh Miller's autobiography, *My Schools and School masters*, after which he plans to edit MacDonald's *Alec Forbes of Howglen*. He is General Editor of the Scottish Classics series and Joint Series Editor of the Scottish Writers series.

1

Introduction

WILLIAM RAEPER

This book could hardly be more timely. George MacDonald is one of the most individual and intriguing of nineteenth-century writers and academic interest in his work has grown considerably over the past ten to fifteen years. The reasons for this are linked to recent developments in criticism, many of which are touched on in the essays in this volume, and which have shown MacDonald's writing as more valuable and important than it was previously held to be.

The aim of this volume is to bring together new essays by leading MacDonald critics in order to show the vitality and depth of current MacDonald criticism. It is hoped that this book will stimulate further research on MacDonald, establishing him more firmly as a subject for serious study. All the essays have been written specially for this book; all deal with some important aspect of MacDonald's writing. As a collection it is the first of its kind.

MacDonald's enduring works have been his children's books – notably *At the Back of the North Wind* (1871), *The Princess and the Goblin* (1872), *The Princess and Curdie* (1883) and the handful of fairy tales collected in *The Golden Key* (1867). MacDonald's two adult fantasy novels *Phantastes* (1858) and *Lilith* (1895) have also remained in print, appearing regularly in new editions since they were first published, and are now recognised as classics of their kind.

Both children's literature and fantasy literature have become established as genres for critical study in recent years, especially in the States. As one of the outstanding children's authors of the nineteenth century and a pioneer of fantasy writing, MacDonald has become the just focus of increased attention. As an acknowledged influence on many authors who came after him – authors such as E. Nesbit, G.K. Chesterton, C.S. Lewis, W.H. Auden and T.S. Eliot – MacDonald is one of those rare writers whose work is a starting point for evaluating the achievments of others. New forms of critical theory – Jungian, psychoanalytic and feminist – turning towards the exploration of sexuality and the fantastic – have also found fitting subjects in MacDonald's texts.

1

Alongside the attention paid to MacDonald as a children's and fantasy writer is the growing acknowledgement that MacDonald was also a Scottish writer and a Victorian. This is a new development. In his *George MacDonald*,[1] David Robb has made a strong case for taking MacDonald seriously as a mid-Victorian Scottish writer and does so again in this volume. Often, and remissly, MacDonald's fairy and fantasy books have been extracted from the body of his work and studied without reference either to his age or to his heritage.

As a Victorian, MacDonald exhibited much of the energy and many of the complexities of his period. He dined with Thackeray and was close friends with John Ruskin and Lewis Carroll; he mixed with the Pre-Raphaelite painters and the Christian Socialists (such as Charles Kingsley), leading a life in the London of the 1860s and 70s which brought him into contact with many of the eminent figures of his day.

MacDonald's upbringing, however, could not have been further from metropolitan life. He was born in Huntly, Aberdeenshire in 1824, the second of six sons. His father was an enterprising businessman who later became a farmer. As such, MacDonald was suited in the first instance to life in the country, not the city, in Scotland not England, to activity, not to literature and reflection.

Despite the tuberculosis which afflicted him on and off throughout his long life, MacDonald was an academically talented boy who won a bursary to study at King's College, Aberdeen in 1840. He chose chemistry and natural philosophy (as physics was then called) as his major subjects of study. These interests have a bearing on his later work as a writer [2] and he may have been influenced towards them as a preparation for an agricultural career. It soon emerged, however, that MacDonald's real wish was to become a romantic poet and this conflicted with his family's ambition for him.

At university, MacDonald was prone to fits of melancholy and was uneasy in the Calvinism of his boyhood. He sought after a more loving God and this led him to Universalism and romantic literature. Both of these gave MacDonald a sense of liberation and a way forward to form his own writing and theology.

MacDonald's immersion in romantic literature seems to have taken place in 1842-43 when, owing to financial difficulties, he missed a session at Aberdeen. He went to tutor and to catalogue a library at a large house or castle in the 'far North'. The whereabouts of this library have never been established, but it was probably Thurso Castle, home of the Sinclair family. In MacDonald's short novel, *The Portent*, the narrator records:

'Now I was in my element . . . I found a perfect set of our poets–perfect according to the notion of the editor and the issue of the publisher, although it omitted both Chaucer and George Herbert. I began to nibble at that portion of the collection which belonged to the sixteenth century; but with little success. I found nothing, to my ideas, but love-poems without any love in them, and so I soon became weary. But I found in the library what I liked far better–many romances of a very marvellous sort, and plentiful interruption they gave the formation of the catalogue.'[3]

The image of the library as a place of sexual adventure and spiritual exploration was to persist throughout MacDonald's career as a writer, culminating in the mysterious library in *Lilith*.

MacDonald graduated in 1845. He briefly considered a career in chemistry, but instead took a steamer south to London where he became tutor to a family in Fulham. Even at this stage his family must have been edging him towards the ministry (they were Congregationalists) and, finally, he entered Highbury Theological College in 1848. That same year he became engaged to Louisa Powell.

MacDonald found himself constrained at Highbury where his teachers' theology conflicted with his own romantic leanings, and he left without taking his degree in 1850. Even so he was 'called' to a small Congregational church in Arundel, Sussex in the autumn of 1850 and in March 1851 he finally married Louisa Powell.

Up until this point, MacDonald had published only one poem, *David*, in the *Scottish Congregational Magazine*.[4] His next public efforts were the translations *Twelve of the Spiritual Songs of Novalis* given to his friends as Christmas presents at the end of 1851. These translations caused suspicion among members of MacDonald's congregation who feared they were tainted with the new German biblical criticism which traditional churchgoers detested. In addition, rumours spread that the young pastor believed animals might share a place in heaven and that a kind of purgatory might exist. As a result, MacDonald's salary was reduced in June 1852–a strong hint for him to leave–though he did not finally quit Arundel until May the following year.

At the insistence of his elder brother, Charles Francis, MacDonald took his growing family to Manchester. There he began his own church and supplemented his income by teaching English literature, mainly to women. In 1855 his first major work, the long blank verse poem *Within and Without* was published. This attracted the admiration of, among others, Charles Kingsley and Lady Byron. The latter became something of a patron to MacDonald. She paid for him to winter in Algiers from 1856-57 before he returned to Hastings where he wrote *Phantastes*, published to mixed reviews in 1858.

The MacDonald family soon moved to London. By now George and Louisa had six children and MacDonald was in demand as a lecturer. He became professor of English Literature at Bedford College (then a college for women) in October 1859.

In the 1860s Lewis Carroll became a familiar visitor to the MacDonald home and John Ruskin became a close friend in 1863. After a difficult start, MacDonald's first novel, *David Elginbrod*, appeared in 1863 and from then on he produced a steady stream of novels. He became popular as a writer and lecturer and was held in high esteem for his religious beliefs. In 1865 he tried unsuccessfully for the Chair of Rhetoric and Belles Lettres at Edinburgh, but in 1868 he was awarded an Honorary Ll d by Aberdeen University in recognition of his own literary achievements.

In 1869 MacDonald accepted the editorship of *Good Words for the Young*, the magazine for children in which *At the Back of the North Wind* and *The Princess and the Goblin* were first serialised.

Mary MacDonald's bad health forced the family to seek a kinder climate in 1877 and they built a house in Bordighera, a town on the Italian Riviera close to San Remo in 1880. Many British people wintered there and the MacDonalds threw themselves enthusiastically into expatriate activities. MacDonald began Sunday evening 'At Homes' where he would preach informally as part of a service arranged by the family.

Bordighera life continued for twenty-five years. MacDonald spent the winters in Italy where he continued to write novels and in the summer months he and the family would travel to Britain where he undertook long, exhausting lecture tours.

Despite literary success. money was still short and Louisa decided to employ her eleven children to stage plays for profit. Their most popular adaptation was *Pilgrim's Progress* in which MacDonald's eldest daughter Lilia showed remarkable talent as Christiana. A religious family on stage was not a common sight in the nineteenth century, but MacDonald believed in the high calling of these performances.

In 1872 MacDonald and Louisa embarked with their eldest son Greville on a lecture tour of the United States. The schedule was punishing and MacDonald suffered frequent bouts of bad health. One newspaper reported perceptively of him: 'In the others we have known the force of great minds, but in him the glow of a great soul.' This 'glow' in MacDonald's imagination is what arrested those who came into contact with him and which is stamped powerfully on all his writings.

After the publication of *Lilith* in 1895, MacDonald's health began to deteriorate. In 1898 he suffered a stroke and barely spoke again for the rest of his life. He outlived Louisa who died in 1902 and, in the final years of his life, was cared for by his youngest daughter Winifred and her husband. He died at Ashtead in Surrey in 1905 and, in a special service, his ashes were put into his wife's grave in Bordighera in 1906.

MacDonald was a striking figure during his lifetime – either wielding a sword as Macbeth or dressed in Mr Greatheart's suit of mail in the family's *Pilgrim's Progress*. Thousands came to hear him preach; tens of thousands read his novels. His was a distinctive, challenging and reassuring voice; his was an individual imagination.

Modern criticism of George MacDonald begins with C.S. Lewis. In an often quoted passage from his autobiography *Surprised by Joy*, Lewis describes the effect of buying a copy of MacDonald's *Phantastes* at Leatherhead railway station in 1916:

> 'It is as if I were carried sleeping across the frontier, or as if I had died in the old country and could never remember how I came alive in the new.'[5]

But it was in the introduction of his *Anthology* of MacDonald published in 1946 that Lewis paid his greatest tribute:

> 'I have never concealed the fact that I regarded him as a master; indeed I fancy I have never written a book in which I did not quote from him.'[6]

Lewis's influence as a critic has waned over the past twenty years and his literary judgements no longer carry the weight they once did. Even so, he had the last word on MacDonald for a long time. He was effusive about MacDonald's power, but critical of his style:

> 'If we define Literature as an art whose medium is words, then certainly MacDonald has no place in its rank – perhaps not even in its second.'[7]

As an enthusiast, Lewis has had an enormous (and not entirely beneficent) influence on *how* MacDonald has been perceived. MacDonald has been read largely for his imaginative theology and symbolical fantasy, certainly not as a Victorian and Scottish novelist of any standing.

In the present volume Catherine Durie's essay on 'George MacDonald and C.S. Lewis' examines Lewis's complex attitude to MacDonald. She shows how Lewis was speaking 'off the record' as a devotee rather than a critic, and how this has affected subsequent approaches to MacDonald. Her essay is a necessary one, helping to clear ground for new approaches to MacDonald.

There was a mixed critical reaction to MacDonald in his own day. Many reviewers thought that he was too prolific and some held his work to be too pedantic and didactic. The *Edinburgh Review* of 1876[8] detected a 'slight smack of the schoolmaster' while the *Fortnightly Review* of 1868, in a survey of MacDonald's books, stated:

> 'Each succeeding volume has become increasingly didactic. From *David Elginbrod, Phantastes*, or the comparatively unknown *Adela Cathcart* to *Robert Falconer*, there is a lamentable falling-off in artistic method and purpose.'[9]

Generally, however, MacDonald's sentiments and morals found favour as did his characters and portraits of life in Scotland. He was recognised as a novelist of power and stature. The *Edinburgh Review*, commenting on 'Recent Scotch Novels' recorded: *'David Elginbrod* is evidently the work of an original mind, we may say of an original genius.' In 1868 the *Athenaeum* commented:

> *'Robert Falconer* is the matured utterance of all the thoughts and aspirations which Dr MacDonald tried to say or sing in his early poems, and the completed picture of what he sent forth in more or less fragmentary form in his previous novels. He has fulfilled all his promises, and this is saying no little.'[10]

What is striking is that MacDonald was taken *seriously* as a popular novelist. His difficult prose style was accepted without murmur as was the dense Scots dialect employed without much concession to the English reader.

MacDonald's adult romances *Phantastes* and *Lilith*, now regarded as two of his most important books, fared less well at the hands of the reviewers. *Phantastes* received mixed notices when it first appeared in 1858. The Athenaeum wryly advised that:

> 'Any one after reading it might set up a confusedly furnished second-hand symbol shop.'[11]

The reviewer went on to comment: 'He seems to have lost hold of all reality.'

Lilith found no favour at all:

> 'That some high purpose prevades this strange mystical farrago we are willing to believe, but its methods of presentment seems to be neither lucid nor edifying.'[12]

By the 1890s MacDonald's novels had lost the popularity they had once held and the name of George MacDonald went into an eclipse.

When MacDonald died in 1905 the obituaries portrayed him as a grand old man, a novelist with spiritual vision, who had gradually withdrawn from the world. The years in Bordighera followed by the stroke and silence had taken MacDonald away from his London acquaintances and literary life and added to the public perception that while MacDonald was still in this life he had somehow passed beyond it.

In 1924, Greville MacDonald, MacDonald's eldest son and biographer, organised celebrations for the centenary of the birth of his father. Several of MacDonald's works (including *Lilith*) were re-issued and, by this time, critical appreciation had changed. MacDonald was no longer seen as the uplifting novelist of the 1860s, 70s and 80s, but as a unique writer of fairy tales whose vision had outlasted his time. In his introduction to Greville MacDonald's biography, *George MacDonald and His Wife*, published in 1924, G.K. Chesterton wrote:

> 'But in a certain rather special sense I for one can really testify to a book that has made a difference to my whole existence, which helped me to see things in a certain way from the start; a vision of things which even so real a revolution as a change of religious allegiance has substantially only crowned and confirmed. Of all the stories I have read, including even all the novels of the same novelist, it remains the most real, the most realistic, in the exact sense of the phrase the most like life. It is called *The Princess and the Goblin* and is by George MacDonald . . . '.[13]

This assesment of MacDonald is one which has lasted up to the present day. As a result, his novels have, until recently, been relegated to dusty shelves and his poetry and theology forgotten. What has been read have been the children's books, the fairy tales and *Phantastes* and *Lilith*.

The first, pioneering study solely devoted to a critical examination of MacDonald's works was *The Golden Key* by Robert Lee Wolff published in 1961.[14] Wolff subjected MacDonald's work to a Freudian analysis and drew a stark sexual interpretation from MacDonald's fantastic images. His approach has been judged too crude by subsequent critics and his final picture of MacDonald as a bitter and disillusioned man is insupportable. However, Wolff *had* studied MacDonald's books, including the novels, and was able to point back expertly to the German romantic sources which MacDonald had used.

After Wolff's *The Golden Key*, the next book to concern itself with MacDonald criticism was Richard Reis's *George MacDonald* published in 1972.[15] In contrast to Wolff's Freudian analysis, Reis offered a suggestive Jungian reading which had been followed up and amplified by succeeding scholars.

Rolland Hein, another American critic, published a useful introduction to MacDonald entitled *The Harmony Within* in 1982.[16] (That
these three critics are American should not go unnoticed—fantasy
literature has gained more respect on that side of the Atlantic and its
study occupies a greater place in university and college programmes).
These books represent the 'first wave' of recent MacDonald criticism and are individual attempts to focus attention on MacDonald as
an author worthy of serious academic study.

In the last fifteen years MacDonald criticism has begun to increase
and diversify. Stephen Prickett, now Regius Professor of English Literature at Glasgow University, has compared George MacDonald to
Matthew Arnold and Charles Kingsley in *Romanticism and Religion*
(1976)[18]. David Robb's *George MacDonald* (1987)[19] has made a
strong case for MacDonald to be taken seriously as a Scottish novelist
and he has written with depth and assurance about the particular
Scottish tradition in which MacDonald was writing.

Colin Manlove has written extensively on MacDonald in his *Modern Fantasy* (1975)[20] and Roderick McGillis's recent articles in various scholary journals have received wide acclaim.[21]

These critics have done sterling work on MacDonald and have
shown him to be a valuable and important writer. All of them have
contributed an essay to this volume.

What has emerged is that MacDonald is a writer of some stature, a
fascinating and important Romantic, Victorian, Scot and Fantasist,
who is worth a great deal more attention than has so far been allotted
to him.

The contributors to this volume have used a variety of critical
approaches. Because of this, the essays do not follow a linear progression, but are concerned with different methods of analysing different
aspects of MacDonald's work. Most notably the essays by Roderick
McGillis and Edmund Cusick use a psychoanalytic and Jungian
approach. These forms of analysis applied to MacDonald's fantasy
writing are particularly fruitful. McGillis's feminist theorising is compelling and Cusick's examination of the major symbols in MacDonald's fantasy writing is an important and new contribution to Mac-
Donald criticism. The point at which MacDonald's fantasy writing
began to be unravelled by critics was the publication of Robert Lee
Wolff's *The Golden Key*. The first links between MacDonald's fantastic images and sexuality were made in that book. Unfortunately this
was done aggressively and there was a resistance to Wolff from many
quarters. Happily, criticism has become more sophisticated since as
McGillis and Cusick both show.

The essays in this book are *academic* essays, but it is hoped that they will challenge and inform the general reader as well as the student and increase enjoyment as well as knowledge of MacDonald's work.

In this book David Robb continues his own work on MacDonald and the Scottish novel found in *George MacDonald*. He takes as his starting-point Douglas Gifford's conjecture that MacDonald's novels are 'novels of mythic regeneration'. Robb's careful examination of Scotland's psyche, culture and history looks at MacDonald's responses to his heritage as a Scot and further uncovers an area of MacDonald studies which has long been neglected. It has (sadly) so often to be emphasised that Scottish writers are not English writers and the Scottish tradition is quite distinct.

From a different historical viewpoint Gillian Avery gives a solid grounding to the fairy tale in the nineteenth century. The importance of her essay is in giving a context to MacDonald's writing for children which points up his achievement and distinctiveness compared with other writers for children of that time. This is a perspective which is sorely needed when so often MacDonald's works are studied in isolation. Colin Manlove gives a closer reading of MacDonald's children's writing, comparing him with Charles Kingsley and amplifying some of Avery's conclusions.

Hal Broome's essay is an original and intriguing piece of work. In it he examines the scientific basis of MacDonald's dream-frame and shows how many of MacDonald's images and sequences are drawn from nineteenth century scientific theory. Broome is able to explain persuasively how scientific thinking fed MacDonald's fantasy writing. In doing he throws fresh light on the complexities of the Victorian mind.

Stephen Prickett's delineates *Phantastes* as the most successful *Bildungsroman* in the English language. Prickett argues a strong case for MacDonald's use of Goethe and highlights the German tradition from which *Phantastes* sprang.

Yet these essays represent at most a 'work in progress' in MacDonald criticism. there is still a great deal to be done. MacDonald's stature as a Scottish writer (and his use of tradition and dialect) has still to be fully assessed. As a Victorian, MacDonald's fantasy writing and novels comprise a collection of texts that must be increasingly valuable to anyone interested in that age. As a fantasy and children's writer, MacDonald's prominence will grow clearer only as these areas of study establish themselves of the Atlantic. MacDonald's romantic theology, forged as it was in the crossover of religion and literature in the nineteenth century, also needs further exploration. And there is still more than this. New forms of criticism have unlocked MacDonald's texts in ways not foreseen twenty-five years ago. It is time that feminist critics discovered MacDonald and his use of the *anima* and complex female imagery, and that romantic critics paid more attention to him. MacDonald's obvious linking of textuality and sexuality makes him an ideal candidate for the major new critical theories developed in the last fifteen years.

The MacDonald who appears in these pages is a curiously modern writer. Like his protagonist Vane in *Lilith* he seems to have passed through a mirror, travelling from the nineteenth century to the twentieth only to discover a surprising reversal of what had formerly been the prevailing critical opinion. MacDonald's fantasy and fairy works, which were either misunderstood or passed over a century ago, now appear as his most important contribution. In the light of recent critical theory they appear modern – even postmodern: of their time, but not contained by their time. As Stephen Prickett writes in his essay in this book:

'MacDonald was one of the few nineteenth-century writers to recognise that realism and fantasy are two sides of the same coin: that realism is as much as arbitrary and literary convention as fantasy, and that fantasy is as much dependent on mundane experience as realism.'

Any critic must believe that MacDonald is ready for an enormous amount of further study in the near future. It is satisfying to present the essays contained in this volume; it is exciting to speculate on what is yet to come.

Reference

1. David S. Robb, *George MacDonald* (Edinburgh: Scottish Academic Press, 1987)
2. See Hal Broome's essay in this volume and David S. Robb, 'George MacDonald and Animal Magnetism' *Seven* 8 (1987), 9-24
3. George MacDonald, *The Portent* (London: Smith, Elder, 1864), 80
4. *Scottish Congregational Magazine* (February 1846)
5. C.S. Lewis, *Surprised by Joy* (London: Geofrey Bles, 1955), 169
6. C.S. Lewis (ed.) *George MacDonald: An Anthology* (London: Geoffrey Bles, 1946), 20
7. ibid., 14
8. *Edinburgh Review* 'Recent Scotch Novels' (April 1876), 336-349
9. A J. Knight *Fortnightly Review* vol 10 (July 1868), 115
10. *Athenaeum* No 2123 (July 4, 1868), 13
11. *Athenaeum* No 1619 (Nov. 6, 1858), 580
12. *Athenaeum* vol 106 (Nov. 9, 1895), 639

13. G.K Chesterton, intro, to *George MacDonald and His Wife* by Greville MacDonald (London: Allen and Unwin, 1924), 9
14. Robert Lee Wolff, *The Golden Key* (Yale: Yale University Press, 1961)
15. Richard Reis, *George MacDonald* (New York: Twayne Books, 1972)
16. Rolland Hein, *The Harmony Within* (Grand Rapids, Michigan: Eerdmans, 1982)
17. Stephen Prickett, *Romanticism and Religion* (Cambridge: Cambridge University Press, 1976)
18. Stephen Prickett, *Victorian Fantasy* (Sussex: Harvester Press, 1979)
19. David Robb op. cit.
20. Colin Manlove, *Modern Fantasy* (Cambridge: Cambridge University Press, 1975)
21. See articles by Roderick F. McGillis cited in bibliography of this volume.

2

George MacDonald's Scottish Novels

DAVID S. ROBB

The story of how MacDonald came to write *David Elginbrod*, the first of his sequence of Scottish novels, has often been repeated. His attempt at drama, a play called *If I had a Father* was refused by the publisher George Murray Smith who then advised him that 'if you would but write novels, you would find all the publishers saving up to buy them of you! Nothing but fiction pays' (MacDonald 1924, p.318). Despite, however, his great need to find anything that would indeed pay, it was not until he encountered the Martin Elginbrodde quatrain, several years later, that he felt able to act on this advice (MacDonald 1924, pp. 320-1). I have argued elsewhere (Robb 1987, pp. 27-8) that this delay suggests that MacDonald was not simply driven by the force of brutal circumstances into a lifelong thwarting of his genius in the uncongenial drudgery of novel-writing. While it is clear that financial necessity drove him to produce, like Scott, the *number* of novels he wrote, it is not inevitable that this, in turn, means that prose fiction was incapable of expressing much of what was important to him or that he was invariably doomed to artistic failure in the medium. On the contrary, his best novels (other than the fantasies) suggest to me that fiction rapidly became an essential medium for him, not just for financial reasons, nor yet simply out of didactic considerations. His Scottish novels, long recognised as containing his best work outside his fairy fiction, afforded him an opportunity for self-exploration and for coming to terms with his Scottish origins. In doing this, they constitute a significant addition to ninteenth-century Scottish fiction.

It has taken a long time to begin to shift the Lewis-derived consensus that MacDonald's novels are to be valued only for what they contain (their Christianity) rather than for what they are. When Lewis, in his famous essay, makes his grudging acknowledgement that there may be readers who might find 'a queer awkward charm in their very faults', it suddenly occurs to him that, along with the other specialist qualifications needed to explain this quixotic taste, such a reader perhaps 'will need to love Scotland too' (Lewis 1946, p. 17).

Experience suggests that Lewis was actually correct, for it seems likely that adequate reassessment of these novels, if it is going to come at all, will come from the perspectives provided by critics consciously working towards a fuller understanding of Scottish literary traditions. One such critic, Douglas Gifford, has recently provided a brief but stimulating account of MacDonald in the course of an elaborate survey of Scottish nineteenth-century fiction (Gifford 1988, pp.227-30). He describes MacDonald's Scottish works as the most thoroughgoing examples of what he terms 'the novel of mythic regeneration'. He means, by this term, those many nineteenth-century novels in which Scotland is portrayed as sick (split, politically unjust, incapable of nourishing its finer spirits, out of touch with its past and uneasy in its Scottishness, etc.) and in which a hero or heroine must bear the responsibility of 'being' Scotland (as, say, Chris Guthrie embodies Scotland in *A Scots Quair*) and of resisting the destructive tendencies in Scottish life. He also recognises the boldness and patriotic ambition implied by MacDonald's Scottish fictions: their very existence implies what their tales so often portray, namely 'a Scottish-based moral regeneration for Victorian Britain' (Gifford 1988, p.227).

What is most striking, however, about Gifford's account is the excitement over MacDonald's fiction which it conveys. It is brief and far from comprehensive, even considering the swift, broad brushstrokes which it employs. In it, nationalism ousts religion from the perceived centre of concern to an extent which seems excessive. Yet it is surely correct in its insistence that these are, to a very considerable extent, novels about Scotland and its implication that, in the best of them at least, MacDonald is far more important than merely deserving 'some merit as a passable mid-Victorian Scottish novelist or as a theological storyteller' (to quote another very recent assessment) (Raeper 1987, p.213). In them, I believe that MacDonald was conducting a sensitive exploration of his Scottish origins, and meditating on the relationship between those origins and the world of urban England where he now found himself. By the time he began writing fiction, MacDonald's experience was rich and full of contrasts. His finest Scottish novels are attempts, I suggest, to bring coherence to that variety; but coherence, in the event, was not achieved at the first attempt. Only as the series of novels progressed—*David Elginbrod* (1863), *Alec Forbes of Howglen* (1865), *Robert Falconer* (1868), *Malcolm* (1875), *The Marquis of Lossie* (1877), *Sir Gibbie* (1879) – was MacDonald able to find what he had to say and how best to say it. It was at first a step-by-step process.

It is not only the delay in the writing of his first non-fantasy

novel which speaks against the notion that MacDonald the novelist
was a mere drudge, performing at the whim of necessity: so also does
the Scottish emphasis of that first novel when it appeared. Its opening
line is not the work of someone playing safe with the sympathy of his
largely English readership. Neither is David's first prayer a few lines
later; nor is the family discussion which closes the chapter. MacDonald's sense of his own temerity comes out in his reassuring translation
of Janet's opening cry (in the novel's fourth sentence), in his comment to the reader immediately after the prayer, and in his attempt to
smooth away his reader's prejudices in his description of Margaret's
utterance as 'musical in spite of the rugged dialect into which the
sounds were fashioned'. He knows he is taking a risk – a foolish thing
for a mere breadwinner to do. (And, indeed, his immense difficulty
in getting the novel published at all is now another solid element in
the MacDonald legend.) Yet his need to challenge his readers with all
this Scottishness strongly prevails, for he does not confine himself to
the forms of Scots dialect to which his readers may have accommo-
dated themselves in the novels of Scott; he writes, rather with the
more colourful but less familiar sounds of his own North-East in his
ear. Another recent writer on MacDonald, Emma Letley, provides a
valuable summary of contemporary attitudes to Scots amongst readers and publishers, attitudes against which MacDonald had to persist
(Letley 1988, pp. 88-92). She also demonstrates the linkage Mac-
Donald makes, in this and subsequent novels, between Scots speech
and the values (of childlikeness, of naturalness, of spiritual rightness
and strength, etc.) which *David Elginbrod* is intended to stress (Letley
1988, pp.93-105). At the outset, MacDonald was writing novels on
his own terms.

Let us consider that famous quatrain once again. What was it
about it which so immediately caught MacDonald's attention? Following Wolff, most commentators seem to assume that it was the
implied theology, of Man's need for a merciful God, which
crystallised something in MacDonald (Wolff 1961, p.191). This was
clearly important, but other qualities, too, may well have played their
part. Surely the Scots utterance, and also what can only be called the
intimacy of address to the deity, helped unlock MacDonald's imagination, as Raeper puts it? (1987, p.178). The naturalness, but also
the boldness, of the plea encapsulates that immediacy and spontaneity of intercourse between man and God which is perhaps more characteristic of Scottish devotional traditions than of English. (A few
decades later, for example, Henry Grey Graham comments at length
and with distaste on the grotesque length and frequency of prayers in

eighteenth-century Scottish life and worship, and on the universal
insistence that these utterances should seem to be spontaneous.)
(Graham 1937, pp.291-3)

MacDonald would have been thoroughly acquainted with previous
literary responses to this Scottish devotional manner in, for example,
the poems of Burns. The following, after the account of peasant family worship in 'The Cotter's Saturday Night', is surely one of the
sources of the novel, along with the Elginbrodde quatrain:

Compar'd with this, how poor Religion's pride,
  In all the pomp of *method*, and of *art*,
When men display to congregations wide,
  Devotion's ev'ry grace, except the *heart!*
The POWER, incens'd, the Pageant will desert,
  The pompous strain, the sacerdotal stole;
But haply, in some *Cottage* far apart,
  May hear, well pleas'd, the language of the *Soul*;
And in His *Book of Life* the Inmates poor enroll.
                                    (145-53)

Burns illustrates, too, the same natural intimacy in prayerful
address to the Creator-but in a different key-in 'Holy Willie's
Prayer'. It is probable, too, that MacDonald knew the comical prayer
of Davie Tait in Hogg's *The Brownie of Bodsbeck*, a passage in which
the pastoral imagery of New Testament tradition is exploded from
within by the earthy detail with which Davie confidently (and confid-
ingly) loads it. Clearly MacDonald had no use for the gleeful bur-
lesque at which both Burns and Hogg were so adept, but nevertheless
the passages were capable of demonstrating to him the powerful literary potential of the elevated confidentiality of spontaneous prayer in
Scots.

In its bold, colloquial and intimate utterance, and in its willingness
to risk apparent blasphemy in the unorthodoxy of both manner and
matter, the quatrain must have seemed to MacDonald to sum up the
best instincts within Scottish religion, in contrast to the rigidly inhu-
man Calvinism which was theologically dominant. (Cf. the right-
hearted blasphemy torn out of the mouth of a strict Calvinist in *Alec
Forbes*, when Thomas Crann urges Alec to risk his life *and soul* to
save two marooned women: 'Better be damned, doin' the will o'
God, than saved doin' noathing!' (ch. 53)). The sense of a buried
ideal of Scottish life and belief, at odds with the visible imperfections
of the place and time, is regularly to be detected in MacDonald. The
Elginbrodde epitaph precipitated more than a theologically partisan
outlook (accounts of the book which, like Wolff's, lay particular

stress on anti-Calvinism seem very unbalanced): it prompted Mac-Donald to attempt a portrait of an ideal Scottish personality, with right religious instinct at its core. Suddenly encountered in the midst of a London literary gathering, the epitaph enabled MacDonald to glimpse the piercing force with which a Scottish grasp of God's truth, expressed in Scottish terms, could shine out in the wider world. His finest Scottish novels grow, variously, out of this insight.

One further line of speculation might be permissible at this point, as we contemplate MacDonald's sudden plunge in 1863, with *David Elginbrod*, into the exploration of Scotland's strengths and weaknesses, and the relationship between Scottishness and the English world of the majority of his readers. The essential character of the Scottish mind and outlook, and especially of the Scottish intellectual tradition in comparison with that of England, had very recently been brought to the forefront of the attention of the reading public by the publication in 1861 of the third volume of Henry Thomas Buckle's *History of Civilisation in England*. This volume was a sustained attack not only on the dominant Scottish religious outlook, especially as embodied in what Buckle presented as the all-powerful clergy, but also and more penetratingly, on what he analysed as the mental tendency of that clergy to move, in any philosophical operation, from theory to facts (i.e. deductively) rather than from observed fact to theory, in the English Baconian tradition. Buckle believed that a resistance to inductive thought–a tendency resulting from the dominance in Scottish mental life of a deductive theology–was the source of the powerlessness of Scottish philosophy to combat and defeat the Evangelical (or, as Buckle saw it, superstitious) forces still very evident in Scotland. Thanks to Buckle, the question of Scottish traditions in theology, learning and moral character was a prominent intellectual issue in the 1860s.

MacDonald's tendency would have been to share Buckle's distaste for the tradition of Scottish clerical thought. After all, it is as an outspoken rebel against Calvinist-derived theological theory that Mac-Donald is primarily thought of. His work is full of eloquence and bitterness against precisely that logical construction of theological doctrine which Calvinism had become and which he regarded as originating purely from men's minds, with little of the divine in it at all. From his days as a student in Aberdeen, when his growing dissatisfaction with the theology offered him caused him to suffer depression, MacDonald was essentially at odds with the world of his origins. Neither of our two main biographical accounts, by Greville MacDonald and by William Raeper, go into much detail as to why he should have gone so swiftly to London as the first step in finding something to do aftergraduating, but Raeper makes clear (1987, pp. 55-6), as Greville MacDonald did not (1924, p. 91), that the move to London *preceded* any word of a possible tutoring post. One can only assume that the unknown world of London appealed to him more, and seemed more promising, than the known world of Scotland. There seems to be an element of rejection in this decisive move south.

It is obviously impossible, however, to paint a picture of MacDonald as one who loathed Scotland. It still harboured a loved family, it was still the scene of childhood and youthful memories which only became more dear with each passing year, and MacDonald clearly regarded his Scottishness as a prized and quintessential element of his very being, as countless indications in the rest of his life (let alone explicit statements in his writing) testify. We might even conjecture that his experience was that of countless other Scots who travel outwith Scotland: it is when living in another country, in England or beyond, that they first fully realise their Scottishness.

Elsewhere, I have suggested (Robb 1987, p. 6) that however individual and unexpected MacDonald's personality and beliefs may seem, he can be seen as a recognisable Scottish personality. He may have rejected the doctrines of the Huntly Missionars but his total unwillingness to compromise with worldliness, and the strength of his moral urgency, suggest that he is their offspring nevertheless, and the child of centuries of vigorous Scottish religious dissent. Within that tradition, there has usually been discernible a trace of nationalist self-consciousness: the belief that Scotland and the Scots are, in some sense, chosen by God is an easy one for the Scottish religious to fall into. Is there not a trace of it in MacDonald's encounter with the world, both in his books and his life? His instinctive method was the communication, not just of his 'message', abstractly considered, but of his own personality. (This was, of course, a favourite technique of Victorian writers.) And in that persona which was so powerfully offered to the world, his Scottishness was both an inevitable and potent element. Furthermore, as Raeper has brought out more clearly than Greville MacDonald did (Raeper 1987, pp. 182-3), Carlyle had a major impact on MacDonald, as on so many others of the time, and, perhaps even more significantly, most of the contemporary religious thinkers with whom MacDonald was variously associated were Scots–Erskine of Linlathen, A.J. Scott, Edward Irving, Norman MacLeod. Only F.D. Maurice was not (Raeper 1987, p.241). It seems perfectly possible that MacDonald felt himself part of a 'a Scottish-based moral regeneration for Victorian Britain'. When he at last saw his way to writing a novel, that was the pattern it expressed. It was to Scotland, and to the possible impact of an elevated Scottish personality on more familiar English fictional landscapes, that he turned.

It is not surprising that MacDonald, in his very first novel, should attempt to articulate this idea in its most complete and direct form. That *David Elginbrod* is weak, despite the strong elements within it, is universally acknowledged; but the reasons usually given for this weakness have to do merely with the early disappearance of the title-character, and with the large-scale shifts of scene. The latter reason is seldom used against *Robert Falconer*, although much the same pattern is to be found in it, while to insist that the novel stands or falls on the personality of David is to underestimate, I think, the quickly established interest and centrality of the triangular relationship between Hugh, David and Margaret, as well as the strong contribution to the sense of region provided by Janet's speech and attitudes, in the first section of the work. Rather, its weakness when compared with the best of the novels which followed is due, I think, to the lack of social depth in its various locations, and to the strong sense of direction which pervades its latter half. (MacDonald, unlike most other novelists, seems at his best and most characteristic when his works progress with a massive, broad, dream-like inconsequentiality. Hugh's entanglement with Euphra, and the ensuing tales of Euphra's salvation and the thwarting of Funkelstein, are much stronger, plot-directing narrative concerns than MacDonald tended to use subsequently. The emphasis on plot narrows rather than strengthens the effect of the work.)

Nevertheless, *David Elginbrod* contains much that is vigorous and enjoyable and, furthermore, reveals with especial clarity the pattern which MacDonald wanted to elaborate. In the tale of Hugh Sutherland and his relationship with David and his family, MacDonald was able to present a powerful picture of Scotland as the cradle of a Christlike force for redemption, a force which, through the accident of personal contact, is capable of touching the innermost being of strangers far away in England. Other essential components of MacDonald's vision as a novelist appear: the journey through life from a type of Eden, through pain, difficulty and moral fall, to a soundly-based (because experience-based) return to bliss. Drawn as he is to versions of pre-lapsarian existence, MacDonald wants the virtue of that state to come into thorough contact with the ordinary, fallen world of men and women. This is partly because the experience of meeting and rising above one's sinfulness is a necessary precondition for the full achievement of moral potential, but also because MacDonald's vision is of a religion which has an impact on the world of sinners. In the long run, MacDonald's interest is less with figures of established perfection like David, secure from the outset in their perfection, but rather with those who have to strive for that perfection, and who go out into the world (of the city, or of England) to encounter evil in others or in themselves.

As we have seen, however, MacDonald's attitude to Scotland is more contradictory than this, and he could not, even in this first Scottish novel, treat it simply as Eden. It is natural that anyone who decisively exiles himself from a childhood domain will tend to one of two attitudes towards it. He will either idealise it, bathing it in nostalgia, seeing it as the home of all that is best, or will tend to denigrate it in comparison with the wider world which he now knows, looking back on the place of his childhood as limited or limiting, a place of unenlightenment where his being was cramped. Perhaps he will go further and pillory it for worse faults still–this is a large part of the attitude to Scotland of such novelists as George Douglas Brown and 'Lewis Grassic Gibbon'. How to bring such attitudes into some stability is a problem with which many Scottish novelists have had to wrestle, and MacDonald was no exception.

There is a further twist still in MacDonald's relationship with Scotland, which has a bearing on his treatment of his homeland in his fiction. In an obvious way, Scotland *is* 'home' to MacDonald, and remained so throughout his life, despite his never permanently living in it after his student days. The permanence of his affections is surely indicated by the exclamation in *Castle Warlock* (1882): 'Oh, that awful gray and white Scotch winter–dear to my heart as I sit and write with windows wide open to the blue skies of Italy's December!' (ch. 13, 'Grannies's Ghost Story'). His regular return to Scotland throughout his life, both in his writing and in actuality, indicates the permanence of its hold on him, and the sense of it as 'home' is strong in most of the Scottish novels, in which it is the scene, time and time again, of the hero's return to origins and to love. He seems to have gone to Huntly for the last time in 1891 when he went to the churchyard at Ruthven where the bells in his story *The Wow o' Rivven* was interpreted by the fool as crying 'Come hame, come hame'. In a letter written during this visit (Raeper 1987, pp.360-1), he suggests that it is the experience of separation, of exile, which creates (at least for him) the sense of this landscape as 'hame'. 'But I see the country more beautiful than I used to see it, *for as a boy it did not much please me*' (my italics). The idea of home only has full reality when one is homeless.

The Victorian concept of 'home' has been illuminated, like so much else, by Walter Houghton (1957, pp. 341-8). In his discussion, Houghton brings out how 'home' was felt as being opposed to the pressures and difficulties of modern life. It was a special place, cut off, associated with the peace and security of childhood. It was a refuge. It took on, in the Victorian imagination, a nostalgic, backward-looking and pastoral quality. It became one of the ideals which the Victorians opposed to the pressures, difficulties, imperfections and materialism of their age. The ease with which MacDonald's Scottish, rural recollections accord with this pattern is obvious. His fictional 'Scotlands', based on his memories of earlier decades (Robb 1988, pp. 279-85), are sometimes used in contrasts of nation and culture ('Scotland' as opposed to 'England'), sometimes in contrasts of mode of life (country as opposed to city), sometimes in contrasts of time ('then' as opposed to 'now'), sometimes in all these together. MacDonald's powerful sense of Scotland as 'home' provided him with a potent earthly type with which to project his overriding sense of heaven as the home of us all.

Only a heavenly home is perfect, however: homes on earth are flawless only in the crudest of imaginations, and in the most pitiably nostalgic of memories. Treating Scotland as 'home' did not require MacDonald to write of it as ideally harmonious and attractive, an earthly parallel of a heaven of eternal harp-playing. Homes have their own difficulties, strains and tensions – fortunately so, from the point of view of a novelist who wishes his readers to turn the page. Yet the strains and difficulties characteristic of domesticity are usually more static than those of the outside world – semi-permanent, the products of personality clashes and long-term situations. Conflicts and stresses tend to evolve, and resolve, more slowly than they do in other spheres of life. By contrast, in the outside world, experience tends to be faster moving, situations change more quickly and social contact is, on the whole, more various and fluid. This broad contrast is one reason why 'home' is a refuge, because it is (with luck) stable and secure. It can be relied upon, in the experience of most people. The world outside the home is faster-moving, more dangerous and less familiar, more capable of producing unexpected pitfalls–but, consequently, it is often more interesting, exciting and challenging.

This difference is the basis for deeper contrasts and rhythms in MacDonald's fiction, and for the need he feels, both as a novelist and as a moralist, to send his characters out into the hurly-burly of worldly experience. When his characters essentially feel themselves to be 'at home', their stories tend to be static, spatial explorations of environment and circumstance. When, on the other hand, they find themselves cast out abroad, either in the city, or in England or yet further afield, their stories become more dynamic, more linear, more obviously plotted. MacDonald believes the former state to be a version of what is most deeply true of our status and experience as creatures of God–heaven lies all about us. On the other hand, the dynamic experience of exile is necessary–necessary to him as a novelist, to make his fictions more interesting, and to all men as children of God, to make them fully conscious of that heavenly omnipresence.

The conflicts of MacDonald's fiction, therefore, vary according to whether they are of home, as it were, or whether they are of the world. When they are of home, they are essentially static and the aim of the fiction is towards the uncovering of the truth. (Nothing essentially changes; it just becomes known better.) When they are of the world at large, they are dynamic and the aim of the fiction is towards the vanquishing of evil. (Change is achieved in the moral balance.)

Perhaps this pattern is most readily to be perceived by considering one of MacDonald's greatest achievements, the two Portlossie novels, *Malcolm* and *The Marquis of Lossie*. In an earlier discussion of these works (Robb 1987, p.71), I differentiated between the two by saying that in *Malcolm* it is evil that has the initiative, while in the sequel goodness goes on the offensive. I still think that to be a fair account, but I should now like to add to it by stressing how the overriding movement in *Malcolm* is towards the revelation of the hero's status, while in *The Marquis of Lossie* the movement is towards the hero's triumph and the rectification of what is wrong in Florimel, the heroine of the earlier book. The first book is deeply static, despite its wealth of character and incident: we *discover* that the hero is not what he seems. The second is deeply dynamic, because we *know* from the outset that the hero is not what he seems, and that the book must be moving towards the public revelation of that fact. It is entirely in keeping with this pattern that the first book confines itself to Scotland–to a part of Scotland, indeed, which formed a distinct and happy portion of MacDonald's childhood memories. The sequel, however, moves the central and decisive part of the action to London and the book is defined by the tension between the two locations.

For there is a further element in the pattern of relationship involving home and outer world, country and city, Scotland and England, in MacDonald's personal mythology of these matters. The city and/or English environment to which the scene often moves, in contrast with the Scottish rural scene which is 'home', is not merely a place of temporary, but obscurely necessary, experience. It is not just where one has to go to know evil. It is from there that the power comes to combat evil and to make the Scottish 'home' an even better place. The outer world demands and stimulates a dynamism which, once contact is established between the two domains, feeds back into the pastoral world, to the benefit of the latter. In London and the south of England, Malcolm, for example, not only finds and protects Florimel, and tricks her home again, but he attains enough experience of the depths of Mrs Catanach's evil to render her henceforth completely harmless in Portlossie and finds a new companion, Clementina, who becomes an essential consort once his rule is established. More broadly, we assume, I think, that it is Malcolm's experience and self-confidence in knowing and mastering (in his own way) the fashionable world of London that enables MacDonald to transform him, with some semblance of credibility, into the gracious, innovative, utterly masterful marquis with which he closes the novel. Malcolm's discovery of the cultural delights of a capital city is one of the prominent features of his stay there. Furthermore, in going to London he is imbibing at the cultural and political sources of his title; after all, he is a marquis and part of the British system of nobility, rather than a purely Scottish notable such as a clan chief or a laird (though it is as an idealisation of such Scottish figures that MacDonald finally depicts him). Nor is it just Malcolm alone (and his northern marquisate) that benefits from the experience of London. It is there that Florimel comes across the man whom it is right that she marry, and it is there (more significantly still) that Graham, the stickit minister and retiring schoolmaster of *Malcolm*, discovers his own potential for dynamism. The departure of many of the principle characters for London seems to have been a vital step in the movement towards the ultimate apotheosis of Portlossie.

We can already find these patterns, however, in *David Elginbrod*, where the contrast between the Turriepuffit portion and the tale of Hugh's adventures in Arnstead and London is marked. The opening book is concerned with establishing David's character and with exploring a set of relationships and a way of life – the 'world' of Turriepuffit. It has a kind of linearity at the heart of it, but it is that natural linearity of growth (of individual maturity, of relationships) which reads quite differently from the marked and dominating linearity of a mystery plot. Its episodes depict a blossoming of relationships, a static unfolding. Even when a painful tension enters, as Margaret is lost in the snow storm and requires rescuing, its import has to do with the relationship of the young man and woman rather than with the narrative excitement which it suddenly seems to want to arouse in the reader. At Arnstead, by contrast, Hugh is steadily drawn into a complex of sensation novel circumstances which erupt into crime, danger and luridness and require the intervention of Falconer, a kind of moral detective. The pattern whereby the values of David's outlook are partially lost sight of and then rediscovered by Hugh, while elsewhere they take root and grow (to the great benefit of the morally ambiguous Euphra), is clear enough. The worldly denizens of contemporary England can be saved by the goodness to be found on a Scottish estate. (Falconer, too, the Scot who operates so effectively in darkest London, illustrates the same pattern in his own rather mysterious way.) The end of the book, too, is built on the hero's return to his spiritual origins, now fully appreciated and dominant for the first time in his life. Scotland's religious authority, and its moral and religious importance for Britain as a whole, seem clearly outlined.

Yet even here a constant undertone of criticism of Scotland is to be found. If Scotland holds the Elginbrods who welcome Hugh into their home, it also contains the laird and his wife who resolutely refuse to make the tutor equally welcome. Scotland is the home of meanness just as it contains generosity, and the matter is compounded by the snobbery shown by the laird's wife in particular. The narrative is liable to be graced by comments such as 'dear old Scotland . . . which has the sweetest songs in its cottages, and the worst singing in its churches, of any country in the world' (Book 3, ch. 6, 'A Sunday's Dinner'). David, we learn, has refused an eldership, a refusal to join a Scottish establishment which further focuses the book's well-known antagonism to the prevailing theological outlook. Hugh experiences antagonism both from a social superior, Mrs Glasford, and from inferiors – his fellow-labourers in the harvest field. And even in the Elginbrods' cottage there is more than a trace of anti-intellectualism in Janet's attitudes. While Scotland is portrayed as the breeding-ground of such moral masterpieces as David and Margaret, it is also, sporadically, seen as being in the grip of established, conventional ideas of value, class, conduct and religious dogma, to an extent and in ways which are in danger of stifling individuality of thought, behaviour and belief. And even David and Margaret, we must believe, are not quite perfect when we first encounter them, for they believe (and the reader seems to be expected to share the belief) that Hugh has something valuable to offer them in his teaching. The mental and cultural isolation of the Scottish countryside is a serious handicap, it seems.

David Elginbrod is thus a book in which the apparent pattern of

values favourable to Scotland is complicated by a more complex, if
less immediately obvious, set of attitudes underlying and contradict-
ing them. MacDonald must have realised that he had more to do in
sorting out his attitudes to Scotland before he could properly handle
his larger theme of defining Scotland's moral relationship with Victorian Britain. Thus, his next book is thoroughly Scottish in setting
and concern, and in it he confronts, unflinchingly, all that he rejects
in his Scottish roots. In *Alec Forbes of Howglen* he finds a much more
subtle, as well as more extensive, way of bringing his conflicting attitudes into stable relationship. No longer is he content with *David
Elginbrod's* simple pattern of Scotland/country/'home' being superior
to England/city/place of exile. Now the focus is almost entirely on
Scotland, which is seen more objectively and truly as a place with as
many weaknesses as it has strengths. He approaches Scotland now in
a basic spirit of criticism, literally from first sentence to last. The
moral values which he believes can be associated with Scotland have
now to be earned, and fought through to. As *David Elginbrod* ends,
Scotland's faults have either been mysteriously cured or are now simply being ignored; the conclusion contents itself with getting Hugh to
make it up with the surviving Elginbrods, and with finally pairing off
hero and heroine. By contrast, the happiness of Alec and Annie is
embedded in a much more full and satisfying dispensation of characters and fates, satisfying because the rewards of the good and punish-
ments of the bad are not massaged into moral simplicity. Scottish
society has not been magically transformed or purified, even though
the immediate travails of the principal characters have been overcome.

The opening of the book is, perhaps, a deliberate contrast to the
opening of the earlier novel and reveals that MacDonald is respond-
ing to Scotland, and recreating it in fiction, with an altogether new
level of artistry. Both works open with Scottish domestic rituals, but
the positives associated with the Elginbrod family worship are very
different from the negative tone of Chapter One of *Alec Forbes*. Mac-
Donald takes the opportunity provided by the necessary plot prerequisite–the death which orphans Annie Anderson–to establish a
distanced, ironical attitude which is capable of transforming a com-
monplace scene into an image of mystery and threat. However freely
the narrator may later comment, and however subjective in character
the story may later become, the sense of a critical, ironical observer is
firmly established at the very outset. This narrator is capable, too, of
unconventional judgement: 'Nothing can be so desolately dreary as
full strong sunlight can be'.

But more is happening here than the establishment of a fictional persona. This opening contains some crucial embryonic elements. These strange men are gathered to celebrate a death, and a sense of what is deadly in Scotland will form a large part of MacDonald's preoccupation in the novel as a whole. *Alec Forbes* explores what is dead in Scotland with a new thoroughness. Nor is it only the ceremonial of the men sitting silent round the table which brings death into focus: the chapter develops into a superficially lively scene of social exchange which nevertheless has death at the heart of it. From here, the book progresses to a copious set of metaphoric variations on the idea of death, whether it is the deathliness of the Missionar theology, or that of Bruce's greedy materialism, or the emotional vampirism of Kate, or the demonic malevolence of Beauchamp, or the paralysing despair of Cupples, or the snobbery of Mrs Forbes, or the moral immaturity of Alec, or the homelessness of Annie.

This last, too, is dimly foreshadowed in this opening, for the banishment of women from these ceremonials is underlined. A major thematic strand of the novel is the treatment of women in Scotland's markedly masculine society, and the horror of what it can turn them into. Annie's homelessness is the over-arching carrier of this theme, though Kate Fraser is destroyed by the cynically manipulative treatment she receives at the hands of Beauchamp. Even Mrs Forbes is oppressed by Bruce. Some women react more radically and terribly to the masculine ethos in which they find themselves. Mrs Bruce is given one of the most horrific moments in the novel when she cuts the child Annie's hair and sells it: 'with a smile to her husband, half loving and half cunning, Mrs Bruce dropped the amount into the till' (ch. 14). Later Alec finds in the brothel some more women who are prepared to do what men want, and the prostitutes are transformed, in Isie Constable's perceptive misapprehensions, into torturers of uncertain sexual status: 'They say they're women; but I dinna believe that. It's no possible. They maun be men dressed up in women's claes.' (ch. 75). Neither Mrs Bruce nor the fallen women are rescued in this novel, but the role of most of the other female characters, especially Annie, is to be the object of rescue for right-thinking men.

The overriding accusation against this Scotland, however, is its greed and meanness, and its key villain is Robert Bruce the shopkeeper. The theological criticisms which were highlighted by Wolff are substantial, but MacDonald introduces softening qualifications into his disapproval of Scotland's religious life which are lacking in his denunciations of its naked materialism. Bruce is partially loathed because his gambit is to link his greed with devotional display and to allow his religious life to be utterly consumed by his mercantile instincts. The Scottishness of MacDonald's concern is perpetually expressed by the constant air of cultural demonstration: the unfamiliarity of the speech and culture of this society is implicitly acknowledged on every page and frequently supplemented by remarks generalising about the Scots. An example is the comment on the lack of spontaneity and the theoretical bias of Scottish women, when Mrs Forbes's maid uncharacteristically leaves Annie's hair unbound: 'Anyone would think such an impropriety impossible to a Scotch-woman. But then she had been handling the hair, and contact with anything alters so much one's theories about it' (ch. 14). (How Buckle might have nodded in agreement over that!) Much later, MacDonald generalises about the differences between Scottish and English girls like Kate's friend Miss Warner – 'English girls being generally more shy than Scotch girls' (ch. 46). This premise notwithstanding, Annie is yet later made to suffer, indirectly, from 'the reticence of Scotch people' when her friends omit to inform her of her true financial relationship with Bruce (ch. 58).

As Douglas Gifford has noted (1988, p. 228), it is no accident that the villain of the piece is named after Scotland's great hero-king. It is part of Bruce's strategy for mercantile dominance that he associates himself with the victor of Bannockburn, but it is MacDonald's passionate irony that has allowed the spider which inspired the wandering king to 'try, try, try again' to consume the hero and transform him into a rapacious shopkeeper: 'He stood on the watch in his shop like a great spider that ate children; and his windows were his web' (ch. 8). Bruce has a patriotism which, curiously, is the one value by which he seriously holds, beyond that of money-making and the welfare of his own kith and kin. Despite his devout protestations, his religion is little more than the primitive desire to placate the divine powers so that he may be allowed to thrive materially (see his fears for his stock when a flood threatens Glamerton). But when Cupples goads him by deriding King Robert and his victory of 1314, 'Bruce hesitated whether to show Mr Cupples out or in. His blue blood boiled at this insult to his great progenitor.' (ch. 79). Bruce's identification with modern Scotland is one of the most telling twists of the novel, as is his reduction of the patriot hero to a crafty digger of pits and sower of coltraps. MacDonald's own Scottish patriotism, based on a firmer sense of Scotland's past glories, is articulated in the same exchange, as Cupples begs the 'shades o Wallace and Bruce' to forgive the apparent insults.

Appropriately, MacDonald's condemnation of Scotland in *Alec Forbes* is far from absolute: indeed, he is occasionally to be found suddenly jumping from a criticism of Scotland to a compensating, and yet more severe, criticism of England. And even when discussing aspects of Scotland which particularly outrage him, such as school cruelty or hell-fire preaching, he will suddenly qualify his denunciations.

Cupples is the key character to whom it falls to checkmate both the main villains, Bruce and Beauchamp. (If Bruce is an embodiment of the worst of the new world of Victorian urbanised Scotland, Beauchamp is an embodiment of the worst of the old, brutal, rapacious, pride-filled attitudes of the phase of aristocratic landed dominance.) Cupples is a figure associated with the city – indeed, he professes to hate the country. Nevertheless, we learn that his origins were rural, and when he is drawn back to the countryside by Alec, he blossoms. In him, the city's association with learning, ideas and high culture is stressed and the best traditions of Scottish antiquarianism represented. He is a distillation – appropriate word! – of the Aberdeen M.A. degree, as his effortless tutoring of Alec in a range of subjects, and his guardianship of the university library, indicate, and he provides a route back to the Scottish past and therefore to the best of Scotland. A good Baconian, he strives to attain a theory of the universe which will combine its beauty and its pain (see the end of ch. 39), but fails until the dynamism of Alec's painful progress through experience drags him along in its wake. Once enlisted again on the side of the angels, however, he is able to offer all the sophisticated knowledge and intelligence which is required to outwit both Beauchamp and Bruce. He ends a creature of both town and country, equally at home in either.

It is one of the marks of this novel's distinction, however, that such concepts as 'home' and 'exile' are no longer simply equated with particular settings in a rigid, clear-cut way. They are reflections, rather, of the situations and states of mind of individual characters. Thus, Glamerton is, for Alec, the secure rural home from which he must sally forth to meet the difficulties and pain of the city. The horrors of Malison's school do not touch him to the quick; for that, he must fall in love, and encounter Beauchamp, and drink. (One notes, however, that Alec's actual home is on a farm on the outskirts of the town: he is making a daily descent into the complexities of urban exile, without being fully conscious of the fact.) For Annie, however, Glamerton is the scene of her exile from the blissful security of her father's farm; to the little girl, the little grey town fully confirms her forebodings as she approaches it, and her story is of how she gradually transforms this place of exile into her home. Thus, Glamerton is, to the reader, at once the setting of a boyhood idyll, and the occasion of some ferocious criticism of aspects of Scottish life. This convincing ambiguity of treatment is repeated when the scene shifts to Alec's student days in Aberdeen. There, however, it is he who is the exile, but he is associated with Cupples who is essentially at home in the city.

MacDonald seems to be implying that the innocent power of the exile figure (Annie in Glamerton, Alec in Aberdeen) must intertwine with the mastery of the place (embodied in Alec in Glamerton, Cupples in Aberdeen). This process is the salvation both of the innocent who needs help, and the worldly-wise denizen who gives it. By this somewhat complex formula, MacDonald found a means of expressing his sense of how, in a real world, the values of an idealised place and time can be intertwined with the terrible imperfections he saw around him, and could remember in his own past.

Alec Forbes of Howglen is the novel analysing and criticizing Scotland which MacDonald had to write. Once it was written, he was able to return with new confidence and understanding to his larger theme of the moral relationship between Scotland and England. The reappearance of Falconer signals that in the third novel he is indeed conscious of returning to the concerns of the first, but *Robert Falconer* shares more than just the title character with *David Elginbrod*. MacDonald is rewriting that first novel, turning once again to the tale of a divine force reaching out from Scotland into England, rescuing, standing out in marked, challenging contrast, bringing Christ where he is absent, checkmating and outwitting the forces of evil. Now, however, Scotland is no longer confidently shown producing, with apparent ease, the figure of divine authority which David had been. No such figure was going to come easily to MacDonald after the harsh examination he had just completed in *Alec Forbes*. In any case, David did not embody that combination of the dynamic instinct for outreach which characterises MacDonald's later heroes, nor that element of strength derived from knowledge of the ways of the city which became so important in the following novel. Morally magnificent as David may be, MacDonald would take some time before trying, once again, to centre his Scottish fictions on such a complete, confident paragon. In *Robert Falconer*, the tale of the hero's life in Rothieden is one of difficulty, disappointment and doubt, and MacDonald's now developed instinct as a writer is sure in selecting from the first novel the character that he really needs as his central figure. He places him in a novel which continues the exploration of Scotland's failings, so thoroughly begun in *Alec Forbes*, this time using man's artistic instincts as symbol of the needs and promise which Scotland strives so hard to thwart (Robb 1988, p. 286). Yet the balance he developed in *Alec Forbes* enables him to make Mrs Falconer, the principal embodiment of what is to be criticised in Robert's Scotland, a deeply sympathetic figure and one of his finest characters. Where Alec had to combine with Cupples so that innocent Scottish country rectitude could be fused with mastery of the world of the city (how fine a symbol of their essential mutal dependence at this level of meaning is their more superficial mutual dependence in the matter of alcoholic reformation), Robert comes to combine the two in himself as he suffers the denial of the woman he loves, and as he develops his role as a social worker in the London slums in his search for his father.

The Portlossie novels represent something of a new beginning in MacDonald's series of Scottish novels. One aspect of this newness is that MacDonald is now able to return to the idea of making his central character a paragon from the outset, as David had been, but Malcolm MacPhail is born with the combination of strong rural innocence and that equally strong instinctive mastery of the ways of the world which had been denied David. This is achieved, of course, by the adoption of the folk-tale ploy of making him an aristocrat in disguise. Thus, when MacDonald takes his country boy to town, there is never any need to show his hero at a disadvantage, despite the culture clash. Indeed, by the adoption of the idea of 'nature's gentleman', MacDonald is able to focus his criticism on the Victorian aristocracy, where indeed he had focused it before, but not with such a sustained attack, nor with such vehemence. (Mr Arnold in *David Elginbrod*, Beauchamp in *Alec Forbes*, and even Baron Rothie in *Robert Falconer* are none of them quite so convincing as Malcolm's aged regency buck of a father, so infuriating as Florimel in *The Marquis of Lossie*, nor so hated by MacDonald as Lady Bellair and Lord Liftore in the same novel.)

The idea of the lost heir is used once again, with great success, in *Sir Gibbie* in which MacDonald once again doubles back on an earlier fictional pattern and completes the possible permutations set up by the earlier Scottish novels. Confined to Scotland, like *Alec Forbes*, the novel straddles town and country once again. As if, however, it did not show sufficient originality by having as its hero the deaf mute Gibbie, it has an equally powerful, if slightly less obvious, originality in making the city the scene of his childhood bliss, in circumstances which would have been used by more conventional novelists to embody a Victorian childhood hell. The relativity of 'home', which we noted in connection with *Alec Forbes*, is here brought to its fullest fruition. The Scottish countryside is where Gibbie is exiled to, and where he finds, first of all, his childhood crucifixion at the hands of the gamekeeper. Of all MacDonald's major characters in these novels, Gibbie is the one who is most at home in the city, and he also embodies the powerful innocence which is usually the prerogative of MacDonald's country children. If Malcolm MacPhail is the country-born Christ-figure whose mastery of city ways is merely latent in him for a long time, Gibbie is the city-born Christ-figure who brings to fruition that paradoxically necessary power for good which is found where men and women are most obviously cut off from their God.

REFERENCES

D. Gifford, 'Myth, Parody and Dissociation: Scottish Fiction 1814-1914', in Gifford, D. ed., *The History of Scottish Literature*, Vol. 3, *Nineteenth Century*, (Aberdeen University Press, 1988).

H.G. Graham, *The Social Life of Scotland in the Eighteenth Century*, 4th ed., (London: Adam & Charles Black, 1937).

W. Houghton, *The Victorian Frame of Mind, 1830-1870*, (New Haven & London: Yale University Press, 1957).

E. Letley, *From Galt to Douglas Brown: Nineteenth-Century Fiction and Scots Language*, (Edinburgh: Scottish Academic Press, 1988).

C.S. Lewis, *George MacDonald: An Anthology*, (London: Geoffrey Bles, 1946).

Greville MacDonald, *George MacDonald and his Wife*, 2nd ed., (London: George Allen & Unwin, 1924).

W. Raeper, *George MacDonald*, (Tring: Lion Publishing, 1987).

D.S. Robb, *George MacDonald*, (Edinburgh: Scottish Academic Press,1987).

D.S. Robb, 'Realism and Fantasy in the Fiction of George MacDonald', in Gifford, D, ed., *The History of Scottish Literature*, Vol. 3, *Nineteenth Century*, (Aberdeen: Aberdeen University Press, 1988).

R.L. Wolff, *The Golden Key: A Study of the Fiction of George MacDonald*, (New Haven: Yale University Press, 1961).

3

Phantastes and *Lilith*: Femininity and Freedom
RODERICK MCGILLIS

The similarity between MacDonald's two great romances, *Phantastes* which inaugurates his career in 1858 and *Lilith* which is its culmination in 1895, was evident to some as soon as the second book appeared. Katherine Pearson Woods, in a review of *Lilith* in the New York *Bookman* (1895), notes that it was 'advertised as being like *Phantastes* and so it is, as the dreams of youth resemble the vision of an age which is not the second, but the first and only, the eternal childhood' (133). Anodos has grown into, she suggests, Mr Vane. More recently, Colin Manlove notices something similar when he suggests that in a sense '*Phantastes* and *Lilith* together make up a single fantasy' (*The Impulse of Fantasy Literature* 75). Pearson also notes the similarity of the Bags in *Lilith* to the Blockheads in *Phantastes*. She might have noted several more parallel incidents in the two works: his Shadow, his own evil self, plagues Anodos in *Phantastes*, but in the later book the universal Shadow who stands, as Louis MacNeice points out, 'to the whole of humanity as the earlier Shadow stood to the hero of *Phantastes*' (100) confronts Vane; in both works the hero mentally 'gives birth' to a beautiful woman in a cave (Mendelson 205); each cave contains life-sustaining water; both heroes undertake journeys of ascent which take them from an unthinking phallocentric acceptance of the material and of the body to a vision of splendour and joy. Both books are about coming of age: the protagonist in each experiences loss of the father who has died and they manage successfully to overcome the hegemony of the male drive for fixity and finality. The quest for identity is a quest for continuous becoming, not to imprint the self on the world, but to achieve that joy which is a going out of the self.

Noting the comparison between the two books, Robert Lee Wolff writes that *Lilith* 'apparently began as a companion-piece to *Phantastes*: the search for a father balancing the search for a mother' (331). Neither book, however, is so much a search for mother or father than it is an attempt to overcome the duality implied in such a search. MacDonald's work exhibits the tendency apparent in

31

romance toward the polarisation of imagery; it often creates a structure of binary opposition: male/female, sun/moon, silver/gold, child/
adult, dark/light, city/country, rich/poor, dream/reality and so on.
Such binary thinking is masculine, aggressive, analytic, and adversarial.
It perpetuates difference based on authority. Where does power lie?
Do the rich control the poor, does man dominate woman, is gold
more valuable than silver, is the moon a reflection of the sun, and so
on? A reverse thinking – one that is feminine, passive, imaginative, and
sacrificing – is equally flawed because one cannot live exclusively in
fairy land where names are unnecessary. MacDonald's contribution to
nineteenth-century narrative is his ability to break the codes of closure. Narrative in its inevitable opening and closing rests on binary
opposition: beginning/ending. Life as narrative has its beginning and
ending: birth/death. MacDonald's vision is romantic in that it presses
beyond binary thinking to posit the possibility of thinking beyond
such opposites. For MacDonald, narrative neither begins nor ends,
life neither begins nor ends. His books press towards a vision of
mutuality in which the divisions of masculine and feminine, life and
death, body and spirit are no more. In short, an eschatological drive
moves MacDonald's work in a traditionally vertical direction.

Anodos' path, as his name indicates, is upwards; his is a successful
journey of regeneration. The mention of old Sir Upward at the
begining of *Lilith* (Chapter I, 190) is a reminder of Anodos' success.
It was Sir Upward who originally taught Mr Raven the means of
entering the imaginative realm, and it is his portrait that initiates
Vane's experience. Sir Upward is Anodos the successful voyager in
life and in the other world, and he serves as a foil to Vane in *Lilith*.
MacDonald stresses the point by making a concrete relationship
between Anodos and Vane: Anodos has an 'old uncle Ralph', and it
is surely more than coincidence that Vane's grandfather is 'old Sir
Ralph'. Both Ralph and grandfather Ralph represent the masculine
scepticism that denies the world of the unseen, and this scepticism is
what the experiences of Anodos and Vane transform.

In several ways Vane and Anodos are similar: both have scientific
casts of mind; both are alone in the world; both have just graduated
from Oxford; both have inherited a large estate; and neither has had
to work for his daily bread. Both are Philistines: money and social
position are criteria of social respectability. They are, in words which
Mr Raven applies to society in general, 'childish' and 'self-satisfied'.
Vane's first thoughts on finding himself in the strange land are concerned with economy, the getting of money and food: 'I have never
yet done anything to justify my existence; my former world was

nothing the better for my sojourn in it: here, however, I must earn, or in some way find, my bread! But I reasoned that, as I was not to blame in being here, I might expect to be taken care of here as well as there! I had nothing to do with getting into the world I had just left, and in it I found myself heir to a large property!' (Chapter IV, 204). Anodos too thinks of money early in the book, inspecting his purse to pay the woman in whose cottage he rests before embarking on his journey through fairy land. This interest in money and what it signifies – accumulation, possession, domination, power, desire, control, retention – diminishes as Anodos and Vane proceed on their journeys.

If there is a difference between the two books, it is in the deepening of the books' imagery; *Phantastes* is a mid-century fantasy influenced by Pre-Ralphaelite medievalism, and *Lilith* expresses the *fin de siècle* mood with its deeper uncertainty. *Phantastes* is self-consciously about poetry. Anodos is a poet, and MacDonald originally planned to make Vane a writer, but he changed his mind when he wrote the second version of *Lilith*. Although both books develop the themes of language and reading, *Lilith* does not deal directly with the poet and art; instead it deals with everyman's life-struggle against an evil that is as much external as it is psychological. The Fairy Palace in *Phantastes* represents the poet's imagination and its dancers are emblems of art. In *Lilith* this place appears as the castle overgrown with parasitic ivy, a hollow shell, and its dancers present a frightening vision of the pre-destined round which all men must take. The image here corresponds to the dancers of Yeats' 'Nineteen Hundred and Nineteen' whose tread 'Goes to the barbarous clangour of a gong'. The dancers are whirled, powerless to control their movements or direction, propelled by time and change. For Yeats, 'Men dance on deathless feet', but MacDonald's dancers will dance only as long as it takes for them to develop 'faces', that is to become pure in spirit. The dancers in *Phantastes* have more in common with the 'Marbles of the dancing floor' that 'Break bitter furies of complexity' in 'Byzantium'. The marble statues that dance in the Fairy Palace inhabit the Byzantium world 'out of nature and life and becoming' where all is symbol, where all is eternal.

Phantastes, which MacDonald subtitles 'A Faerie Romance for Men and Women', contains a genuine fairy land: it begins with the conventional fairy story motif that has the main character confronted by a fairy who will grant him a wish, and the animistic world of the tale contains humanised trees, enchanted gardens and woods, nasty goblins, old witches, and gallant knights. The plot is loose and diffuse like that of *Thh Faerie Queene,* and the prose is highly metaphoric.

Lilith, on the other hand. has the haunting quality of a dream. The prose is much tougher, reflecting the barren landscape. The plot is concentrated and the whole more dramatic with a great deal of dialogue. Vane, unlike Anodos, is constantly asking questions and struggling to understand the world in which he finds himself. A greater sense of urgency pervades this book. Colin Manlove, in his perceptive discussion of the similarities and differences between these two books, says *Phantastes* is centrifugal and implies that *Lilith* is the opposite: centripetal (*The Impulse of Fantasy Literature* 85). In terms of Manlove's focus on Anodos' roughly linear journey and Vane's corresponding non-linear journey, his observation is surely neat. From the point of view of structure, however, *Phantastes* is a rigorously centripetal book.

I have written elsewhere of the centred structure of *Phantastes*, and John Docherty has noticed a similar centering structure. The book moves inward to the story of Cosmo von Wehrstahl in chapter thirteen, the middle chapter of twenty-five, and outward to the entrance to and exit from fairy land. What MacDonald refers to as the 'community of the centre' is an experience of liberation from binary thinking and from linear narrative based on the beginning/ending duality. This is why the two halves of the book radiate outward from the story of Cosmo who goes out from himself, loses himself in fact—he dies in an act of self-sacrifice – in order to find himself. For MacDonald, paradox is the necessary condition of existence: within is without, east is west, fairy land is quotidien life, evil is good, and so on. Truly, opposition *is* friendship if only we can break the code of adversarial thinking. Anodos begins by thinking everything exists to satisfy his desire; his is a narcissistic attitude that does not see the other as important as itself. For example, much of the book recounts Anodos' desire to touch, to claim a woman for himself. Eventually he comes to realise that desire only satisfies as an index of heterogeneity. The drive of the text into its centre, the drive of the text's intertextuality into the centre of literary experience, takes Anodos and the reader – who are the same person – into an understanding that functions through feeling: 'I began to feel in some degree what the birds meant in their songs, though I could not express it in words' (Chapter V, 42).

Phantastes, then, centers on the polysemous word, the endlessly suggestive text. The quotation from Novalis that serves as epigraph to the book speaks of the fairy tale as 'musical fantasy', wonderful and fragmented. At the end of the book, Anodos rests beneath a great beech tree and listens to the leaves overhead: 'At first, they made sweet inarticulate music alone; but, by and by, the sound seemed to begin to take shape, and to be gradually moulding itself into words; till, at last, I seemed able to distinguish these, half-dissolved in a little ocean of circumfluent tones: "A great good is coming–is coming–is coming to thee, Anodos"; and so over and over again. I fancied that the sound reminded me of the voice of the ancient woman, in the cottage that was four-square' (Chapter XXV, 182). Anodos hears words which remind him of the woman who was so like his mother, the woman whose voice is the voice of a soul 'full of all plenty and bounty' (Chapter XIX, 135); he hears these words sounding from the branches of a tree, and consequently echoing the voice 'like a solution of all musical sounds' (Chapter IV, 38) which come from the maternal breech tree that protects Anodos from the horrid and paternal Ash early in the story. Such echoes and re-echoes through the book haunt the mind mysteriously; like music', *Phantastes* does not give its meaning clearly, despite the sprinkling of epigrammatic utterances which appear through the text. The book's discourse combines feminine musicality and suggestiveness with masculine assertiveness; this apparent 'split' leads Manlove to imagine MacDonald creating the book in two stages and using two 'different areas of his mind' (*Modern Fantasy* 77): his imagination and his intellect. The impulse of the book, however, is to draw these two apparently opposed faculties together.

At the center of *Phantastes* is a library containing books of all kinds: metaphysics, travel, history, fiction. The metaphor draws all knowledge, all types of discourse together. But rather than aggressive male appropriation of these books, Anodos experiences personal release in reading them. He becomes the traveller, the metaphysician, the historical character in the books he reads. Fusion of subject/reader and object/character takes place as Anodos enters the embrace of the book. He experiences an erotics of reading, throwing himself onto 'one of the many sumptuous eastern carpets' which lay on the library floor and reading until he is very weary with a 'faintness of rapturous delight' (Chapter XI, 81). He loses himself in reading. Something similar happens at the end of the book when Anodos dies into the embrace of the earth: 'Now that I lay in her bosom, the whole earth, and each of her many births, was as a body to me, at my will. I seemed to hear the great heart of the mother beating into mine, and feeding me with her own life, her own essential being and nature' (Chapter XXIV, 178). This experience of the mother leads him to conclude that 'it is by loving, and not by being loved, that one can come nearest the soul of another; yea, that where two love, it is the loving of each other, and not the being beloved by each other, that originates and perfects and assures their blessedness. I knew that love gives to him that loveth, power over any soul beloved, even if that soul know him not, bringing him inwardly close to that spirit; a power that cannot be but for good; for power in proportion as self-ishness intrudes, the love ceases, and the power which springs there-from dies' (Chapter XXIV, 170). The masculine power associated with 'lands and moneys' (Chapter I, 16), with the grasping voraciousness of the Ash, and with the desire to touch, to possess and own, here is replaced with a notion of power based on renuncia-tion. Power is, we might say, joy or *jouissance*; it is polymorphous. Anodos returns to the mother. His aphoristic style is not so much a reflex of partriarchy's didactic urging of proper behaviour as it is a reflection of a fragmented and orphic prophecy.

Lilith, too, forces us beyond binary thinking. In his strange experi-ences in the mirror world, Vane meets Mr Raven who is at one and the same time a bird, and a man. He is Adam the old and the new man. He is a librarian and a sexton, a guide and a teacher. His method of teaching is to bewilder Vane, to force him to answer rid-dles and to reassess his view of reality. Vane, who believes (as does Anodos) that 'touch would correct sight' (Chapter III, 193) is a materialist, and by implication – 'I know this seems nonsense' (Chap-ter III, 196) Vane tells his skeptical audience – so is the reader. The reader will undoubtedly echo Vane's puzzled query when finding himself in strange territory: 'How am I to begin (making myself at home) where everything is so strange?' (Chapter III, 195). However, strangeness can free the reader, and the infuriating paradoxes and rid-dles of Mr Raven can serve to wake the reader's imagination. Mean-ing must be felt and thought in each person and cannot be given. 'You bewilder me,' Vane says to Raven, whose reply is: 'that's all right!' (Chapter VI, 210). Mr Raven is intent on breaking down old categories of thought.

As a librarian, Mr Raven says he was a 'bookworm', but once he 'came to know it', he 'woke among the butterflies'. Now, as sexton, he has 'given up reading'. The riddle is that sexton and librarian are 'much the same profession' To a reader like Vane, 'books are but dead bodies'; Mr Raven's vocation is not to bury these books, but rather, to give them a new life (Chapter IV, 204, Chapter VI, 210). This involves giving readers, including Vane, glimpses of meaning in order that mystery and wonder may remain to encourage a continu-ation of reading. The metaphor of the half-book is relevant here. Vane finds a half-book in his library. The words of this volume are only partially available to him, yet what he reads wakes in him ideas and feelings he has never before had. Its effect precedes understanding and hints at a more powerful understanding than can be obtained through reason alone. This book refuses to give up its meaning, and consequently it may be read over and over again. The reader who touches a book, finishes with it the way Vane touches and finishes with a splendid butterfly, finding only 'a dead book with boards outspread' where once had been a thing of beauty (Chapter X, 228). The book's beauty can only be a joy forever while it remains mysterious; the open book is uninteresting.

This helps to explain the ending of Vane's adventures. As he approaches the throne of the Ancient of Days with Lona, Vane feels a hand reach out to him from a cloud. It leads him to 'a little door with golden lock', through which he passes. Once through, Vane turns to see 'the board of a large book in the act of closing behind me' (Chapter XLVI, 419). He is in his own library. The point here is not only that his experience is derived from a book, that books open up fantastic worlds, but also that imaginative books remain in one sense closed. The echo is from the last chapter of Daniel, where Daniel receives instruction to 'shut up the word, and seal the book' (12:4). Only at 'the time of the end' will the book be unsealed; in other words, in the book of Revelation. Implied here is the notion of 'the endless ending' (the title of the last chapter of *Lilith*), of stories whose endings do not bring closure. Also implied here is the idea of necessary mystery; the book remains to be read again. The reader will profit from rereading the book recently closed. To delight in mystery without an irritable reaching after fact and reason is to live in everything and have everything enter and live in us. *Lilith*, which begins ostensibly as a search for the father, ends with a vision of maternal comfort. As Vane lies on his bier, he hears Eve, referred to as the mother, singing a sweet song, one which the comforting old woman in *Phantastes* sang to Anodos. Vane lies beside his mother. As he and the children approach the heavenly city, angel-mothers descend to meet them and take the children home. Back in this world, Vane waits for his return to the heavenly-city, to 'that life, which as a mother her child, carries this life in its bosom' (Chapter XLVI, 420). The mother, then, liberates us from paternal meaning.

But how easily things go wrong. In both *Phantastes* and *Lilith*, as well as in his work generally, MacDonald tries to go beyond traditional thinking. His attempts must fail since the idea of androgynous thought was for MacDonald impossible to maintain in an imperfect world. In the perfect world, we will be the books we now read, and meanings will be clear. Until we reach this unmediated perfection, we must accept what we have: a fallen world. Both Anodos and Vane return to this world and wait with melancholy hope for the new day.

Phantastes: Erotics of Imagination

To Love is to survive paternal meaning–Julia Kristeva

MacDonald claimed that *Phantastes* took him 'two months to write without any close work' (*George MacDonald and his wife* 290). It was published on October 28, 1858 and the immediate reaction was not encouraging. The *Athenaeum*, in a review on November 6, called it 'an allegory in prose, which reads as though it had been written after supping too plentifully on German romance, negative philosophy, and Shelley's "Alastor", and then instead of his having mounted his Pegasus to ride it off, he seems to have been ridden off himself by a nightmare' (580). In a letter to Mrs A.J. Scott, MacDonald objected to the review's use of the word 'allegory': 'I don't see what right the *Athenaeum* has to call it an allegory and judge or misjudge it accordingly–as if nothing but an allegory could have two meanings' (*George MacDonald and His Wife* 297). Throughout his career, MacDonald speaks disparagingly of allegory and privileges symbolism. In this he followed his romantic precursors, especially Coleridge; but more to the point, his dislike of allegory indicates his dislike of binary thought. Near the end of his career he writes: 'A genuine work of art must mean many things' (*A Dish of Orts* 317). It must be symbolic. Mac-Donald argues in one of his sermons that 'we must beware of receiving . . . any symbol 'after the flesh', beware of interpreting it in any fashion that partakes of the character of the mere physical, psychical, or spirituo-mechanical. The symbol deals with things far beyond the deepest region when symbols can be drawn' (*Unspoken Sermons*, Third Series 53). Consequently, when the *Athenaeum* reviewers calls *Phantastes* a 'wilderness of wilderment' and a 'riddle that will not be read' he is hardly off the mark.

That readers may respond favourably to such a bewildering text is evident in the reviews which appeared in the *Spectator*, the *Leader*, the *Globe*, and the *British Quarterly Review*. MacDonald successfully tapped into a desire felt by many Victorians to maintain amid the smoke stacks of Coketown a sense of faerie. Two years before the publication of *Phantastes*, Frances Browne remarked that 'the fairies dance no more. Some say it was the hum of schools – some think it was the din of factories that frightened them '(*Granny's Wonderful Chair* 150). She also holds a hope that some time the fairies will return to the world. This belief that fairy land is not something confined to fiction is evident in MacDonald's work. As usual, MacDonald breaks down the opposition between fairy land and reality. Anodos has fairy blood. The farm he visits early in his travels is on the borders of fairy land, borders which he indicates in 'Cross Purposes' neither mortal nor fairy can locate. The two worlds, as Stephen Prickett has noted, interpenetrate.

Phantastes contains chapter headings from a variety of texts which signify the sources for MacDonald's imaginative vision. Collectively, these citations from precursor texts draw attention to a variety of forms MacDonald brings together in *Phantastes*. In other words, just as he breaks down binary thinking (classificatory thinking) generally, MacDonald also breaks down/generic/genre/gender categories by generating a new kind of text. The reviewer in the *Globe* notices this play with genre. '*Phantastes* . . . is in some respects an original kind of thing. We know nothing with which it can be fairly compared. It is not like Fouque's *Undine*, nor Tennyson's '*Princess*'; it is not like the old tales of King Arthur's 'Round Table'; it is not like the *Faerie Queen*; nor is it like the German popular and supernatural tales, yet it is not unlike all of these.' What many of the works cited have in ·common is an interest in the artist. *Phantastes*, like Novalis's *Heinrich von Ofterdingen*, is a *Kunstlermärchen*, a fairy tale that depicts the unfolding of artistic potential within the mind of a young person. Anodos's journey takes him into the realm of the imagination in all its enticing and alluring forms. Although MacDonald values the imagination, he also follows Shelley in stressing the dangers inherent in the pursuit of the image for its own sake. MacDonald is quick to seize on the implications of Shelley's *Alastor*; he focuses on the danger of 'the Poet's self-centred seclusion' which Shelley speaks of in the preface to *Alastor*. The avenging spirit of the poem is the self, and in MacDonald's romance Anodos' Shadow plays the same role. Anodos, as his Shadow signifies, is a Philistine and a rationalist; he is also a sensualist. Anodos's sensuality is apparent from the first pages of the book.

From the secretary in which Anodos finds his father's papers and some withered rose-leaves, comes a 'tiny woman form as perfect a shape as if she had been a small Greek statuette roused to life and motion' (Chapter I, 16). The animated statue anticipates the marble lady whom Anodos pursues later in the story. Once the fairy stands before Anodos in human size, 'a tall, gracious lady, with pale face and large blue eyes' (Chapter I, 17), he is drawn towards her by an attraction as 'irresistable as incomprehensible'. His passion, a force he cannot understand let alone control, leads him to reach out in an effort to embrace her, but she steps back with a reprimand. She refers to forbidden relationships, reminding him that one cannot make love to one's own grandmother. She provides Anodos with a vision of the maternal sea; she displaces the erotic urge from body to imagination. Her beautiful blue eyes in their effect on him are like the blue flower of Heinrich von Ofterdingen's dream or the blue eyes of Serpentina in Hoffmann's *The Golden Pot*. Anselmus, in *The Golden Pot*, looks into the elder tree and sees 'a pair of marvellous blue eyes looking down at him with unspeakable desire, so that an unknown feeling' and an 'intense longing' possess him (*Selected Writings*, 64). In *Phantastes*, the fairy's eyes fill Anodos with 'an unknown longing' and create the impression of a maternal sea:

> I remembered somehow that my mother died when I was a baby. I looked deeper and deeper, till they spread around me like seas, and I sank in their waters. I forgot all the rest, till I found myself at the window, whose gloomy curtains are withdrawn, and where I stood gazing at a whole heaven of stars, small and sparkling in the moonlight. Below lay a sea, still as death and hoary in the moon, sweeping into bays and around capes and islands, away, away, I knew not whither. Alas! it was no sea, but a low fog burnished by the moon. 'Surely there is such a sea somewhere!' I said to myself. (Chapter I, 18)

The sea represents not only the comfort and protection of the womb, but also death, a comforting easeful death watched over by the beneficent moon and stars. The vision is marked contrast to the room with its darkness and gloomy curtains. Anodos then hears a voice that assures him that such a sea exists in Fairy Land. MacDonald has set up a tension between physical and spiritual desire, a tension he will reconcile during the course of Anodos' travels. The maternal voice which beckons Anodos is not, then, a sign of MacDonald's Oedipal complex, as Wolff maintains (47). This voice, as Keith Wilson notes, draws attention to the 'distinction between imaginative vision and scientific analysis' (143), but in doing so it draws attention to a mode of thought other than the male analytical thinking which weighs and measures, which separates in order to systematise experience. The mother draws Anodos into an experience of totality of being. Feminine thinking takes us out of the self and into the joy of participating in all things. That this feminine principle arrives at a crucial time in Anodos' life is apparent from the fact that, at twenty-one he has just come of age; he is about to enter the male world, the world of finance. Early in his journey, Anodos meets the vampire Ash tree and the protecting Beech. The male Ash clearly represents the grasping desire to possess, the will to power associated with a sexuality based on violence, represented by the Alder-maiden. The Beech, on the other hand, represents the male ideal of woman as self-sacrificing nurturer. MacDonald tries to overcome the stereotypes of angel and whore, but first he must confront them. Until late in the book, the females Anodos meets – Alder-maiden, beech, marble lady, country maiden, old crone, and elderly lady – fall into these categories; either they offer Anodos beauty, gratification, protection, service or they threaten him with emasculation, loss of identity, pollution, enslavement. As Kathy Triggs notes, 'Victorian culture encouraged (MacDonald) to idealise woman and to see her as something better than man' (28). In his *Reminiscences of a Specialist*, Greville MacDonald recalls that the

first social axiom I was taught to express in words was 'Ladies first!' My parents' intimacy with such protagonists of the feminist movement as the beautiful and devoted Josephine Butler, Madam Bodichon of Girton renown, Mrs Reid, Principle of Bedford College . . . Anna Sidgwick, Miss Buss and Miss Beale, no doubt made deep, if forgotten impression upon me . . . I distinctly remember wondering how it could be that my adored mother had ever married my father who, in spite of his splendour, was only a man! (29)

Greville repeats this last line in his biography of his father where he also notes that 'I am still crushed at times by the conviction . . . that I, as a male, am still a worm,' (*George MacDonald and His Wife* 300). In *Lilith*, Adam tells Vane that 'Men are not coming home fast; women are coming faster' (399). In *Phantastes*, MacDonald offers the usual Romantic and Victorian set of angel women and demon women.   Passive and sacrificing women such as the beech lady are reminiscent of Romantic anima figures such as Sophia in Novalis's 'Kingsohr's Marchen'. Sophia is eternal wisdom; through her man can find eternal truths and a prefiguration of the spiritual world. Another echo sounds from Heinrich's rapturous apostrophe to Matilda in *Heinrich von Ofterdingen*: 'You are the saint through whom I offer my prayers to God, and through whom he has revealed his love. What is religion but the complete union of loving hearts? You are a manifestation of eternal love in its sweetest forms' (131). Matilda is 'the very spirit of song' and the beach lady's own song carries Anodos back to his childhood innocence and oneness with nature. Anodos perceives the woman he meets not so much as angels as extensions of himself, property upon which he may perpetrate his designs. In short, these women have no room to roam, but rather are confined to cottages, to blocks of alabaster, to infancy, or to the ground. Anodos' desire, the male desire, is to free the female in order to reconfine her to his wishes.

For example, when Anodos enters a 'rocky cell' and finds a block of alabaster inside of which reclines a beautiful lady, he remarks that her face was 'more near the face that had been born with me in my soul, than anything I had seen before in nature' (Chapter V, 44-45). Later, this marble lady is explicitly called Isis, an allusion no doubt to Novalis's story of Hyacinth and Rosebud in *The Disciple at Sais*. Hyacinth's search for Isis, the Holy of Holies, a search which takes him away from his youthful and earthly love, Rosebud, ends when he stands before the 'Celestial Virgin', the veiled goddess. He draws aside the veil and finds Rosebud. Anodos too must learn to value earthly woman for what she is. Now, however, his creative act, freeing the lady from the marble prison, serves his selfish desire to appropriate her for himself; he desires that she 'might glorify my eyes with her presence' (Chapter V, 45). With knife, gaze, and song he penetrates the marble which encases her. His imagination is thoroughly phallic. The strength of Anodos' confused, selfish and even perverted sexuality is apparent as he follows the white lady.

He enters a forest as night falls, and the pleasures of this forest enrapture him. The sound of birds and scent of the woods lull him. Winged creatures–bats, owls, and a night-hawk–and the active verbs 'rose', 'uplifting', 'crossed', and 'clasped' add an interesting sexual aura to the setting. Traditionally, the demon Lilith has associations with the birds mentioned. Be this as it may, Anodos does not sense the liberating possibilities of this demon, nor does he sense the dangers she poses for male aggression. Instead he pursues his phallocentric thoughts:

> Numberless unknown sounds came out of the unknown dusk; but all were of twilight-kind, oppressing the heart as with a condensed atmosphere of dreamy undefined love and longing. The odours of night arose, and bathed me in that luxurious mournfulness peculiar to them, as if the plants whence they floated had been watered with bygone tears. Earth drew me towards her bosom; I felt as if I could fall down and kiss her. I forgot I was in Fairy Land, and seemed to be walking in a perfect night of our own old nursing earth . . . Great boughs crossed my path; great roots based the tree columns, and mightily clasped the forest, perfect in forest ways and pleaure. And when, in some close canopy of leaves, by some giant stem, or in some

mossy cave, or beside some leafy well, sat the lady of the marble, whom my songs had called forth into the outer world, waiting (might it not be?) to meet and thank her deliverer in a twilight which would veil her confusion, the whole night became one dream-realm of joy. (Chapter VI, 50)

The sexual implications are clear, and the desire to gratify his own senses marks Anodos' failure, both as an artist and as a human being. He sings a song, a paean to illicit love and a hoped-for assignation, to the 'Queen of Night'. Unable to sublimate his sexual fervour, Anodos falls prey to the only other vision of the female he can imagine: the fatal woman. He encounters the Alder-maid – and loses his manhood. Anodos, at this point, can only conceive of woman as dominated or dominating.

Perhaps an even clearer example of the book's interest in freeing the female from male domination and formulation is the country maiden Anodos meets shortly after acquiring his Shadow in the cottage of negativity. This child-maiden carries a 'small globe' which emits both radiant colours and beautiful sounds; it is the globe of poetry and faith. Anodos finds the maiden attractive, as she does him. They travel together by day, but part discreetly at night. Finally, Anodos' libidinous nature gets the better of him and he feels the globe. His Shadow self asserts its phallic aggressiveness and shatters the globe and with it the young girl's faith, joy, and innocence. He departs from her, leaving her bemoaning the loss of her globe. When next he meets her, after his sojourn in the fairy palace and while he is imprisoned in a tower, she sings a song that arouses the sensations of the maternal. The song is like 'a living soul, like an incarnation of Nature . . . like a caressing bird . . . like a sea . . . like a long draught of clear spring-waters . . . like essential sunlight . . . like a mother's voice and hand' (Chapter XXII, 162).

Drawn by the song, Anodos leaves the prison. The singer is the little girl whose globe he had broken; she is now a 'beautiful woman'. Her experience is a paradigm for the attainment of the joy of poetic vision. She now has no need for the globe, a childish crutch; she has attained a far more precious childlikeness. Her suffering has 'uplifted' her into the realm of joy, and she has become a complete poet singing songs which 'do good, and deliver people' (Chapter XXII, 163). She is in touch with her own unconscious, that limitless country where the repressed – women and fairies – manage to survive. She offers Anodos an example of the female poet, one who, as Hélène Cixous suggests, 'couldn't care less about decapitation (or castration), adventuring, without the masculine temerity, into anonymity, which she can merge with, without annihilating herself: because she's a giver' (259). She travels here and there through the dark forest singing her songs, a 'radiance' in a dark world.

The quest in *Phantastes* is to slay the phallus, to relinquish the desire for ownership. This is the significance of the story of Cosmo as it is of Anodos' attempt to get rid of his Shadow. The first half of the book presents attempts on the part of phallocentric desire to take control of Anodos: the Ash tree's attack, the coming of the Shadow. The second half, after Anodos' stay in the Fairy Palace where he reads stories which concern desire and its perversion, presents Anodos' attempts to quell phallic desire, to overcome the will to ownership and property. His brief stay in the cottage with four doors brings him to the maternal hearth where he has a four fold vision which reconciles past and present, life and death, body and spirit. On leaving this cottage, Anodos encounters two athletic young brothers who are preparing to battle three evil giants. Work, play, and song go together here in companionship; Anodos participates in a common enterprise: the quelling of masculine violence. The giants come and the battle ensues. MacDonald provides one perspective on this incident in his sermon, 'True Christian Ministering':

> So with the Christian man; whatever meets him, obedience is the thing. If he is told by his conscience, which is the candle of God within him, that he must do a thing, why he must do it. He may tremble from head to foot at having to do it, but he will tremble more if he turns his back. You recollect how our old poet Spenser shows us the Knight of the Red Cross, who is the knight of holiness, ill in body, diseased in mind, without any armour on, attacked by a fearless giant. What does he do? Run away? No, he has but time to catch up his sword, and, trembling in every limb, he goes on to meet the giant; and that is the thing that every Christian man must do. (*A Dish of Orts* 309)

The two brothers, along with the giants, die in the battle indicating the death of manhood without song. Ministering is not the prerogative of angelic womanhood. In *Phantastes,* the idea is clear after Anodos meets for the second time the maiden whose globe he had broken. Seeing her and hearing her songs, Anodos finds humility. No resplendent knight, he doffs his armour and his pride and sets his course eastward with no heroic pretensions, but certain that 'he that will be nothing but a doer of his work, is sure of his manhood' (Chapter XXII, 165).

Following this incident, Anodos meets Sir Percival who relates a story of a little girl who tries to gather a pair of wings for herself while wooden men buffet and trample on her. The wooden men refuse the girl flight; they are inflexible, robot-like creatures with no eyes, nose or ears. Their desire is to assert, rather than create. The girl, however, desires to be what Cixous calls an 'airborne swimmer'. Woman, 'in flight . . . is dispersible, prodigious, stunning, desirous and capable of others, of the other woman that she will be, of the other women she isn't, of him, of you' (260). The airborne state is what Anodos achieves after slaying the monstrous wolf who represents the death-impulse of the people of the settlement Anodos and Sir Percival happen upon. In death, Anodos finds life, a condition of blessedness. He learns that 'it is by loving, and not by being loved, that one can come nearest to the soul of another' (Chapter XXIV, 179). I wish to equate this with Cixous's sense of female power: 'to watch-think-seek the other in the other, she'll get back even some unexpected profit from what she puts out. She gives that despecularize, to unhoard'. The woman gives 'with no assurance that she'll get back even some unexpected profit from what she puts out. She gives that there might be life, thought, transformation' (264). For MacDonald, to achieve this state is to feel, as Anodos does, 'the great heart of the mother beating into mine' (Chapter XXIV, 178). His imagination fills all things, luxuriates in the earth and in the sky. Pleasure is complete.

As we would expect, MacDonald's vision presents a possibility rather than an actuality. A 'writhing as of death' comes over Anodos, and he returns to the 'more limited . . . bodily and earthly life' (Chapter XXIV, 180). He returns home where his sisters greet him warmly. The book ends with kinship and sisterhood and exhortation. Fairy land is no longer on the margins of Anodos' life, but central to his existence. The great good that he feels is coming is the liberation from an economy based on proprietorship and power. The only power worth having is the power to give love.

Lilith: *Imagination Emasculated*

He had the Word,
had it from on high, while I,
previous to alphabets, superfluous as ampersand,
curled on chaos still my edges blurred.
                    Pamela Hadas

Whereas *Phantastes* suggests that each person must become a living text, poem, or song, *Lilith* reverts to the insecurities of the masculine ego which desires fixity. The books in the Fairy Palace library in *Phantastes*, like visions of beauty, truth and goodness, offer what

MacDonald's character Malcolm calls in *The Marquis of Lossie* (1877) 'revelation before mystery'. Malcolm goes on to explain: 'mystery is what lies behind revelation, that which as yet revelation has not reached. You must see something–a part of something, before you can feel any sense of mystery about it. The Isis forever veiled is the absolutely unknown, not the Mysterious' (117). The meaning of the books Anodos reads, the meaning of *Phantastes*, cannot be fixed. The edges blur; they coordinate rather than subordinate. In *Lilith*, however, the mysterious half-book in Vane's library which wakes feelings and spiritual sensations in him is opened by the patriarchal Mr Raven who is also Adam. Adam reads this book in order to reassume control over his first wife Lilith, to put an end to her protean behaviour. The book contains a poem which is apparently a rendering of Lilith's own words, and these Adam uses against her. Her words, previous to alphabets, are now written on parchment and bound; Adam tosses the book in which they appear between Lilith who has taken the form of a Persian cat and her escape route up the chimney. The book which contains her words is used to control her. Earlier in the book, Vane had seen a beautiful bird-butterfly, reached out to touch it, and found 'a dead book with boards outspread' (Chapter X, 228). Books create bookworms, and the phallic image nicely expresses the patriarchal view of the world in this book. We might recall that a worm is the instrument responsible for Lilith's purgation in Mara's House of Sorrow.

Vane's whole experience in the seventh dimension turns out to be an experience of textuality; he must succumb to the authority of the word as text: his father's in the manuscript Vane finds; that of Mr Raven, who is among other things a librarian; and that of the Ancient Days, who speaks from the Book and who is the Word. Vane explicitly accepts God's word as text when he recites it at the end of the book: 'All the days of my appointed time will I wait till my change come' (Chapter XLVII; Job 14:14). The word, however, is not easily fixed, and, Lilith (both the book and the character) slips away from masculine authority. MacDonald cannot fail to subvert his own desire. Perhaps this very tension between the masculine drive to certainty and regulation and the feminine acceptance of openness and mystery is what bewilders many of the book's readers. *Lilith* is between two worlds, one patriarchal and resistant to change, the other subversive and mercurial; one text-based and authoritarian, the other previous-to-text and dynamic. *Lilith* is distinctly *fin de siècle*; it signals the end of the world and heralds the coming of another yet powerless to be born.

MacDonald worked for five years–1890-95–writing this book; it gave him more difficulty than any of his other books. He suffered from depression during these years caused by, among other things the death of his dearly beloved eldest child Lilia Scott MacDonald, a strained relationship with the eldest son Greville, and doubts as to his ability to write the 'one *great* poem' he had in his mind (*George MacDonald and his Wife* 518). In September 1894, he wrote his son Greville to say that *Lilith* 'is not to be a success in the money way', and that he doubts 'if I shall ever write another book'. He speaks of mental and spiritual trials (*Reminiscences* 321). He expresses the same doubts to his friend Lady Mount Temple when he writes to her in December of the same year, and he predicts that she 'will not quite like' the book he is writing (MS. 9745, National Library of Scotland). In *Lilith*, MacDonald tries to reassert the authority of masculine control which, over thirty years earlier, he had undermined in *Phantastes*. Put another way, he tries to tame a figure who has haunted his imagination since at least 1864. In that year, MacDonald included the story 'The Cruel Painter' in his novel *Adela Cathcart*, and one of the story's three principle characters is Lilith. She also appears, displaced into the figure of a horse, in *Wilfrid Cumbermede* (1872), and she is present throughout MacDonald's work in various guises. In *Lilith*, he tries to return this freeborn spirit to the father; he tries to domesticate her. Lilith and her erotic energy come under censure as a desire for power; her history receives a masculine reading from Adam. However, she does not accept patriarchal authority easily, and the book manages to break free of masculine control. In it sexuality defers eschatology.

In short, *Lilith* is a troubling book. This was apparent from the beginning; before it appeared MacDonald gave it to his wife to read, and she 'found the narrative often distressing, its hidden meaning too obscure, and she feared lest it should be taken as evidence of weakening power, rather than the reverse' (*Reminiscences* 320). She called it 'a terrible book', and she 'could not be happy over its publication' (321). Although Greville deeply admired the book and referred to it as 'the Revelation of St. George the Divine' (321), he admitted that it 'attracted little notice' and that even MacDonald's 'multitude of followers and disciples . . . hardly cared or dared to listen to his messengers, however arresting, when they appeared in unexpected habiliments' (*George MacDonald and His Wife* 547). Indeed, the reviews were largely unfavourable. *The Pall Mall Gazette* believed 'that Mr. George MacDonald's new romance will not only puzzle but disappoint his admirers'. The reviewer then admits to his failure 'to find *Lilith* either amusing or instructive – anything, indeed, but a wild phantasmagoria of nonsense' (9). Several reviewers suggest that MacDonald's age has affected his creative powers. The writer in the New York *Critic* drily comments that he is disinclined 'to write precisely what we think'. The book, he continues, raises a 'sadly familiar query', and he 'looks up a biographical date or two, and answers the questions affirmatively: *Fuit Ilium*' (58). The *Athenaeum* laments 'to find the sweet bells jangled, and the imagination once lofty and penetrating, declined to the incoherent and grotesque' (639).

Even MacDonald's friend William Robertson-Nicoll feels constrained to criticise. As Claudius Clear, he writes in the *British Weekly*:

> I leave to the last a book which on every account I should have been delighted to praise, Dr. George MacDonald's *Lilith*, published by Messrs. Chatto and Windus . . . *Lilith* is a romance somewhat in the style of *Phantastes*, and it contains much that is beautiful and noble. But it will never have the success of *Phantastes*, and it does not deserve it. It is obscure, here and there it is almost unpleasant, and the general impression is not satisfying or restful. Still, it will quicken thought and faith. (395)

Robertson-Nicoll is perhaps more right than he knows: the average reader desires satisfaction and rest from books; that is, he likes his reading to confirm what he already knows and to quiet his mind. Yet this is hardly true of all readers, since the very impetus to read suggests a dissatisfaction with the present from which the book removes the reader. In short, a contradictory impulse motivates us to read: we look for certainty and we look for wonder.

In *Lilith* certainty and wonder, or what I call here the masculine drive for control and the feminine openness to change, are disfigured. Vane, as we might expect, constantly seeks for certainty; instead he finds riddles. Mr Raven/Adam speaks with authority and moral certainty; yet he often casts his words in paradox and riddle. Vane, as a latter-day Adam finding his first wife Lilith, seeks to possess her and when this proves impossible, he castigates her as power-hungry. Lilith is clearly a threat to children and young men, yet she is undoubtedly beautiful and liberating. The ideal is a virginal femininity which includes the maternal, and is represented by Eve, Mara and Lona; yet the book makes clear that virginity is aridity. The erotic is a vampirish lust for power; yet without sex there is no progression. Nothing in the book is stable, although stability is what everyone seeks. The Little Ones fear growth and yet they must grow if they are to become spiritually strong; Mara, Adam, Eve, and Lilith are capable of metamorphosis, yet each in his or her own way desires an end to change; Vane wishes to know the meaning of things and is constantly bewildered; and the distinction between dream and reality becomes so blurred that at the ending of the book (which is not an end) we do not know whether Vane is dreaming or whether he is, in actuality, back in his own home.

The confusion between dream and reality at the end of the book leads Wolff to conclude that the last six chapters are 'bad art' (369). He argues that the story 'ought to end' after Vane takes bread and wine with Adam, Eve, and Mara in Chapter 42 (365). The only reason for MacDonald continuing the story, he says, is to extricate himself from the dilemma of having a dead narrator. But MacDonald faced the same problem at the end of *Phantastes*, and he must surely have been aware of what he was doing. Anodos and Vane pass out of their visionary worlds as easily as they enter them. To have them wake as from a dream like the narrator of *Pilgrim's Progress* would create too great a separation between the real and the ideal. MacDonald believed that the vision was co-existent with the concrete; our life is no dream, but it can become one at any moment.

Wolff further remarks that 'we have in fact already reached the end of Vane's education' (365), but Vane is a slow learner. Unlike Anodos, Vane does not lose his Shadow self. In his dreams he performs magnificent deeds of atonement, but he rises suddenly in the darkness. Once again, as he had earlier, Vane flees the chamber of death. He meets Adam who comforts him, but tells him that trials lie ahead. Instead of accepting his dream, Vane now tries to escape it by casting himself down a hole. Leaving the dream that had been given to him, Vane 'left the holy sleep itself behind' (Chapter XLIII, 406), and he finds himself back in his own garret. Desperately he tries to return to the world. He grieves not for his error, but because he has lost Lona: 'My heart died within me. I had lost Lona!' (Chapter XLIII, 407). He now wonders whether she may not simply be a figment of his imagination, and if she is he will tell God, 'Even thou canst not help me,' (Chapter XLIII, 407). He asks not for goodness or mercy, but for Lona.

On the fourth night he wakes in Adam's cemetery, but the question is whether this is just another dream of his own making. Mac-Donald's intention is clear in a cancelled passage in the second of the eight pre-publication versions of *Lilith* in the British Library. In this passage Vane says that after he awoke in his house he struggles vainly 'like Sterne's starling' to go back, and 'At length . . . I did have a dream concerning the house of the dead and something else, with which I shall end my narrative. My reader may leave my book here if he have read this far, for what follows is only a dream' (247). Vane's wish is to find Lona and he dreams; his wish is fulfilled and

Lona appears in her beauty. It is, we read in the published version, 'a glorious resurrection-morning' (Chapter XLV, 414). Wolff asks why this is not the final resurrection day (367), but MacDonald writes in the first manuscript version, 'All mornings are resurrections.' Each day people are up and away, yet others such as Lilith herself or Lord and Lady Cokayne have a longer period of suffering to endure. Everyone will be saved, but some sooner than others.

Of course, MacDonald cancelled the passage which suggested readers may stop reading before the end of the book because it offered both certainty of meaning – 'what follows is only a dream' – and the appearance of inessential material. Why read on if what follows is not necessary? By removing the passage, MacDonald created uncertainty at the end of the book. The uncertainty as to what is and what is not a dream conforms to the book's drive beyond closure. *Lilith*, as the title of the final chapter indicates, has an 'endless ending.' The final things are put aside as Vane returns, at least apparently, home. Lona has entered heaven, but her mother Lilith has yet to rise from her couch of death and Vane too waits for his time. *Consummation*, whether devoutly to be wished for or not, has yet to take place. Ripeness is all.

Vane's experience in the final pages of this book is somewhat similar to Anodos' experience of death in *Phantastes*, except that here the echoes of Dante's *Paradiso* inform us that Vane's quest is for the heavenly city and that he can only accomplish this with the assistance of a woman. His journey heavenward is in the company of the children and Lona, who is now associated with Eve, whom Vane refers to throughout the book as the mother: 'It was dark . . . but I saw her (Lona): *she* was not dark! Her eyes shone with the radiance of the Mother's, and the same light issued from her face – nor from her face only, for her death-dress, filled with the light of her body now tenfold awake in the power of its resurrection, was white as snow and glistening. She fell asleep a girl; she awoke a woman, ripe with the loveliness of the life essential. I folded her in my arms, and knew that I lived indeed' (Chapter XLIV, 407). Lona has replaced Eve, the mother, who had served as something of a Beatrice for Vane.

When he first meets Eve in the cottage, her eyes impress him: 'The life of her face and her whole person was gathered and concentrated in her eyes, where it became light' (Chapter VI, 209). These are the 'shining eyes' of Beatrice which Dante first sees in Canto 31 of the *Purgatorio* and which fill his soul 'with wonderment and glad' and give it 'that food which, satisfying of itself, causes thirst of itself' (Dante 381). Like Beatrice, Eve is heavenly beauty and holy communion. She gives Vane 'the perfect meal' of bread and wine. Later, inside the cemetery, Eve's whole face flashes 'with a loveliness like that of Beatrice in the white rose of the redeemed. Life itself, life eternal, immortal, streamed from it, an unbroken lightning. Even her hands shone with a white radiance, gleaming like a moonstone. Her beauty was overpowering' (*Lilith*, Chapter VII, 203). This change in Eve parallels the change in Beatrice from the *Purgatorio* to the *Paradiso* where she appears 'as a sudden flash of lightning which so shattereth the visual spirits as to rob the eyes of the power to realize e'en strongest objects'; she is a 'living light' (Dante, 586). MacDonald's allusions to Dante–Mara too has her parallel in Mathilda who prepares Dante for the vision of Beatrice in the *Paradiso*–show how deeply he wished to idealize woman, to desexualize her. All three ideal women–Eve, Mara, and Lona–are virginal mothers who willingly submit to male authority. Of the three, Lona is the palest, a weak figure who passively follows where man leads. Vane describes her as a 'tender grandmother', and through her he prepares to fulfil, as William Raeper notes, Anodos' wish to marry his grandmother (368). Lona is mother, grandmother, sister, and loved one; she is innocence, Beulah, without identity, unlike her mother who knows who she is and what she wants.

Lilith is the woman who refuses to be written. Unlike her daughter Lona, Lilith lives in the city and has economic and political power. She also has sexual power. She is the book's figure of evil, ostensibly because she desires to perpetuate her own life at the expense of others. Yet MacDonald's sympathy, even admiration, for her is apparent in the firmness of her resolve, her magnificent defiance of anyone who would deny her identity, equality, and liberty. She is, as Vane readily admits, both attractive and repulsive. In terms of the book's plot the reader has no doubt but that she is a terrible mother, the fatal woman, the vampire who offers nothing less than death-in-life. She is the Whore of Babylon (in this case Bulika); she is chaos since she has gathered up the waters of the land; she is selfishness since she wants all things for herself. Her source in Sumerian and Jewish mythology are well documented (e.g. McGillis 1979; Koltuv), but I take her genealogy here from Frye: 'The Great Whore of the Bible is the Medusa who turns men to stone, the *femme fatale* of the romantic poets whose kiss is death, whose love is annihilation' (140). She blocks our view of the unfallen world and initiates us into generation, the experience of sexuality. From the book's point of view, from the male point of view, she is responsible for man's fall from grace. Leaving Adam, Lilith inaugurated the cycle of pain and suffering associated with childbirth, work, tyranny, and death.

Yet, Lilith herself, so the patriarch Adam states, is redeemed through childbirth–'for even Lilith will be saved by her childbearing' (Chapter XXIX, 323). This is, however, a male fantasy: the female as mother must be safe and unthreatening. But Lilith the sexual being–never mind motherhood–is necessary to Vane's passage into maturity; indeed, she is in part created by his own desire. As the words of her own poem indicate, she works her will in the brain of the man who desires:

'But if I found a man that could believe
   In what he saw not, felt not, and yet knew,
From him I should take substance, and receive
   Firmness and form relate to touch and view;
Then should I clothe me in the likeness true
   Of that idea where his soul did cleave!' (Chapter XXIX, 319)

Lilith appeals to man's weakness by assuming the firmness and form he most eagerly imagines, but she remains all the while in control. She clothes herself; she takes substance 'from him'. She needs him on her side. Without him she becomes a demon, a Circe, a lone woman who must confirm or suffer for her independence. Vane has first-hand evidence of this when he finds himself inside Lilith's brain, seeing the events of the story from her perspective. He follows her into the black hall of her palace:

The instant the princess entered, I heard a buzzing sound as of many low voices, and, one portion after another, the assembly began to be shiftingly illuminated, as by a ray that went travelling from spot to spot. Group after group would shine out for a space, then sink back into the general vagueness, while another part of the vast company would grow momently bright.

Some of the actions going on when thus illuminated, were not unknown to me; I had been in them, or had looked on them, and so had the princess: present with every one of them I now saw her. The skull-headed dancers footed the grass in the forest-hall: there was the princess looking in at the door! The fight went on in the Evil Wood: there was the princess urging it! Yet I was close behind her all the time, she standing motionless, her head sunk in her bosom. The confused murmur continued, the confused commotion of colours and shapes; and still the ray went shifting and showing. It settled at last on the hollow in the heath, and there was the princess, walking up and down, and trying in vain to wrap the vapour around her! Then first I was startled at what I saw: the old librarian walked up to her, and stood for a moment regarding her; she fell; her limbs forsook her and fled; her body vanished. (Chapter XXVII, 312)

Vane reviews the scenes he had experienced earlier in his travels towards Bulika and learns that Lilith too had been present at the ruined castle with its frantic dancers and in the Evil Wood with its wild battle of skeletal armies. But why would she recall these incidents? And why enter the black hall now when she has just been wounded by a white leopard? Why tell Vane she wants him to get something for her scratches and then leave him? Does she not know he will follow her? I do not know the answers to these questions, but we might surmise that Lilith's conscience is at work, that she is not as vile a body as the men in the book would have us believe. In any case, Vane also sees Mr Raven/Adam disembody Lilith. He effects a dispersion of the lady. Adam's power over Lilith is the power to control her body, to make it disappear. He de-sexes her with a vengeance. At the end too, I might add, he cuts her hand off with a sword drawn from a scabbard of vellum. The vellum connects with the manuscript book with the vellum cover from which Adam reads the poem that controls Lilith. Sword and manuscript emasculate Lilith. In fact, the pressure on her is so great that by the end Lilith pleads with Adam to cut off her hand.

In *Lilith*, little pleasure derives from the text; the imagination is castrated. Vane returns home to wait until he is called to his final journey home. No sisters greet him, although in the first manuscript version Vane returns to a sister and her friend. But this first version did not include Lona. Lona remains Vane's longed-for lover, but her virginal and tepid nature are uninspiring; Vane describes her love for him as the 'devotion of a divine animal' (Chapter XXIV, 347). In contrast, Lilith remains strongly fascinating. The scene in which she confronts Mara is profoundly moving. Lilith asserts her independence: 'I will be myself and not another.' She defies God to 'unmake me from a free woman' (Chapter XXXIX, 371). The cards are, of course, stacked against her; she must capitulate. MacDonald attempts fairness by adding that the great Shadow who has haunted the book and who is the Cabbalah's Sammael (Samoil as MacDonald has it in Chapter XIX, 284), will 'lie down and sleep also' (Chapter 388). This is the story as told by the angels. We might say, however, that MacDonald was the Devil's party without knowing it. *Lilith* survives as a great book not because of its emasculating strictures against changing sex roles, social dislocation and individual identity, not because of its eschatological vision, but because of the subversive power of its mysterious images. The book resists systematisation; it delights in paradox, in synecdoche, in riddle, in metaphor, in pleonasm, in oxymoron, in change.

Finally, both *Phantastes* and *Lilith* express things that are 'inexpressibly different from any possible events of this economy' (*Lilith* Chapter IX, 227). The word 'economy' has to do with managing the house, with managing state finances and resources, and with the divine government of the world. 'This economy' refers to the patriarchal world with its 'records of lands and moneys' (*Phantastes* Chapter I, 16), but the world MacDonald creates in his two fantasies presents a different economy, one presided over by the feminine spirit of love, mystery, and generosity. Managing the household is managing the home, and home, as Mr Raven says in *Lilith*, 'is ever so far away in the palm of your hand' (Chapter IX, 225). Homes in the economy Vane experiences are presided over by females: Eve and her cottage, Mara and her cottage, Lona and her bucolic forest of little people. Hospitality and care are what greet the visitor to these homes. To the female who presides over the home, names are unimportant; when Vane discovers that in Mara's cottage his name 'was gone from me', she replies, 'Never mind . . . it is not wanted. Your real name, indeed, is written on your forehead' (Chapter XV, 253; cf Revelation 2:17). And when the name becomes clear, there will be no need to proclaim it because the person 'is the name' (*Unspoken Sermons*, First Series 108). Mr Raven/Adam asks: 'Why know the name of a thing when the thing itself you do not know' (Chapter V, 207). The thing itself, not its outward appearance or its name, is what matters. Lilith is woman, leech, moon, serpent, Hecate, bat, leopard, tree, and wolf; the old librarian is sexton, raven, Adam, an angel of the resurrection, and the new Adam. Their appearance or their name are ways of containing what cannot be contained. In the new economy there will be no naming and homes will not confine.

References

Athenaeum, Review of *Phantastes*, November 6, (1858), 580.
———, Review of *Lilith*, November 9, (1895), 639.
British Quarterly Review, Review of *Phantastes*, 29 (1859), 296-297.
Frances Browne, *Granny's Wonderful Chair* (London: Dent, 1963 (1856)).
Hélène Cixous, 'The Laugh of the Medusa', Elaine Marks and Isabelle de Courtivron, eds., *New French Feminisms* (New York: Schocken, 1981), 245-64.
The Critic, Review of *Lilith*, 25 (1896), 58.
Dante, *The Divine Comedy*, Carlyle-Okey-Wickstead translation (New York: Random House, 1950).
John Docherty, 'A Note on the Structure and Conclusion of *Phantastes*, *North Wind: Journal of the George MacDonald Society*, 7 (1988), 25-30.
Northrop Frye, *Fearful Symmetry* (Boston: Beacon Press, 1967 (1948)).

The Globe, Review of *Phantastes*, December 30, 1858.

E.T.A. Hoffmann, *Selected Writings*, ed. and trans. by Leonard J. Kent and Elizabeth C. Knight, Volume 1 (University of Chicago Press, 1969).

Barbara Black Koltuv, *The Book of Lilith* (York Beach, Maine: Nicolas-Hays, 1986).

The Leader, Review of Phantastes, November 13, (1858), 1222.

George MacDonald, *Adela Cathcart* (London: Hurst and Blackett, 1864).

————, *A Dish of Orts* (London: Sampson, Low, Marston, 1895).

————, *Letters*, MS. 9745 Letters and Poems, 1862-1900, National Library of Scotland.

————, *Lilith* MSS, British Library: BM Add. Mss. 46187 *Lilith.*

————, *The Marquis of Lossie* (London: Kegan, Paul, Trench, 1887 (1877)).

————, *Phantastes and Lilith* (Grand Rapids, MI: Eerdmans, 1968).

————, *Unspoken Sermons* (First Series. London: Alexander Strahan, 1867).

————, *Unspoken Sermons* (Third Series. London: Longmans, Green, 1889).

————, *Wilfrid Cumbermede* (New York: George Routledge, n.d. (1872)).

MacDonald, Greville, *George MacDonald and His Wife* (London: Allen and Unwin, 1924).

————, *Reminiscences of a Specialist* (London: Allen and Unwin, 1932).

Louis MacNeice, *Varieties of Parable* (London: Cambridge University Press, 1965).

Colin Manlove, *The Impulse of Fantasy Literature* (Kent, Ohio: Kent State University Press, 1983).

————, *Modern Fantasy*. (Cambridge University Press, 1975).

McGillis, Roderick. 'The Community of the Centre: Structure and Theme in *Phantastes*', in *For the Childlike: George MacDonald's Work Children* ed. Roderick McGillis (forthcoming).

————, 'George MacDonald and the Lilith Legend in the Nineteenth Century', *Mythlore*, 19 (1979), 3-11.

Michael Mendelson, 'George MacDonald's *Lilith* and the Conventions of Ascent', *Studies in Scottish Literature*, 20 (1985), 197-218.

Novalis, The Disciples at Sais and other Fragments, translated by F.V.M.T. and U.C.B. (London: Methuen, 1903).

————, *Heinrich von Ofterdingen*, Trans. by Palmer Hilty (New York: Frederick Ungar, 1964).

Pall Mall Gazette, Review of *Lilith*, October 18 (1895), 9.

Stephen Prickett, *Victorian Fantasy*, (Bloomington, IN: Indiana University Press, 1979).

William Raeper, *George MacDonald* Tring: Lion Publishing, 1987.

William Robertson-Nicoll (Cladius Clear), 'Dr. Parker's New Novel–and Others', *British Weekly*, October 10 (1895), 395.

Spectator, Review of *Phantastes*, December 4 (1858), 1286.

Kathy Triggs, 'Worlds Apart: the Importance of Double Vision for Macdonald Criticism', *Seven: An Anglo-American Literary Review*, 5 (1984), 26-33.

Keith Wilson, 'The Quest for 'The Truth': A Reading of George Mac-Donald's *Phantastes*', *Etudes Anglaises*, 34 (1981), 140-52.

Robert Lee Wolff, *The Golden Key: A Study of the Fiction of George Mac-Donald* (New Haven: Yale University Press, 1961).

4

MacDonald and Jung

EDMUND CUSICK

for Josephine

> We have often found that a poet who has gone out of fashion is
> suddenly rediscovered. This happens when our conscious devel-
> opment has reached a higher level from which the poet can tell
> us something new. It was always present in his work but was
> hidden in a symbol. C. G. Jung

In this essay I will discuss the way in which the theories and insights
of Carl Gustav Jung can aid the understanding of George MacDonald's fiction. Parts one and two are a survey of relevant critical work
on MacDonald, and a study of Jung's own account of literature.
Through these studies I develop a schema for understanding Mac-
Donald's work in terms of the unconscious.

Parts three and four put this theoretical understanding into practical effect. I first deal with the most important unconscious archetype
in MacDonald's work, the anima, studying both the explicitly fantastic works and the realistic novels. I then undertake a detailed study
of the way that unconscious content appears in a single passage of
MacDonald's fantasy.

In my conclusion I refer to the more general implications of
approaching the unconscious through symbolic art.

References to Jung's work are to the standard edition of the *Collected Works* in 20 volumes, edited by William McGuire and translated by R. F. C. Hull, and to *Man and his Symbols* edited by Jung and
Marie-Louise Von Franz.

1. Fantasy and the Unconscious

Modern critics have come increasingly to recognise the importance of
the unconscious psyche to fantasy writing. To understand and to
interpret material which derives from the unconscious it is necessary
to refer to its proper discipline, namely that of psychology. Psychology, in its various schools, has explored the unconscious through the
analysis of the dreams and fantasies of patients.

As Rosemary Jackson writes in *Fantasy: The Literature of Subversion*
(1981): 'Fantasy . . . deals so blatantly and repeatedly with unconscious material that it seems rather absurd to try to understand its significance without some reference to psychoanalysis and psychoana-

lytic readings of texts. (40). The centrality of the unconscious in MacDonald's fantasy in particular is now also acknowledged. The subject matter of works such as *Lilith* is so far removed from waking experience that few twentieth-century critics would venture to account for it in terms of conscious invention. It has been recognised that dream, the product of the unconscious, is crucially important to MacDonald's fantasy. In his introduction to *The Visionary Novels of George MacDonald* W.H. Auden Writes: 'But his greatest gift is what one might call his dream realism, his exact and profound knowledge of dream causality, dream logic, dream change, dream morality: when one reads him, the illusion of participating in a real dream is perfect . . . '. Again and again MacDonald's work itself makes reference to dream to explain its meaning. The marvellous journey of 'The Golden Key' begins with a boy dreaming of the golden key. *Phantastes* is prefaced by Novalis' manifesto for a new kind of art which would be like dream, and which *Phantastes* amply fulfils. *Lilith* becomes a series of dreams,and ends with the words: Our life is no dream, but it should and will perhaps become one.' In MacDonald's realistic novels such as *Wilfrid Cumbermede* (1882) and *Donald Grant* (1883) dreams, and series of dreams, are convincingly reproduced (and seriously considered) in a way that is unique in Victorian fiction. Further, we see these dreams shaping and developing the conscious lives of the characters. In such novels the reader is continually made aware of the two worlds which his character inhabit: the 'real' world of waking life, and the dream-world of the unconscious. To do justice to MacDonald's writing in all its depth, an understanding of the unconscious world which his characters enter would seem helpful, if not vital.

Recent critical work on MacDonald has to varying extents recognised this, employing either Freudian or Jungian terminology to refer to the unconscious. Wolff's *The Golden Key* (1961), whilst acknowledging no formal psychological structure (other than the help of 'a practicing analyst' is based on Freudian dream analysis. This involves a distinction between 'manifest content' and 'latent content' – a reduction of the individual form of the dream to general rules of psychic expression, and indeed of psychic content. It is in this 'latent dream content' (the dream's message as deciphered or 'unmasked' by the analyst) that the dream's significance lies, not in its individual expression. Thus, for example, Wolff unmasks the manifest content of the moss around cottage in 'The Golden Key' to reveal the latent content of pubic hair. The cottage is exposed as the female genitalia. Not surprisingly, the 'Golden Key' which Mossy grasps, and on which Wolff bases his study, turns out to be the penis. However unsatisfactory are Wolff's attempts to deal with the symbols of MacDonald's fantasy, he has forced the issue of the psychological origin of the fantasy into prominence. Subsequent critics have responded in different ways: Rosemary Jackson conducts a post-Freudian study of MacDonald's fantasy, finding in it a reversion to infantile fantasies and fears, including the destruction of the self. Other critics have turned to Jungian psychology.

I believe that Jungian models are far more suited to MacDonald's work. In Freudian psychology the unconscious is seen as the repository of conscious content that has been repressed, while in Jungian psychology the collective unconscious affords access to a spiritual realm which has never been conscious. The difference between the two psychological schools is, very crudely (though Wolff's work, in its distance from the complexities of clinical case studies seem to invite such crudeness), that one views the unconscious as biological, deterministic, and negative, while the other sees it as positive, spiritual and timeless. By 'negative' I mean that Freudian psychology is primarily concerned with unconscious manifestations in so far as they are pathological. The Jungian (who also proceeds from the starting-point of the neurosis) sees the unconscious as a source of energy, perception and creativity, that may usefully be sought by any individual, not just the neurotic or schizophrenic.

The difference between the two approaches may be illustrated by two quotations from Jung:

> The view that dreams are merely the imaginary fulfilments of repressed wishes is hopelessly out of date. There are, it is true, dreams which manifestly represent wishes or fears, but what about all the other things? Dreams may contain ineluctable truths, philosophical pronouncements, illusions, wild fantasies, memories, plans, anticipations, irrational experiences, even telepathic visions, and heaven knows what besides. (16:137)

> Freud takes the neurosis as a substitute for a direct means of gratification. He therefore regards it as something inappropriate – a mistake, a dodge, an excuse, a voluntary blinding. To him it is essentially a shortcoming that should never have been. Since a neurosis, to all appearances, is nothing but a disturbance that is all the more irritating because few people will say a good word for it. And a work of art is brought into questionable proximity with the neurosis when it is taken as something which can be analysed in terms of the poet's repressions. In a

sense it finds itself in good company for religion and philosophy are regarded in the same light by Freudian Psychology. (15: 156)

A choice is demanded betweeen the two psychological approaches. One can either work forward from a symbol, seeking to discover what meaning it may hold as an encapsulation of some greater truth; or one can work backward from it, reducing it to its sources in the anterior psychic condition of the author. The question is posed of whether the only significance of art is as a clue to the psycho- pathology of the author.

One's approach to unconscious material in literature is in turn dependent on whether one accepts the Freudian or the Jungian definition of the unconscious. If the art of unconscious is the art of the artist's repressions, then the greatest value that can be gained from it is to identify the personal content that lies at its source. If, however, 'unconscious' art arises from the collective unconscious, then it taps the same collective sources as myth and religion, and demands the same sort of consideration that is given to religious experience. Our criticism of visionary art will depend very largely on our attitude to visions. It is an issue which one would expect to encounter in a study of Blake or Yeats, but which is no less pertinent to our reading of MacDonald. *Lilith* can be taken as the revelation of an unconscious order which sounds echoes in every psyche, or as merely the product of MacDonald's personal neuroses.

I believe that the Jungian approach will prove more helpful in assessing the unconscious dimension than would Freud's. Whereas Freudian approaches seek to discover 'latent content' within the work, Jung argues that 'the work of art exists in its own right and cannot be got rid of by changing it into a personal complex' (15:147). Thus Jung's analysis allows us to treat the subject matter of symbolic art seriously, as a record of psychic experiences that are beyond reduction.

Furthermore, there are some remarkable correspondences which make MacDonald's fantasy and Jung's psychological theory compatible. I will consider these in more detail in the following section. One can note, however, that both systems are Platonic, in that they postulate a transcendant realm (the spiritual world or the collective unconscious) which can manifest itself in, and affect, the individual psyche.

Several of MacDonald's critics have referred to Jung's theories of the unconscious. In the Introduction to his *Modern Fantasy* (1975) Colin Manlove employs the Jungian concept of archetypes to explain the origin of the female figures in fantasy: 'It is true that in fantasy the supernatural may in part belong to our reality by being a disguised physical, moral or mental phenomenon, but it is never more than partly these things . . . George MacDonald's North Wind, Mara, and the grandmother in the 'Curdie' books are mother surrogates or even versions of the Jungian *anima.*' (6) Manlove raises the issue of the origin of MacDonald's fantasy figures in the collective unconscious only to drop it again in the space of a phrase. Yet if this is their origin, it will have profound consequences for the criticism of MacDonald's work.

In *George MacDonald* (1972) Richard Reis offers a brief analysis of MacDonald's work in loosely Jungian terms, while deliberately distancing himself from Jungian theory and clinical practice. Reis sees an archetypal dimension to many of MacDonald's characters and identifies some of them as figures originating in the collective unconscious: 'George MacDonald's symbolic fantasies are, then, full of archetypal characters, all of which may be identified with those which Jung has catalogued by collating the dreams and fantasies of his patients.' (116). In particular, Reis identifies 'the shadow' who appears in both *Phantastes* and *Lilith* with the shadow figure which Jung observed in his studies of dreams. Marie-Louise Von Franz outlines the nature of the shadow in *Man and His Symbols* Part Three, 'The Process of Individuation' (171-85). The shadow is the personification of all those negative traits belonging to the ego–cruelty, cowardice, selfishness and so on–which we deliberately exclude from consciousness because we would rather not be aware of them. In dreams, however, the unconscious compensates for our conscious attitude by the generation of the shadow figure. The shadow is thus part of ourselves. In dreams the shadow can take the form of a person whom we know (and dislike intensely) or appear as a strange unknown opponent.

The shadow in *Phantastes* and *Lilith* does resemble the shadow in both nature and behaviour and, as Reis comments, the coincidence in naming seems remarkable. But while MacDonald's fantasy work reveals the unconscious form naked and undisguised, the influence of the underlying archetype is also cast over the apparently 'real' conscious world of his realistic novels.

The manifestations of the unconscious in MacDonald's work are not restricted to his fantasy, though they may be most obvious there. In the other world that MacDonald names Faerie or the Seventh Dimension, the shadow appears as an unearthly, supernatural figure. The shadow also appears in the 'realistic' fiction, however, in the guise of 'real' characters. Such figures nonetheless are a little too intense to be ordinarily credible, but we believe in them because, as Reis notes, they strike some inner chord of recognition that has nothing to do with our waking experience.

A case in point occurs in one of MacDonald's most closely autobiographical novels, *Alec Forbes of Howglen* (1865). The aristocratic villain Patrick Beauchamp who appears at each crisis to thwart Alec's purpose is, curiously, described in the same terms that were applied to George MacDonald when he (like Alec) was at Aberdeen University. He is marked out by his adoption of the ostentatious finery that MacDonald was noted for at University. He and his mother are obsessed with their Highland ancestry, as was MacDonald. Beauchamp wins over the affections of Alec's lovely cousin Kate, and corrupts her by reading Byron to her. MacDonald (as William Raeper's biography, *George MacDonald* indicates (53-54)) was strongly attached to his own cousin, Helen MacKay, while at university. Alec and Beauchamp battle for some time (Beauchamp almost drowns Alec) but when Beauchamp is vanquished Alec himself undergoes a rapid moral decline. Beauchamp appears to be a shadow cast by the author's own unconscious self, a figure somewhere between that of Hogg's Gilmartin in *Confessions of a Justified Sinner* and the shadow in *Phantastes*.

The second figure from the unconscious which Reis, like Manlove, identifies in the fantasy is the anima. The archetype of the anima is of such crucial importance to MacDonald's fantasy that I wish to study it in depth in part three.

To sum up, Reis has, if only tenatively, taken the critical step of regarding the fantasy work in the same light as one would regard a dream. This dream-like fantasy is MacDonald's natural element, he suggests. MacDonald's imagination was: 'at home in fantasy and lost or incongruous or banal in the world of the novel, the rational re-creation of waking life.'

MacDonald's natural gift is, then, his access to the unconscious, a gift which could only, or only fully, be expressed in fantasy writing. Yet the unconscious function may operate in apparently realistic fiction also, and when figures from fantasy appear in his novels, conscious reality appears to be subverted by inner, psychic, order. C. S. Lewis observed in his introduction to *George MacDonald: An Anthology* (1946) that MacDonald's realistic novels depart from realism to move towards fantasy or to preaching, and comments that they are at their best when they do so. Rosemary Jackson provides a rationale for this. The conscious or realistic mode may be unable to prevent

unconscious material from 'usurping' the narrative: 'The centre of the
fantastic text tries to break with repression, yet it is inevitably constrained by its surrounding frame. Such contradictions emerge in
graphic form in the many Gothic and fantastic episodes which break
into nineteenth century novels . . . ' Building on Lewis and Reis, it
is possible to chart the appearance of fantastic elements in MacDonald's realistic novels.

The way in which fantasy enters the realistic novel is through fantastic images. In *Victorian Fantasy* (1979) Stephen Prickett discusses
the importance of visual images to fantasy literature. He writes of
Frankenstein: 'What we are apparently faced with here is a very peculiar paradox: a literary medium that doesn't tell us a story, so much as
offer verbal *pictures.* The Gothic did not work by sequential arguments . . . but by flashes that haunt the waking mind like the images
of dreams.' (10-11). The Fantastic retained this propensity to form
images as it developed from the Gothic, and MacDonald's fantasy,
too, works by a series of images. In Fantastic works these images
appear in vivid and living form: a panther leaping through a mirror,
skeletons dancing by night, a woman whose eyes hold the starry heav-
ens within their depths. When fantasy enters the novels, it does so by
means of images. These are either introduced, at the level of suggestion, by means of similes and metaphor, or through dreams, or
through interpolated stories of the supernatural. A case in point
comes in *Malcolm* (1875) when Malcolm meets the woman he
believes to be his mother: '. . . a lady tall and slender, with a well-
poised easy carriage, and a motion that suggested the lithe grace of a
leopard. She greeted him with a bend of the head and a smile, which,
even in the twilight and her own shadow, showed a gleam of ivory.'
(2:189).

To a reader familiar with *Lilith* the allusion to Mrs Stewart as a
leopard, followed by the image of teeth gleaming from shadow, cannot fail to recall Lilith herself. Elsewhere, Mrs Stewart is described as
a 'vampire demon', (3:299) a unique phrase in MacDonald's realistic
fiction, but one that is brought to fulfilment in Lilith, who is both
vampire and demon. This is only one instance, but there are more
than twenty other examples of the content of *Lilith* turning up in
novels, some written almost thirty years before *Lilith* itself. This is the
main evidence for the existence of an unconscious function within
the novels: the images of the novels often seem to have an 'inner' or
unconscious reference that becomes apparent when they are related
either to other images in the novels, or to the fantasy. It is as though
underlying MacDonald's exterior creative purpose of writing Chris-

tian novels was another creative purpose which finds its natural language of expression in images. This purpose twines its course restlessly beneath the surface of the realistic novels, only infrequently finding unfettered expression in explicitly fantastic works, often in the guise of fairy tales or children's fiction.

The division between these two functions in MacDonald's writing is nowhere more starkly illustrated than in the reactions of two modern critics to his fantasy. In his introduction to *George MacDonald, an Anthology*, C. S. Lewis argues that the central element in MacDonald's thought is the father-son relationship, which binds together MacDonald's own life experience and his Christian faith. On the other hand, David Holbrook, in his Introduction to the Everyman edition of *Phantastes*, argues that the most important element of the fantasy is the relationship of the protagonist with the mother and interprets *Phantastes* in particular as a series of encounters with mother figures. Whereas Lewis cites MacDonald as a case that disproves Freudian dogma, Holbrook finds the Oedipus complex alive and well in *Phantastes*: the father is present only in threatening form. To some extent both arguments hold some truth. The idea of a dual text within the works would explain this contradiction. The conscious world of the novels is dictated by MacDonald's conscious, Christian beliefs. It proceeds through reasoned argument, appealing to the conscious mind of the reader. In this world the fatherhood of God is paramount. The conscious text, however, is interrupted by an unconscious one, which appears through images and metaphors, and which bears little allegiance to the purposes of the conscious text. It is, on the contrary, dominated by various feminine complexes, of which the mother complex is one. This is in keeping with Jung's assertion that the unconscious of a man is feminine. Thus Lewis, in his anthology, selects a series of conscious 'preachments' (as he calls them) from the sermons and the novels. Holbrook illustrates his argument with the feminine images of *Phantastes*.

So far, I have studied the role of the unconscious in MacDonald's work from a literary critical perspective. In the next section I will turn to Jung's own writings for a psychological view on the subject.

2. Jung and Visionary Art

Jung's account of literature is chiefly set out in two essays: 'On the Relation of Poetry to Analytical Psychology' (1922) and 'Psychology and Literature' (1930, revised 1950).

Jung divides literature into two categories. The first of these he terms 'psychological'. This accounts for almost all literature, both

popular and literary. 'The psychological mode' he writes, 'works with
materials drawn from man's conscious life' (15:139). It thus includes
comedy and tragedy, most poetry and novels dealing with love, the
family, crime and society.

The other class of literature is the 'visionary', represented by only a
handful of literary works, yet amongst them are some of outstanding
genius, notably Dante's *Inferno*, Blake's poetry and the second part of
Goethe's *Faust*. These works are generated by the emergence of
material from the collective unconscious. Jung carefully distinguishes
such collective unconscious content from repressed personal content,
upon which Freud's work is based. The visionary work has its source:

> . . . in a sphere of unconscious mythology whose . . . images
> are the common heritage of mankind. I have called this sphere
> the *collective unconscious*, to distinguish it from the personal
> unconscious. The latter I regard as the sum total of all those psy-
> chic processes and contents which are capable of becoming con-
> scious and often do, but are then suppressed because of their
> incompatibility and kept subliminal. Art receives tributaries
> from this sphere too, but muddy ones; and their predominance,
> far from making a work of art a symbol, merely turns it into a
> symptom. We can leave this kind of art without injury and with-
> out regret to the purgative methods employed by Freud.
> (15:125)

Jung describes the characteristics of visionary art thus: 'We would
expect a strangeness of form and content, thoughts that can only be
apprehended intuitively, a language pregnant with meanings, and
images that are true symbols because they are the best possible
expressions for something unknown–bridges thrown out towards an
unseen shore.' (15:116)

This summary seems to be a remarkably apt description of works
such as *Lilith* and 'The Golden Key'. Jung's comments strike a
remarkable resonance with the quotations from Novalis that precede
Phantastes:

> The whole of nature must be marvellously mixed with the
> whole of the world of spirits: here the time of anarchy, lawless-
> ness, freedom, of nature in its natural state, the time before the
> world, comes in . . . the world of fairytale is the exact opposite
> of the world of reality, and for that very reason is as thoroughly
> like it as chaos is like completed creation. (*Phantastes*, epigraph)

Here everything is reversed. The experience that furnishes the
material for artistic expression is no longer familiar. It is some-

thing strange that derives its existence from the hinterland of man's mind, as if it had emerged from the abyss of prehuman ages . . . The primordial experiences rend from top to bottom the curtain upon which is painted the picture of an ordered world, and allow a glimpse into the unfathomable abyss . . . Is it a vision of other worlds, or of the darkness of the spirit, or of the primal beginnings of the human psyche? (15:141)

Similarly, Jung's remarks on visionary art seem to describe *Lilith*: 'We are reminded of nothing in everyday life, but rather of dreams, night-time fears, and the dark, uncanny recesses of the human mind' (15:143). He continues:

. . . it is a vision 'as seen in a glass, darkly'. It is nothing but a tremendous intuition striving for expression. It is like a whirl-wind that seizes everything within reach and assumes visible form as it swirls upward . . . The poet must have at his dispo-sal a huge store of material if he is to communicate even a fraction of what he has glimpsed, and must make use of diffi-cult and contradictory images in order to express the strange paradoxes of his vision. Dante decks out his experience in all the imagery of heaven, purgatory, and hell; Goethe brings in the Blocksberg and the Greek underworld; Wagner needs the whole corpus of Nordic myth . . . Blake presses into his serv-ice the phatamagoric world of India, the Old Testament, and the Apocalypse . . . Nothing is missing in the whole gamut that ranges from the ineffably sublime to the perversely grotesque.

There are clear connections here with *Phantastes*, which employs the varied material of the Victorian novel, nursery ryhme, fairy tale, med-ieval romance, and primal religion. Even more relevant to Jung's description is *Lilith*. Here MacDonald uses Adam and Eve from Christian mythology, the raven from both Christian and pagan myth, and Lilith herself from the Caballa. Lilith's identity is itself 'an intui-tion striving for expression' and in this struggle she assumes shapes from across the range of European fairy story and occult lore: as bat, leopardess, princess, vampire, cat, and snake. Yet at no one stage is this realisation complete. Vane's physical pursuit of Lilith is at the same time a psychic pursuit-a quest to apprehend her nature, to cap-ture her through these 'difficult and contradictory images'. The 'strange paradoxes' of MacDonald's vision are evident. Lilith is a demon, yet she is also Vane's female self. She is Vane's seducer, and the mother of his bride. She is Adam's wife, though Adam represents love and wisdom.

Jung's account of visionary art also cites 'the proliferation of monstrous, daemonic, grotesque and perverse figures'. (15:144). This too
finds a set of parallels in MacDonald's fantasy. There are the goblin's
animals of the 'princess' books–bizarre crosses between men and
beasts, the giants, goblins and ogres of *Phantastes*, the mutated animal
forms of *The Princess and Curdie* 'Wilder and more grotesque than
ever ramped in nightmare dreams' (194) and the horrifying creatures
who inhabit the burrow of *Lilith.* Jung continues: ' . . . what appears
in the vision is the imagery of the collective unconscious . . . In
dreams and mental disturbances psychic products come to the surface
which show all the traits of primitive levels of development . . . so
that we might easily take them for fragments of esoteric doctrines.
Mythological motifs frequently appear, but clothed in modern dress.'
(15:152)

MacDonald's fantasy does include episodes which could be taken
for fragments of esoteric doctrines. 'The Golden Key' depicts the
spiritual journey of two souls, to the eventual destination of the rainbow, where they join beautiful beings ascending to heaven. On the
journey, Mossy bathes in death and afterwards walks on the sea. In
Phantastes Cosmo works ritual magic, and in *Lilith* Vane meets God,
albeit breifly. All three books are concerned with death and intima-
tions of the afterlife, as a glance at their final pages will show.

In MacDonald's realistic work these esoteric fragments appear
intersected with the incidents of a modern novel. The magical cave,
with its dual significance of both womb and tomb, in which a character undergoes an initiation through 'death' and rebirth, occurs in several works, the most remarkable being in *Heather and Snow* (1893)
and *What's Mine's Mine* (1886). In the latter, the two Christian
heroes are carving a giant serpent twining across the roof of their
cave. When the heroine awakes there she believes herself to be in
hell and the two brothers to be spirits (2:305).

To sum up, Jung describes the appearance of the archetypes, normally encountered only in dream or vision, within a literary text in
what he terms visionary art. This confirms the strategy adopted by literary critics of regarding the text as one would regard a dream. The
idea that collective unconscious contents can appear, in a less sustained way, in the fabric of a supposedly 'realistic' novel also gains
some support from Jung. He refers to Rider Haggard's work, which
occupies a 'middle ground' between the realism of 'psychological' and
the marvels of 'visionary' art. Jung writes: 'In more restricted and suc-
cinct form, this primordial experience is the essential content of
Rider Haggard's *She* and *Ayesha*' (15:142).

The archetype which appears in *She* and its sequels is the anima, as Jung indicates elswhere (see 7:297-301), and 17:339). In the following section I will study in detail the appearance of the anima in Mac-Donald's work.

3. The Anima in MacDonald

The anima is the feminine element in the personality of a man. She is an 'autonomous psychic complex' – that is, she represents a part of the unconscious psyche which can exert its sway over consciousness. This is an archetype with its own unconscious personality, which must be faced and come to terms with when a man embarks on the individuation process – the process of sustained intercourse with the unconscious. As Jung writes, recognition of the personality of the anima is the first step to forming a relationship with the archetype and thus integrating the personality. 'The more personally she is taken the better', he comments (7:321-3220).

The character of the anima is to some extent collective, and thus can be recorded and described. In Part Three of *Man and His Symbols*, 'The Individuation Process' Marie-Louise Von Franz sketches the nature of the anima as she appears in both the collective symbols of myth and folktale, and the dreams of individual patients. The anima has two aspects, reflecting both the dangers and the rewards of engaging with the unconscious psyche. The negative, destructive aspect of the anima is portrayed in stories of women with an irresistible and fatal charm, such as the Greek Sirens or the German Lorelei.

In her more benign aspect she serves as a guide in dreams. She plays the same role in visionary art: 'Many examples from literature show the anima as a guide and mediator to the inner world . . . Rider Haggard's *She* or the 'eternal feminine' in Goeth's *Faust*' (Von Franz p. 186). While these are examples of the unconscious archetype appearing 'naked' as it were, in art, there are many more examples of women in fiction who are to some degree coloured by the same underlying archetype. As with all unconscious content, the anima tends to be projected. Thus men perceive and respond to her 'through' a real woman who accountably develops a mysterious allure. Jung describes the classic focus for the anima projection, the woman who embodies the unconscious femininity in the men who fall for her:

> The so-called 'sphinx-like' character is an indispensable part of their equipment, also an equivocation, an intriguing elusiveness . . . an indefiniteness that seems full of promises, like the speaking silence of a Mona Lisa. A woman of this kind is both

old and young, mother and daughter, of more than doubtful
chastity, childlike, and yet endowed with a naive cunning that is
extremely disarming to men. (17:339 and note)

Ayesha, the heroine of *She*, certainly exemplifies this type of
woman, but there are many other examples: Sara Woodruff from
Fowles's *The French Lieutenant's Woman*, Sue Bridehead from *Jude
the Obscure*, Florimel from George MacDonald's *Malcolm*, Elvira in
Coward's *Blithe Spirit*, and Nicole in Fitzgerald's *Tender is the Night*.
All of these heroines can be seen, in the light of Jung's theories, to
possess an attraction arising from the appeal of the unconscious
anima complex, and their stories depict the effects of such attractions.

Visionary art does not merely depict the psychological effects of
the influence of the anima complex, but differentiates (that is, brings
to consciousness) the inner form of the anima herself. In this sense
She is a revelation of the 'primordial experience' of the collective
unconscious described by Jung. *She*, and the other novels in which
Ayesha appears, refer inwards to the unconscious psyche. Whereas
works such as *Jude The Obscure* may depict projections of the anima
complex, and the women who naturally attract such projections, *She*
brings forth the goddess-like figure within the psyche who is the
source of these projections. This confers on *She* the status of 'visionary art'. The power of this figure over consciousness is expressed in
fiction by recourse to the supernatural. Ayesha is not just a woman,
she is a Goddess, necromancer and sorceress. She is a creature of
myth. There are obvious correspondences here with Lilith, who is
vampire, shape-changer and Queen of Hell.

MacDonald's work reveals the presence of the anima complex at
both levels: direct revelation and indirect suggestion. *Lilith* is a
glimpse into the dark world of the threatening aspect of the anima;
while the novels show the influence of the anima in their presentation of 'real' women. I shall examine these two levels of penetration
by the unconscious separately, beginning with *Lilith*.

Lilith

Whenever the unconscious finds expression in art it will exert an
influence over the work of art, pulling it towards the primal modes of
expression natural to the unconscious. Thus character moves towards
archetype (Eve appears in *Lilith*), action moves towards ritual (in
Phantastes Cosmo casts a magic circle, and in *Lilith* Vane has a communion supper with Lilith), and plot tends towards myth (Vane
revives the dead land by bringing it water). This leads to art which is
fraught with a peculiar resonance, its forms and symbols sounding

echoes across a spectrum of culture, religion and myth. The symbolic form-the archetype-holds an inexhaustible wealth of meaning. To the extent that the author has realised the expression of that archetype, the same wealth of meaning is held within the work of art. Jung's comments on the anima make clear the difficulties of dealing with archetypal figures: 'Rider Haggard's *She* gives some indication of the curious world of ideas that underlies the anima projection. They are in essence spiritual contents, often in erotic disguise, obvious fragments of a primitive mentality that consists of archetypes, and whose totality constitutes the collective unconscious.' (17:341)

To study Lilith herself is to study a series of mythic symbols rather than a woman. Lilith, Queen of Hell, is referred to as a fallen angel, as a Goddess, and as Hecate. Like MacDonald's Eve, she does indeed 'embody spiritual content in erotic disguise'.

Lilith's nature is never explained, expressing itself, rather, through haunting images-of serpents, of leopardesses, of a princess-which seize the imagination but which defy rational comprehension. One clue to her nature comes in the mysterious volume which links the two worlds of Victorian England and 'the region of the seven dimensions' (25). Adam reads from it a poem which offers a poetic account of Lilith's history. Lilith, it reveals, embodies all womanhood:

'In me was every woman. I had power
  Over the soul of every living man,
Such as no woman ever had in dower-
  Could what no woman ever could, or can;
  All women, I, the woman, still outran,
Outsoared, outsank, outreigned, in hall or bower.' *(Lilith,* 201)

Lilith, in clear resemblance to the anima, is the one lens through which all women are perceived, the inner form through which they find (emotional) meaning in the psyche of the man who perceives them. That she is in an inner form is not in doubt. The magical book locates Lilith's origin within the hero, Vane:

'But if I found a man that could believe
  In what he saw not, felt not, and yet knew,
From him I should take substance, and receive
  Firmness and form relate to touch and view;
  Then should I clothe me in the likeness true
Of that idea where his soul did cleave !' (201)

Vane himself begins to recognise Lilith as familiar from his own dreams, dimly and reluctantly available to consciousness:

At length she began what seemed a tale about herself, in a language so strange, and in forms so shadowy, that I could but here

and there understand a little. Yet the language seemed the prime-
val shape of one I knew well, and the forms to belong to dreams
which had once been mine, but refused to be recalled. (282)

Lilith herself is not the only expression of the anima complex in
Lilith, however. The number of female figures in the narrative points
to the presence of the anima throughout *Lilith*. In particular, Eve,
Mara and Lona each bring to expression elements of the anima.
While these figures appear as separate characters in the conscious
order of plot, the language of the unconscious–that of images–links
them to Lilith. The clearest example of this is Mara, who is, like
Lilith, a cat-woman, and is feared to have cat's claws (268). Lona in
particular has a collective or universal quality that mirrors that of
Lilith. Again, it is interesting to compare a passage from Jung with
one from MacDonald:

> The projection can only be resolved when he comes to realise
> that in the realm of his psyche there exists an image of the
> mother and not only of the mother, but also of the daughter,
> the sister, the beloved, the heavenly goddess, and the earth
> spirit . . . It is his own, this perilous image of woman . . . she
> is the vital compensation for the risks, the struggles, the sacri-
> fices which all end in disappointment; she is the solace for all
> the bitterness of life. Simultaneously, she is the great illusionist,
> the seductress who draws him into life . . . (9 (ii):100)

> . . . she was become almost a woman, but not one beauty of
> childhood had she outgrown . . . To see her with any . . . little
> one, was to think of a tender grandmother. I seemed to have
> known her for ages–for always–from before time began! I
> hardly remembered my mother, but in my mind's eye she now
> looked like Lona; and if I imagined sister or child, invariably she
> had the face of Lona! My every imagination flew to her; she was
> my heart's wife!

One could hardly have a better account of the anima: in her is com-
bined the whole range of experience of and perception of woman.
She is grandmother, mother, sister, lover and daughter. Lona's identity cannot be disentangled from that of Lilith's–both are expressions
of one figure, the woman within.

The division between Lilith and the other feminine figures appears
at first to be a moral one–Lilith is evil, while the other figures represent good. Probing more deeply, however, it appears that Lilith represents all the forces of woman that are deliberately excluded from
consciousness: chiefly, violence and sexuality. She is the 'Vilest of

God's creatures, she lives by the blood and lives and souls of men'
(*Lilith*, 205). The name and the myth of Lilith underline this. Lilith is
all that is occult, hidden, and fearful in woman. Cast out from the
garden, Lilith is the shadow of Eve. *Lilith* presents the whole spectrum of the anima's aspects through four female figures: Eve, Lona,
Mara and Lilith. Lilith herself is the dark, or unacknowledged, aspect
of the anima. She has one brief moment of entrancing beauty as the
child-bride in her palace: 'She greeted me with the innocent smile of
a girl–and in face, figure, and motion seemed but now to have
stepped over the threshold of womanhood' (176). This offers a
glimpse of a wholeness, a reconciliation of good and evil in one figure, that remains elusive. Elsewhere in *Lilith*, the anima is split. This
is most vividly illustrated in an image: the image not of one leopardess, but of two. One is white, the other spotted, and they are locked
in conflict. A similar dissociation in the anima is evident in the novels.

The Novels

One does not have to read far in MacDonald's 'realistic' novels to
discern evidence of the anima complex operating simply at the level
of character. Both the positive and the negative aspects of anima projection come to play, resulting in women who are to be worshipped
or abhorred. These two aspects of the anima can be illustrated by two
quotations:

> Yet is there testimony only too strong and terrible to the demo-
> niacal power, enslaving and absorbing . . . of an evil woman
> over an imaginative youth. Possibly did he know beforehand her
> nature, he would not love her, but knowing it only too late, he
> loves and curses; calls her the worst of names, yet cannot, or will
> not, tear himself free; after a fashion he still calls love, he loves
> the demon, and hates her thraldom . . . Tom basked in a light
> that was of hell . . . (*Mary Marston*, 2:293)

He had a grand idea of women. He had been built with a Goddess-niche
in his soul, and thought how he could worship the woman that could fill
it. Only pure as snow she must be . . . (*Paul Faber, Surgeon*, 1:239)

Everywhere the anima appears, the woman who is the object of the
unconscious projection develops a fantastic, even a religious aura.
She becomes the vehicle for 'spiritual content in erotic disguise'. This
content manifests itself in images, in the form of the woman-angel. In
the novels, twenty-seven of MacDonald's heroines are compared to
angels: clearly the complex is an important one. The emotional force
which this image carries can prove devastating, if the object of it
should reverse her aspect. In *Mary Marston*, Geoffrey finds himself

disappointed in Letty: 'He had been silently worshipping an angel
with wings not yet matured to the spreading of themselves of the
winds of truth; those wings were a little maimed; and he had been
tending them with precious balms, and odours, and ointments: all at
once she had turned into a bat, a skin-winged creature that flies by
night, and had disappeared in the darkness!' (1:293).

It may be noted that the shattering of the angel image does not return
her to reality, but rouses another image from the unconscious. This is
the bat, one of the forms in which Lilith, the dark anima, appears (see
Lilith Chapter 10).

When the anima is present, she exerts an irresistible hold, or fixa-
tion, over consciousness. Jung writes of

> one aspect of the archetypes which will be obvious to anybody
> who has practical experience of these matters. That is the arche-
> types have, when they appear, a distinctly numinous character
> which can only be described as 'spiritual', if 'magical' is too
> strong a word . . . It can be healing or destructive, but never
> indifferent . . . This aspect deserves the epithet 'spiritual'
> above all else. It not infrequently happens that the archetype
> appears in the form of a spirit in dreams and fantasy products, or
> even comports itself like a ghost. There is a mystical aura about
> its numinosity, and it has a corresponding effect upon the emo-
> tions. (8:405)

The 'heavenly' quality of MacDonald's heroines can thus be related
to the same unconscious complex which generates Lilith. The operation of this complex is illustrated in *Malcolm*, where Malcolm, who is
falling in love with the fickle and beautiful Florimel, compares himself to a man who has fallen in love with a mermaid, an angel or a
ghost (1:149). In reality there is only Florimel, but in Malcolm's psyche Florimel (perceived through the anima complex), arouses
another form, which is more, or less, than human. It is this shape
which the fantastic forms of mermaid and angel partially express. This
inner form is more fully revealed in the fantasy: in *Phantastes* the
hero meets a race of angel women, and sees mermaids.

So far, I have considered the 'indirect' appearances of the anima in
realistic fiction, chiefly through metaphor. She is more immediately
evident in two novels where the unconscious archetype intervenes in
the course of a real relationship. These are *Thomas Wingfold, Curate*
(1876) and *Wilfrid Cumbermede* (1872).

Thomas Wingfold, Curate tells the story of Leo, a young student
who experiments with drugs, eventually becoming an addict. He falls
in love with Emmeline, a heartless flirt who toys with his affections until

he is completely obsessed with her. While waiting for her at a ball Leo takes drugs, and, in a trance, encounters the anima, the woman within. She manifests herself through two of the images that appear in MacDonald's fantasy, the woman-tigress and the woman angel:

> He thought he was lying in the Indian jungle, close by the cave of a beautiful tigress, which crouched within, waiting the first sting of reviving hunger to devour him. He could hear her breathing as she slept, but he was fascinated, paralysed, and could not escape, knowing that, even if with mighty effort he succeeded in moving a finger, the motion would suffice to wake her, and she would spring upon him and tear him to pieces. Years upon years passed thus, and he still lay on the grass in the jungle, and still the beautiful tigress slept. But however far apart the knots upon the string of time may lie, they must pass: an angel in white stood over him, his fears vanished, the waving of her wings cooled him, and she was the angel whom he had loved and loved from all eternity, in whom was his ever-and-only-rest. She lifted him to his feet, gave him her hand, they walked away, and the tigress was asleep for ever . . . they wandered away into the woods, to wander in them for ever, the same violet blue, flashing with roseate stars, for ever looking in through the tree-tops, and the great leafy branches hushing ever hushing them, as with the voices of child-watching mothers, into peace, whose depth is bliss. (1:234-35)

The hallucination propels Leo into the same realm of fantastic images which Vane enters in *Lilith*. Emmeline is a tigress, as Lilith is a leopardess. Then she is an angel, as angel mothers greet Vane on his arrival at the heavenly city. Both images are aspects of the feminine complex in the unconscious: that is, of the anima.

This vision from the realm of fantasy has violent consequences in reality. As the narcotic wears off Emmeline becomes all too wordly, and Leo, realising her true nature, stabs her to death. The power the archetype can exert over consciousness is grimly illustrated. As Leo flees to Helen, his sister, 'the one thought in his miserable brain was his sister. Having murdered one woman, he was fleeing to another for refuge. Helen would save him'. (1:28).

Helen takes over the role of angel for Leo, but he cannot escape the threatening aspect of the anima. Emmeline, transformed from angel to corpse, appears to him in his mirror, crawling with worms (see *Thomas* 2:197). The more strenuously the dark aspect of the anima is resisted (as Leo resists the image of Emmeline) the more threatening she becomes.

Leo's vision shows the instability inherent in the worship of woman – the glorious image of the angel will inevitably cast a shadow, gaining its substance from all that is denied in woman. As with Geoffrey's image of Letty, the angel reverts to a creature of horror. Evidence of a more general polarisation of the anima surfaces in hints, suggestions and images throughout the realistic novels. *Lilith* is prefigured by hints of its content (like that quoted from *Malcolm* earlier) written up to thirty years previously. Almost all of MacDonald's 'good' heroines are referred to as angels, but eleven of his women characters are referred to as leopardesses. Ten are described in feline terms. The image of the cat is, for MacDonald, one resonant of evil: ' . . . a lamb, be he black as coal, must still be a more Christian animal than a cat as white as snow. Under what pretence could a cat be used as a Christian symbol?' (*The Vicar's Daughter* 1:234).

A more benign example of the intervention of the anima archetype in a relationship comes in *Wilfrid Cumbermede* (1872). Throughout his life, Wilfrid's affections are drawn to two women: the pretty and bewitching Clara Conningham, and the pure Mary Osborne. Both are foci for the anima projection. As a child, Wilfrid spends a night in a chamber in Mary Osborne's castle. That night Wifrid awakes to see an apparition of a knight emerging through a tapestry on the wall. The spectre steals Wilfrid's sword (a family heirloom) and departs. Many years later, Wilfrid sleeps again in the same chamber, and wakes to find himself in bed with Mary Osborne. Her face is marvellously transfigured, and between them lies Wilfrid's sword. This remarkable turn of events is never explained, although it is hard not to interpret it in the Freudian terms that it seems to invite.

In place of a practical explanation, however, MacDonald supplies a fantastic one, in Wilfrid's dreams. Wilfrid, Mary and the castle are transposed into inner figures in the psychic world. In the unconscious, Wilfrid undertakes a spiritual quest, wandering through a huge palace searching for a woman called Athanasia. In each room he enters he finds some token of her – a veil, a glove, and an entrancing scent. At length he finds himself in a chapel like that of Mary's castle, Moldwarp Hall. Behind the altar he sees a veiled female figure whom he knows as death. Wilfrid follows her down a flight of steps, then 'through passages like those of the catacombs' to a door (2:290). Beyond the door extends a beautiful landscape over which the sun is rising. The woman unveils – revealing herself to be the beautiful Athanasia. She steps through the door and closes it, leaving Wilfrid weeping on the other side.

Wilfrid's dream changes the course of his life. It may well be a disguised expression of the apparent, but implicit, sexual encounter, but, for MacDonald, the events in the dream world are of greater significance than those that take place in the physical bedroom. The anima that has at first appeared to him as Death now turns on him the face of divine beauty. Anathasia means 'deathless' in Greek. The experience of the anima is greater than the individual woman, Mary, but it surrounds her and transforms her, in Wilfrid's eyes. He wakes: 'On the other pillow lay the face of a lovely girl. I felt as if I had seen it before–whether only in the just vanished dream, I could not tell. But the maiden of my dream never comes back to me with any other features or with any other expression than those which I now beheld.' (2:294)

Mary herself has been transfigured: 'There was an ineffable mingling of love and sorrow on the sweet countenance. The girl was . . . evidently dreaming, for tears were flowing from under her closed lids . . . All at once the face of Mary Osborne dawned out of the vision before me–how different, how glorified from its waking condition! It was perfectly lovely–transfigured by the unchecked outflow of feeling.' (2:294).

A mysterious and supernatural realm is in evidence, one to which both Wilfrid and Mary have access in dreams. It establishes a bond between them even while Mary is spurning Wilfrid. Wilfrid sees the night as a glimpse of 'that region of the supernatural in which . . . Mary Osborne certainly lived, if anyone ever lived' (2:235). Having fallen in love with the heavenly rather than the earthly Mary, she appears to him more and more frequently in his dreams. The inner figure, the anima, almost seems to replace the outward one of Mary. The novel ends with Wilfrid apparently delaying his marriage to Mary and reflecting instead on a dream in which he sees that Mary and he need not be wed on earth because they are united by God.

The entry of fantasy images into realistic texts enables them to be studied more or less in isolation. Their natural element, however, is the fantastic medium. In the next section I will study a sequence of images as they appear an explicitly fantastic work, in *Phantastes*.

4. Three Images: Light, Water and the Forest

Light

I awoke one morning with the usual perplexity of mind which accompanies the return of consciousness. As I lay and looked through the eastern window of my room, a faint streak of peach-colour, dividing a cloud that just rose above the low swell of the horizon, announced the approach of the sun. As my thoughts, which a deep and apparently dreamless sleep had dissolved, began again to assume crystalline forms, the strange events of the foregoing night presented themselves anew to my wondering consciousness. (*Phantastes*, 1)

These three sentences are the first words of MacDonald's *Phantastes*, and, arguably, they inaugurate the genre of prose fantasy in English literature. They describe a man entering a world which is alien and mysterious. It is not the fantastic world of fairyland or of heaven, but that of consciousness, of 'normal' everyday life. They are remarkable lines because they hint at what lies before them, unwritten, on the other side of the frontier of his 'apparently dreamless' sleep. This world is perplexing because Anodos is born into it from the other world, the unconscious.

Phantastes is the story of one who is drawn into that other world, the realm of his own unconscious self, still waking. Anodos' passage through the curtain of consciousness into the deeper regions of the psyche is signalled by the transformation of the world that he perceives around him. This transformation is communicated to the reader by a number of images. In the following sections I wish to study these images in depth.

Individual images from MacDonald's fantasy, taken into isolation, may seem baffling or obscure, or their inner significance may be overlooked entirely. However, if series of images are studied together – that is, if one studies the occurrence of one image throughout his work – the significance of the image will emerge. This technique was employed by Jung in individuation studies. The individuation process, involving the continuous recording and analysis of dreams over a prolonged period, allows the analyst to piece together the underlying meaning. Jung writes:

Every interpretation is an hypothesis, an attempt to read an unknown text. An obscure dream, taken in isolation, can hardly ever be interpreted with any certainty. For this reason I attach little importance to the interpretation of single dreams. A relative degree of certainty is reached only in the interpretation of a series of dreams . . . the basic idea and themes can be recognised much better in a dream series. (16:322).

Anodos awakes to see 'a faint streak of peach colour' in the sky. The reader is at first as unaware as is Anodos of the significance of this omen, but it is this sign which initiates the inner journey into the unconscious. All of MacDonald's fantastic journeys begin with the appearance of this 'visionary gleam'. The sudden dawning of light

represents the coming to consciousness of elements which were previously unconscious. In Jung's words, 'light always refers to consciousness' (12:259). Elsewhere he writes, 'The central mystical experience of enlightenment is aptly symbolised by Light in most of the
numerous forms of mysticism' (11:828). Julian, the monk-hero of
the early verse drama *Within and Without* (1855) opens the action
with a poetic invocation of the same image:

Evening again, slow creeping like a death
And the red sunbeams fading from the wall . . .
Soul of my cell, they part, no more to come
And yet they strangely draw me, those faint hues
Reflected flushes from Evening's face,
Which as a bride, with glowing arms outstretched,
Takes to her blushing Heaven him who has left
His chamber in the dim deserted East.
Through walls and hills I see it! The rosy sea!
The radiant head half sunk! A pool of light,
As the blue globe had by a blow been broken,
And the insphered glory bubbled forth!

The glow begins Julian's spiritual quest, one which ends, in the final
act, beyond death in a misty celestial realm. The last lines of the play
announce that the entire drama has been a dream.

Mossy's journey in 'The Golden Key' is likewise initiated by a red
glow. The first visual image of the story depicts the red light opening
the way into fairy land: 'The forest lay to the east, and the sun, which
was setting behind the cottage, looked straight into the dark wood
with his level red eye . . .   The trunks stood like rows of red col-
umns in the shine of the red sun, and he could see down aisle after
aisle in the vanishing distance.' ('The Golden Key', p.3.) The coloured light symbolises a more intense mode of perception than the
grey or transparent light of conscious thought. It is as if a wave of
energy from the unconscious floods the sight of those who are beginning the inner journey, and thus the world seems flushed with the
richness of visionary perception. The same red glow appears at the
start of *Lilith*: 'It had rained the greater part of the morning and after-
noon, but just as the sun was setting, the clouds parted in front of
him, and he shone into the room. I rose and looked out of the window. In the centre of the great lawn the feathering top of the fountain column was filled with his red glory' (*Lilith* 3).

One consistent web of symbolism is woven into all that MacDonald writes, and hence the more one reads of his work the clearer and
more meaningful each element of that mesh becomes. The ray of rich

red light also appears in MacDonald's 'realistic' novels, his poetry and fairy tales. It comes at times of heightened emotional intensity and accompanies the fantastic images rising from the unconscious. It falls, for example, on Malcolm and Florimel as they plight their troth at the end of *The Marquis of Lossie* (1877), on the pigeon that Curdie shoots in *The Princess and Curdie* (1883), and in several novels, on the heroine, clothing her with the glory of the other world. The glow of coloured light upon these subjects can be illuminated by reference to Jung: 'Since this function results in an increase of consciousness (the previous condition augmented by the addition of formerly unconscious contents) the new condition carries more light.' (11:828).

In *Castle Warlock* (1882), Cosmo, who has 'the power to read the hieroglyphic aspect of things' articulates the significance of this image: ' . . . The glowing beams of the setting sun . . . fell on her hands, and her hands reflected a pale-rosy gleam on her face. "How beautiful you are in the red light, Joan!" said Cosmo . . . 'It shows you as you are–even more than in the common light . . . your beauty needs a beautiful light to show it!"' (*Warlock* 2:195-96).

It is interesting to compare the red ray of MacDonald's novels with the green ray of Jules Verne's novel *Le Rayon Vert* (also published in 1882) in which the green ray imparts wisdom to the one who sees it.

In the poem 'My Room' (1857, revised in 1893) MacDonald deliberately creates the red light in order to open the visionary world to him.

> Close the eyelids of the room,
> Fill it with a scarlet gloom . . .
> See in ruddy atmosphere
> Commonplaceness disappear!
> Look around on either hand–
> Are we not in fairy land?
>   On that couch inwrapt in mist
> Of vapourised amethyst,
> Lie as in a rose's heart:
> Secret things I would impart:
> Anytime you would believe them–
> Easier, though, you will receive them
> Bathed in glowing mystery
> Of red light shadowy;
> For this ruby hearted hue,
> Sanguine core of all the true,
> Which for love the heart would plunder
> Is the very hue of wonder;
> This dissolving dreamy red

Is the self same radiance shed
From the heart of poet young . . .
If in light you make a schism,
Tis the deepest in the prism.

   This poor seeming room, in fact
Is of marvels all compact,
So disguised by common daylight
By its disenchanting grey light
Only eyes that see by shining,
Inside pierce to its live lining. (*Poems* (1893) 13-15)

By the light of the red glow the room is transformed to reveal a marvellous landscape of caverns and woods, peopled by nereids, oreads, and a sorceress. Are we not in fairy land? The touch of the amethyst light allows access to the spiritual dimension – the room's 'belongings cryptic' can be understood by the 'light apocalyptic'. Magical ciphers, hints of the unconscious, are written on conscious reality for those who have eyes to see – those who, like Cosmo in *Castle Warlock*, can read the hieroglyphic aspect of things.

   In the three fantasy quests which comprise the inner journey, the heroes not only observe the ray, but follow it, entering into the country from which it shines. Once Anodos is in fairy land, the light continues to manifest itself. It shines on the armour of Sir Percivale, displaying both his glory and his shame. The cavern of the Alder maiden who seduces Anodos is lit by 'rosy light' and the same light shines from her eyes. In the romance of the angels, the red ray shines across the sea, pointing the way to the cave of the heroine. The halls of the Fairy Palace are bathed in a red glow. In the library, Anodos becomes Cosmo, who lives on the borders of the unconscious in a perpetual dream, seeing everything 'as through a rose-coloured glass'. Cosmo's fantasies are brought to pass by magic, and his lady appears to him 'as through a purple vapour in the gathering twilight' (*Phantastes* 130). The significance of this colour is more than atmospheric, and can be related to records of other colours in visions. Jung comments: 'Violet is the 'Mystic' colour and it certainly reflects the indubitably mystic or paradoxical quality of the archetype' (8:414). Here the amethyst light, like the red glow in *Lilith*, precedes the appearance of the anima archetype.

   Everywhere the light bears on its beams further manifestations of the spirit world. In each of the incidents above, the red light inaugurates a new phase of Anodos' experience, but he does not recognise its significance. Conscious awareness of the red light and its purpose is only given to him after his 'death' by drowning, when he is resur-

rected on an island. There the wise woman tells him of the ways that
lie between the worlds:
'. . . whenever you wish to come back to me, enter whenever you see
this mark.'
      She held up her left hand between me and the fire. Upon the
palm, which appeared almost transparent, I saw, in dark red a
mark like this ⌐, which I took care to fix in my mind. *Phantastes*,
235.
Now the red fire is intelligible. Anondos can read the cryptic sign
wherever it appears, glowing red, in the world around him, and so is
able to pass between the worlds. It is this knowledge of the red sign,
only won after he has renounced his desire for life, which redeems
him from death and the fear of death: 'the way back . . . is through
my tomb. Upon that the red sign lies, and I shall find it one day, and
be glad.' *Phantastes*, 322.
      Before the glory of the other world fell upon him, from beyond.
Now the red glow has become meaningful to him. As in a 'fragment
of esoteric doctrine', Anodos now has the 'gnosis' to return to the
spiritual home he has won, though it lies on the farther side of death.
This inner transformation has been accomplished by a series of
encounters with archetypal forms from the collective unconscious, of
which light is one. Anodos progresses from merely passively observing the manifestation of the unconscious to following it, recognising
and understanding it, and forming a psychic relationship with it. This
is the pattern of individuation, of reconciliation with the unconscious. It underlies much of MacDonald's fantasy.

Water

The second intimation of the unconscious, or Fairy Land, which
Anodos becomes conscious of is water: ' . . . I suddenly . . .
became aware of the sound of running water near me; and looking
out of bed, I saw that a stream of clear water was running over the
carpet . . . ' (*Phantastes*, 9). The stream is preternaturally alive, sup-
porting living flowers within it: 'And, stranger still, where this carpet,
which I had myself designed to imitate a field of grass and daisies,
bordered the course of the little stream, the grass-blades and daisies
seemed to wave in a tiny breeze that followed the water's flow; while
under the rivulet they bent and swayed with every motion of the
changeful current . . . ' (9-10). This is the river of life, the same
river (as MacDonald tells us in *At the Back of the North Wind*, where
it also appears) that Dante saw in his visions. It is also the river that
flows from the Holy City in the Book of Revelations. The association

of water with spiritual life is a common one in religious and occult symbolism. Jung observes: 'In the language of the alchemists . . . spirit and water are synonymous, as they are in the language of the early Christians, for whom water meant the *spiritus veritatis*. (11:354). In *Lilith*, Vane too follows this river as he approaches the New Jerusalem: 'With silent, radiant roll, the river swept onward, filling to the margin its smooth, soft, yielding channel. For, instead of rock or shingle or sand, it flowed over grass in which grew primroses and daisies, crocuses and narcissi, pimpernells and anemones, a starry multitude, large and bright through brilliant water.' (345)

The stream Anodos finds leads him not to the City of God but to the Fairy Palace, the domain of the Fairy Queen. There Anodos finds the nexus of Fairy Land, the magical pool. The pool is perhaps the most perfectly imagined of all MacDonald's fantastic symbols. It is the point of confluence of two different dimensions. Its apparent limitation, and its bottomless depths, symbolise the relation between consciousness and the unconscious. From above, its waters mirror the starry constellations of the Faery skies, picturing the whole universe in its reflection. The floor of the pool appears to be formed from a mosaic of gems. When Anodos dives into the pool, however, he finds that its waters open into another dimension. Two worlds meet through the one element of living water, the one held, invisible, within the other:

> Then, with open eyes I dived, and swam beneath the surface. And here was a new wonder. For the basin, thus beheld, appeared to extend on all sides like the sea, with here and there groups as of ocean rocks, hollowed by ceaseless billows into wondrous caves and grotesque pinnacles. Around the caves grew sea-weeds of all hues, and corals glowed between; while far off, I saw the glimmer of what seemed to be creatures of human form at home in the waters. I thought I had been enchanted; and that when I rose to the surface, I should find myself miles from land, swimming alone upon a heaving sea; but when my eyes emerged from the waters, I saw above me the blue spangled vault . . . (*Phantastes*, 127-28)

The baptism of Faery is not just the outward sign of a spiritual transformation: it accomplishes the transformation. As though born anew, Anodos finds and penetrates the hidden space of a world previously unknown to him.

Again, the fantasy symbol can be further explored by a study of other inner journeys. In 'The Golden Key' Mossy's immersion in a bath ushers him over the threshold of death. There is an even closer parallel in *Lilith* where Vane (who has also followed a guiding stream) bathes in the palace of Bulika. 'Clear as crystal, the water in the great white bath sent a sparkling flash from the corner where it lay sunk in the marble floor, and seemed to invite me to its embrace ... It looked a thing celestial. I plunged in. Immediately my brain was filled with an odour strange and delicate, which yet I did not altogether like ... I remembered the crushed paw of the leopardess, and sprang from the bath.' (177-87). Vane has been bathing in Lilith's blood. Though he is struck with horror at what he has done, the wider corpus of MacDonald's work suggests that this bathing is inevitable. It is the symbolic fulfilment of a deep desire for union with the anima. Each questing hero is driven along his quest by his pursuit of a mysterious woman, and the longed-for union constellates itself in an image of bathing, one which surfaces elsewhere in MacDonald's work.

In *Wilfrid Cumbermede* (1872), Wilfrid invokes a dream image as he tries to slake his spiritual longing in the flirtatious but shallow Clara: 'For with regard to her my soul was like one who in a dream of delight sees outspread before him a wide river, wherein he makes haste to plunge that he may disport himself in the fine element; but wading eagerly, alas! finds not a single pool deeper than his knees.' (2:264). This longing for submersion – a baptism in the feminine – represents a desire for a union closer than that of sexual intercourse – to dissolve spiritually into the being of woman, or rather, with the anima. Here, union with the feminine is enacted through the symbolism of water. When Anodos tries to kill himself, he finds the ocean of his destruction is another mediating channel to the feminine:

> I ... plunged headlong into the mounting wave below. A blessing, like the kiss of a mother, seemed to alight on my soul; a calm, deeper than that which accompanies a hope deferred, bathed my spirit. I sank far into the waters, and sought not to return. I felt as if once more the great arms of the beech-tree were around me, soothing me after the miseries I had passed through, and telling me, like a little sick child, that I should be better tomorrow. The waters of themselves lifted me, as with loving arms, to the surface. (*Phantastes*, 221)

At the heart of the inner journey lies the relation with the anima. This is enacted through numerous female figures: the 'Grandmother' of 'The Golden Key' Anodos' Grandmother, The White Lady, the Beech and Alder women, the wise woman, Lilith, Mara and Eve. Each new crisis of the psyche is likely to constellate the anima afresh, for it is through the feminine – the unconscious, the unknown – that the complexes of the unconscious psyche find expression, and through these female dream-figures that inner struggles may be resolved.

The Forest

> Great boughs crossed my path; great roots based the tree columns, and mightily clasped the earth . . . . It seemed an old, old forest, perfect in forest ways and pleasures. And when in the midst of this exstacy, I remembered that under some close canopy of leaves, by some giant stem, or in some mossy cave, or beside some leafy well, sat the lady of the marble, whom my songs had called forth into the outer world . . . the whole night became one dream-realm of joy, the central form of which was everywhere present, although unbeheld. (*Phantastes* 69-70).

The third element of the unconscious world which appears to Anodos' dawning awareness is the forest. The forest is an ancient symbol for the unknown regions of the unconscious. Jung writes: 'As at the beginning of many dreams something is said about the scene of the dream action, so the fairytale mentions the forest as the place of the magic happening. The forest, dark and inpenetrable to the eye, like deep water and the sea, is the container of the unknown and the mysterious. It is an appropriate synonym for the unconscious.' (13:241).

The forest spontaneously generates itself around Anodos as he penetrates deeper and deeper into Fairy Land. This emergence is rapid, but progressive. It begins with the products of Anodos' own imagination, the flowers which he has designed on his carpet, and which come to life. From the flowers his eyes are led to the newly awoken clematis and ivy, and from these to 'a great tree'. Following the rivulet from the tree, he finds himself in a dense forest, the forest of Fairy Land. The sequence of symbolic forms leads from waking consciousness deeper and deeper into the unconscious. The image came at first from his own imagination, but the unconscious complex underlying the image – the forest – is deeper and stranger to him than he could guess. Not surprisingly, the character of this forest reflects the inner struggle. Again there is a progression through a sequence of images as Anondos' inner sight is awoken, from the infantile mass of 'flower fairies' to seeing men as trees, walking: the terrifying (and male) ash tree, the maternal beech tree and the bewitching Alder maiden.

Again the unconscious form lying beneath conscious thought emerges in metaphor in the novel. When Wilfrid glimpses Clara she

seems to him to be 'A humanised Dryad!–one that had been caught
young, but in whom the forest sap still asserted itself in wild
affinities with the wind and the swaying branches . . . ' (*Wilfrid*
2:126). What Wilfrid's eyes see is a girl riding a horse. What his psyche perceives , through the lens of the anima, is a Dryad. The woods
occupy the very edges of the unconscious, and, like the ocean, are
feminine. When in *Thomas Wingfold, Curate* Leo crosses the psychic
frontier in his hallucination, he finds himself in thick woods where
the trees have 'the voices of child watching mothers'. The inner
form comes to life again in *Lilith* chapter 11, ('The Evil Wood')
where Lilith manifests herself in the leaves of a tree. In 'The Golden
Key', too Mossy and Tangle must find their way through a forest of
sentient trees.

I have surveyed some of the forms which greet Anodos as he
crosses the frontier from waking consciousness to the unconscious.
Anodos experiences a multitude of revelations and adventures, as do
the other travellers on the inner journey. A book remains to be written about heroes' experience there. I hope I have in this essay given
some indication of the richness and complexity of the symbolic forms
in MacDonald's fantasy.

Conclusion

'A sign is always less than the thing it points to, and a symbol is always
more than we can understand at first sight. Therefore we never stop
at the sign but go on to the goal it indicates; but we remain with the
symbol because it promises more than it reveals.' (*Man and his Symbols*, 66).

MacDonald's fantasies deal with the unconscious, touching his
readers at an unconscious level. Hence, as Reis notes, they have a
peculiar emotional power over the reader, leaving a lasting impression which is nonetheless hard to articulate precisely.

The 'mysterious' hold exerted by MacDonald's fantasy is in a sense
understandable. The symbols of his work touch on unconscious elements within us, and exert an unconscious response. But the unconscious cannot be rationalised or reduced. It is, by definition, an emotional rather than an intellectual aspect of the psyche. It cannot
meaningfully be reinterpreted in terms of ideas, for it does not per-
tain to ideas. It resists expression in terms of words, and instead presents us with strange and paradoxical images. Rather than attempting
to seek a 'universal' meaning for these symbols, we should value Mac-
Donald's work the more, in that it finds an individual, personal,
meaning in his readers. In Jung's words:

A great work of art is like a dream; for all its apparent obvious-ness it does not explain itself and is always ambiguous. A dream never says 'you ought' or 'this is the truth'. It presents an image in much the same way as nature allows a plant to grow, and it is up to us to draw conclusions . . . . To grasp its meaning, we must allow it to shape us as it shaped him (the artist). Then we also understand the nature of his primordial experience. (15:161).

References

Works by George MacDonald

All works published in London; see p. 186 for complete bibliographical details.

(1865)	Alec Forbes of Howglen, 3 vols.
(1871)	At the back of the North Wind.
(1883)	Donal Grant, 3 vols.
(1905)	'The Golden Key', in Greville MacDonald, ed.
	The Fairy Tales of George MacDonald. A. C. Fifield.
(1895)	Lilith.
(1875)	Malcolm, 3 vols.
(1877)	The Marquis of Lossie, 3 vols.
(1881)	Mary Marston, 3 vols.
(1879)	Paul Faber, Surgeon, 3 vols.
(1858)	Phantastes.
(1857)	Poems.
(1893)	Poetical Works, 2 vols.
(1883)	The Princess and Curdie.
(1876)	Thomas Wingford, Curate, 3 vols.
(1872)	Wilfrid Cumbermede, 3 vols.

Secondary References

W. H. Auden, Introduction to The Visionary Novels of George MacDonald, ed. by Anne Freemantle (New York: Noonday Press, 1954).

David Holbrook, Introduction to Phantastes, (Everyman Edition, London: Dent, 1983).

Rosemary Jackson, Fantasy: The Literature of Subversion (London: Methuen, 1981).

Carl Gustav Jung, Collective Works of C. G. Jung, 20 vols., ed. by William McGuire, trans. by R. F. C. Hull (London: Routledge and Kegan Paul, 1953-1979).

Carl Gustav Jung, Marie-Louise Von Franz, et al., Man and His Symbols (London: Pan, 1980).

C. S. Lewis, Introduction to George MacDonald: An Anthology (London: Geoffry Bles, 1946).

Colin Manlove, Modern Fantasy: Five Studies (Cambridge University Press, 1975.)

_____, The Impulse of Fantasy Literature (London: Macmillan, 1983).

Stephen Prickett, Victorian Fantasy (Hassocks, Sussex: Harvester, 1979).

William Raeper, George MacDonald (Tring: Lion, 1987).

Richard Reis, *George MacDonald* (New York: Twayne, 1972).

Robert Lee Wolff, *The Golden Key: A study of the Fiction of George Mac-Donald* (New Haven: Yale University Press, 1961).

Other Works

Rider H. Haggard *She* (London, 1886).

_____, *Ayesha: The Return of She* (London: Ward Lock, 1905).

James Hogg, *The Private Memoirs and Confessions of a Justified Sinner: Written by Himself,* John Carey, (Oxford University Press, 1969).

5

The Scientific Basis Of George MacDonald's Dream-Frame

F. HAL BROOME

According to the sourest of the critical judgements, George MacDonald was an overly conservative, even reactionary, man clinging desperately to religion as the modern world passed him by. He produced some pleasant children's fiction, but sermonised endlessly in his novels. He had an uncanny prescience of both Freudian and Jungian theory, but this was merely the lucky by-product of a strong allegorical streak. He was so engulfed in ideology that the real world was of secondary concern to his religious allegories; master of fantasy by default because he was the paramount escapist.

This was overly harsh criticism: theologians found his New Light leanings advanced for the time and scholars of fantasy have looked up to him as the first modern practitioner of the art. H. G. Wells placed MacDonald's last novel above Jules Verne's fantastic assumptions.[1] But still the view has held that religious allegory tainted MacDonald's fantasy; the secondary world of dreams groaned under the weight of religious didactics, distorting the children's literature with its supernatural message so that no ties to the real world remained.

But according to T. E. Apter's *Fantasy Literature: An Approach to Reality*,[2] comparisons between dream and allegory show 'not the dream's essential differences from literature, but its peculiar relationship with fantasy'. Apter believes that fantasy literature depends upon 'a peculiar, unexpected mingling of internal and external reality'[3] and, furthermore, sees these inner and outer realms bridged by transitional phenomena of which the dream-frame, a device once common to medieval literature of dream and vision, is part. Far from being escapist, a dream-frame allows the primary fantasy of the writer to be worked on with secondary processes such as thought, 'endowing the primitive fantasy with reality-tested derivations'. Zahorsky and Boyer remark that such 'scientific portals' – as accurately depicted dreams would have to be – cause healthy questioning over what is real, since the outer and inner states (called primary and secondary by the authors) are intermingled by these bridges.[4] Zahorsky and Boyer postulated four categories of transitional phenomena from the primary 'real' world into the secondary, internal world: 1) conventional (mirrors, the back of closets), 2) magical and supernatural, 3) Platonic shadow-worlds, and 4) scientific or pseudo-scientific.[5] They consider George MacDonald's works to fall solely within the third category, but they are only partially correct; e.g. conventional frames such as mirrors are found in both *Phantastes* and *Lilith* as both a supernatural device for the student of Prague and a mesmerising device for the self-reflective Mr Vane. The neo-Platonic idea of 'shadows' from the short story of the same name falls within the third category, but it has been overlooked that MacDonald also used the current Victorian biochemical and medical knowledge of sleep to shape his dream frames realistically. In fact, only the cognitive features of the dream-frame, shaped by current science, were common to the majority of MacDonald's fantasy writings. Would this truly be a feature of a man unaware of or even rejecting wholesale the science of his day?

Greville MacDonald's biography of his father revealed MacDonald's early interests in chemistry and natural philosophy (as physics was known at that time).[6] Joseph Johnson, in his early biography of the writer, stated that MacDonald was 'a common-sense mystic, rationalistic rather than fantastic, thinking logically and philosophically in the presence of advancing science . . . for whatever science revealed as true must be in harmony with all truth.'[7] But apart from this early remark there has been a general belief among critics that MacDonald, after earning his MA degree (including chemistry and natural philosophy) at King's College, Aberdeen, in 1845, later rejected science altogether. The fact that MacDonald continued to lecture occasionally on these topics at Bedford College in the 1860s – a period by which it was generally agreed that his theological beliefs had been firmly formed – spoke otherwise. This caused a peculiar problem in classifying MacDonald as simply a fantasist: there was a demonstrable element of current scientific theory in his writings, and he therefore fell within the rather dubious literary subgenre of science-fantasy.

Darko Suvin finds few if any redeeming features in such 'A misshapen subgenre' as science-fantasy, 'organized around an ideology unchecked by any cognition' with 'its narrative logic . . . simply overt ideology plus Freudian erotic patterns'. More heinous a crime to Suvin is the resulting 'unsubstantiated promise that the oscillation between SF and fantasy does not matter since we are dealing with full-blown allegory anyway.'[8] It is Suvin's view that SF is the 'literature of cognitive enstrangement';[9] his peculiarly modern bias against the type of estrangement shown in such fantasies as MacDonald's is that it included elements of the supernatural and metaphysical. Yet the dream-frame present in the majority of MacDonald's works of fantasy cannot be dismissed as non-cognitive; MacDonald was conversant with scientific theories of dreaming, and his religious training even upheld their theological validity.[10] That such works as MacDonald's contained the suspect elements of allegory and the supernatural did not seriously degrade the genre; after all, as Casey Fredericks has shown, myth pervades science-fiction as thoroughly as science-fantasy, and we could therefore have to discount other 'serious' works as well.[11] Casey speaks of science-fantasy as the '"dreaming" pole of science-fiction . . . in such "science-fantasy", man's scientific and technological extensions – man's own creations, fashioned from his own ever-increasing scientific knowledge – provide him with powers and capacities equivalent to his primitive deities.'[12] He also cites the Superhuman theme, '(which) depicts the heroic development of a modern protagonist within the conventional mono-mythic initiatory pattern, but with the result that the modern man rediscovers and recovers an older identity in himself which is that of some superhuman being.'[13] Certainly this theme is found in MacDonald's *Lilith* (1895), wherein Mr Vane meets his earliest relation, the shape-changing Adam, as the result of self-hypnosis, a popular research topic of scientists of the day.[14] That this novel has links with those of H. G. Wells, who has been called a classic writer of science-fantasy, strengthens MacDonald's position as a science-fantasist; but even the earlier *Phantastes* (1858) evokes the same Superhuman theme since the protagonist Anodos, in a somnambulent trance considered by Victorian medicine as conducive to the beholding of phantasms and visions, discovers his relationship with a fairy knight and lady.[15] In consequence, any dealings with MacDonald's fairy land must critically view his use of the dream-frame as a cognitive element and explore its place within the use of myth or myth-like features. No easy task: MacDonald was remarkably knowledgeable about not only biochemistry but also various fields of medicine, including the study of dreams, phantasms, and visions. Furthermore, he went afield into what today would be considered pseudo-science: this included mesmerism and homeopathy.

The most salient point mentioned by Greville on MacDonald's view of science was MacDonald's continual longing to study under the organic chemist Justus von Liebig in Giessen, Germany, a path not taken because of lack of money. Greville reported that as late as 1850 his father still wanted to go to Liebig, but left unmentioned was the man who undoubtedly encouraged MacDonald's attempts, William Gregory. He was Professor of Medicine and Chemistry at King's College during the first four years that MacDonald studied there. Professor Gregory, who later took the Chair of Chemistry at Edinburgh (1844), was a most interesting teacher, the last of a long line of Gregories as recounted by Agnes Granger Stewart in her *The Academic Gregories*.[16] Gregory himself had studied under von Liebig and had edited the British editions of Liebig's main works. And while the cataloguing of the mysterious northern library was cause in part of MacDonald's subsequent interest in Romanticism, it must be questioned whether Gregory, too, did not play a part, for Stewart says of him: 'There is a continual atmosphere of table-turning, mesmerism, and magnetic flames in the tales extant about him, and though the narrators are tender in the memory, they have perforce to take up the attitude of counsel for the defense.'[17] Gregory must have been in the back of MacDonald's mind when he wrote *David Elginbrod* (1863), for the main character, Hugh Sutherland (the last name suspiciously like the area of the catalogued library), met Count von Funkelstein, a follower of Mesmer, in circumstances mediated by a thunderstorm and a lecture in biology.[18] Biology was not quite a common word of the day, and one character of refinement has to ask its meaning. Hugh, admittedly ignorant himself, scornfully replies 'a science, falsely so called',[19] for until Robert Falconer has distinguished the field from mesmerism, or animal magnetism, public opinion incorrectly links the two. Biology proper was a topic familiar to MacDonald, however, precisely because of his knowledge of von Liebig.

A. W. Hoffman, in the Faraday Lecture of 1875 on von Liebig (who died in 1873) gives us some of the points about the chemist which most impressed his contemporaries.[20] Liebig discovered 'radicles (*sic*)',[21] was prone to making 'chemical analogies'[22]–as was Macdonald, who made Swedenborgian transformations of chemical equations for his classes at Bedford College–and provided the process which led to the silvering of mirrors, an important image in MacDonald's works. But most significantly, Liebig was a key figure in the synthesis of organic compounds, a breakthrough which deeply upset religious Victorians. MacDonald, in naming the morally corrupt Count 'von Funkelstein', was making a pun on a more famous natural philosopher and chemist who dabbled fiendishly with biology: von Frankenstein.[23] Mrs Shelley, when she was 'indulging in waking dreams'[24] to find the horror tale *Frankenstein*, relied on rumours that Dr Erasmus Darwin had animated a piece of spaghetti.[25] Mrs Shelley, to her credit, does not seemed to have believed that, and while this public opinion seems silly now, such was the climate of the times. Liebig shared Frankenstein's belief that the life force was analogous with electricity, but he should not be confused with von Funkelstein; MacDonald was simply criticising the exploitation of the ignorant populace by men posing as scientists. The one telling complaint that he had against science was the approach of the scientists themselves, experimenting on people like the witch Watho, blind to the moral questions involved. If we search the adult non-fantasy novels of Mac-Donald, we find that his beliefs differed from the mainstream of science only in perceiving God's hand in the actions of Nature. He did not deny the evidence of its workings, only the argument that Nature was from the beginning unthinking and without plan or order.[26]

Of the editions of Liebig available to MacDonald, the 1842 *Animal Chemistry* had the most profound influence. Prepared by Gregory, it contained a view of 'the intersection of chemistry and physiology' which may be discerned in MacDonald's early work. While technically learning toward logical induction (a trend noticeable in Mac-Donald but repudiated later by Liebig himself in an edition put out after MacDonald's school days), the book was a monument in early biochemistry, reworking the old medieval concept of vitalism within the framework of the quantative approach.[28] Living things were endowed with *'vital force'*,[29] and in ova and seeds this was in either rest or static equilibrium. In Liebig's view its main influence came from external forces which the living thing either resisted in its growth or succumbed to in death. This type of the vital force was known as the vegetative, which women supposedly had in greater measure than men. But there was another internal force as well, the animal, which had volition through the nervous system. Liebig's particular contribution was the awareness of nutrition as a chemical process; the nervous system, or animal vitality, put ingested organic matter (food) through a quantitative change. In fact, the 'vital force does not act . . . at infinite distances, but, like chemical forces, it is active only in the case of immediate contact. It becomes sensible by means of an aggregation of material particles'.[30] Only organic matter could replenish other living matter, rebuilding tissue, and voluntary mechanical effects such as action during the day wasted tissue. So voluntary motions had to be checked at night in the process called sleep, which replenished these tissues. In judging the effect of the outer atmosphere on this inner vital process, Liebig believed that 'the intensity of the vital force diminishes with the abstraction of light; that with the approach of night a state of equilibrium is established . . .'[31] Any disruption of the equilibrium prodded the inner state into action, and unless the inner vitality successfully counteracted external forces, disease resulted. Oxygen in the atmosphere was deemed responsible for

most organic changes, and its action of separation and resistance was
lost at night. In alliance was cold which checked vitality aʳ well; as
temperatures lowered, voluntary motion subsided, resultinᵷ in sleep,
and then, if unchecked, death. MacDonald made the most of this
point in *At the Back of the North Wind*, wherein the protagonist, a
poor boy named Diamond, sleeps freezing in an open stable. The
cold North Wind visits him in his sleep at night, disrupting his vitalic
equilibrium, thus producing his disturbed dreams and edging him
closer to death.[32] In fact, the revitalising property of sleep was in
earlier days equated with dreams, but, in the period that MacDonald
wrote, it was beginning to be recognised that the dreamer was only
imperfectly sleeping: indeed; actions made in sleep–such as Diamond's sleepwalking, or Anodos's–reflected the dreamer's thoughts
and responses to the external stimuli which disrupted the balance of
equilibrium.

In dismissing the germ theory of contagion in favour of his atmospheric theories, Liebig was obviously wrong, as even MacDonald
acknowledged,[33] but in researching the equilibrium between external
and internal that had living tissue in between, Liebig stumbled across
a more sound theory, that of exosmose and endosmose. His
Researches on the Motion of the Juices in the Animal Body, initiated as a
study of potato blight, dealt in part with the effects of external factors
such as weather and time of day on the internal vitalic force.[34] That
MacDonald had studied this work is evident in one of his earliest
poems, the semi-autobiographical 'A Hidden Life', which later
appeared in a collection along with an interestingly titled poem called
Within and Without from the same period.[35]

In MacDonald's poem, 'A Hidden Life', the scholar–interested in
natural philosophy and chemistry–is ordered to bring in crops after
night and before a storm, a very dangerous period according to Liebig
because the electrically-charged stormy air disrupted the normal
equilibrium of night. While the scholar does not 'favour such head-
long race / with Nature',[36] he obeys his father and consequently falls
deathly ill. Initiating his disease is a simultaneous act of both inner
and outer Nature: a lightning flash 'Met by some stranger flash from
cloudy brain' reveals a vision to him. This is just a local lady seen by
the scholar as supernatural. She provides an external image which has
been ingested internally, and the disrupted inner vital force of the
scholar treats her with his imagination. There is something wrong
with his inner vital force, though, for

His spirit was a chamber, empty, dark,
Through which bright pictures passed of the outer world;

The regnant Will gazed passive on the show;
The magic tube through which the shadows came,
Witch Memory turned and stayed [37].

MacDonald here equated the inner force with the Will, and in its passivity it no longer counteracted the external forces acting upon the scholar, and with deadly result. This, too, was found in *At the Back of the North Wind*, for Diamond only succumbs to the North Wind when he actively desires the country at the back of the North Wind.

The presence of the local maiden in the dream vision also accorded with Liebig's theories. 'Everywhere, when two dissimilar bodies come in contact,' he wrote, 'chemical affinity is manifested.'[38] The attraction of the two in a healthy relationship should have brought the scholar's inward-looking focus outward again; the fact that it did not–and that she was not in immediate contact–killed him. Liebig's later distaste for analogy prevented him from studying the equilibrium between the sexes, but MacDonald went afield from his scientific hero in taking human relationships as a serious, affective force. As late as 1891 he wrote: 'Possibly, a spiritual action analogous to exosmose and endosmose takes place between certain souls.'[39] The man-woman equilibrium with its effect on not only the physical health but the spiritual too seems to have fascinated him most of all. Therefore it was common to find couples in his science-fantasies representing balancing attributes: an example would be Richard and Alice in 'Cross Purposes' (1867), who enter fairy land through opposite means of dreaming.[40] Richard leaves the market-place by day-dreaming and Alice, in accordance with Victorian theory that women at puberty are more prone to drowsiness, leaves her home in night-dream. These polar characteristics are kept in fairy land, wherein the pair go deeper in sleep, Richard above the water and Alice below the water, with a living tissue, a leaf, between them. MacDonald was able to demonstrate exosmose and endosmose through living tissue without belabouring the scientific principle, or pointing out that the leaf represented vegetative vitality.

Liebig was highly influential in Victorian medicine, a field which also interested MacDonald. J. Müller's *Elements of Physiology*,[41] a classic German text of the time, exhibited many of Liebig's views by acknowledging that exmosos and endosmos were also applicable to animal tissue[42] and that the imponderables 'Light, heat, and electricity . . . influence the compositions and decompositions going on in organic matter'.[43] Vitality itself prevented decomposition, and water was a prerequisite for maintaining vitality.[44] Because of the importance of water and light, MacDonald's science-fantasies started at the time of receding or approaching equilibrium (the periods of daybreak of gloaming) when both light and water had an enhanced effect. Anodos watched the peach colour of the sun and the far-off sea from his window; Vane stared at the light of the setting sun which played off a fountain. Richard and Alice entered at dusk (Alice in fact gazing at the red light on her wall, looking inward) and bathed in the stream and pool entering fairy land. The most famous of MacDonald's short stories, 'The Golden Key', had as its main symbol the rainbow, the last rays of daylight reflected on water.[45] Such external forces were the stimuli 'necessary for the developed and active life.'[46] In *The History of Photogen and Nycteris*, MacDonald not only has the developing central couple in direct opposition (day and night), but shows how they have to overcome the artificial environment of the witch which has withheld half of the world from them.[47] Indeed, Nycteris finds the most pleasure and influence from not only diluted light but the water from the fountain.

The polar opposition of the various couples was again underscored for that other imponderable, electricity: men were more likely positive and women negatively electrical,[48] and there was more electricity at night, the equilibrium period when the two met. As for sleep, this created a state in which 'the influence of the central organs on the peripheral parts of the system is lowered,'[49] again echoing Liebig's loss of vitality at night. MacDonald even mentioned this as a cause for Miss Cameron's sleepwalking in *David Elginbrod*.[50]

Medical understanding of the sensorium and sleep formed the most important aspect of the dream-frame, for here was the key to what happened between the within and without, the inner and outer, the micro- and macrocosms and the images which inhabited both. The very word 'fantasy' was linked with this, as Gary Kern remarks: 'It is from the Greeks that we get the word fantasy. Generally speaking, they understood φαντασια to refer to images retained in the mind after perception: these night appear haphazardly (what we would call *day-dreaming*) or intentionally (what we would call *imagining*). In either case the images are presented before the mind's eye'[51] Kern remarks that 'aesthetic fantasy' gave consciously-shaped images, and in these deliberately-chosen images we find reality-tested derivations that Apter granted fantasy. In 'A Hidden Life', MacDonald had displayed a theory of perception and cognition of the mind's eye which resembled in some aspects a telescopic vision, with the added medieval distinction of 'Witch Memory'. Müller too stated that the dark called up the imagination from the memory; its images were products of experience, but were reshaped and reformed by the imagination (which readers of *Phantastes* will recognise from P. F.

Fletcher's earlier theory.) [52]

The fact that images inhabited both the inner and the outer called for a system of judging between the two, since it was good medic:! knowledge of Victorian times that there were occasions when one could not tell them apart. Not that the function changed dramatically – Müller believed 'it is indifferent whether a sense be excited to action from within, or from without; in no sense do we perceive an essential difference between the sensations thus produced'. [53] Yet vision was considered the most affecting of the senses, bringing in objects of nature which were influenced and modified by the imagination. [54] Light and colour, two main components of vision, were innate endowments of Nature. [55] These properties were marked by an accumulation of blood within the brain, an internal excitement (the condition later known as 'erethism'). Red, the most excitatory colour, was also the most common colour described by MacDonald as preceding his characters into fairy land, the reversed world which of course had green – the optical opposite of red – as its main colour. [56]

Another peculiarity of the concept of within and without was that in the state of ego-loss the boundaries between the two became obscure; this was common to young children, as Müller indicated by commenting that self-awareness was a product of experience and that the newly-born babe could not easily tell inner from outer. [57] Here then was the scientific basis for MacDonald's known propensity for urging ego-loss, common to religious states but found in various medical states, such as illness, the drugged state, the hypnotised state, and the sleeping state. We may easily point out all of these in MacDonald's works – and the word 'ego', by the way, was known in MacDonald's student days, with Müller explaining that the 'Ego' or 'self' was indistinguishable between inner and outer at first, creating an initial division of the self. Jackson observed this among 'the many Victorian voices which apprehended a polypsychic identity as lack of self'. [58] In order to have a rational and scientific foundation for his tales in which internal imagery was projected upon the external world, MacDonald had a difficult task – he had to ask his reader to go against experience, and it must be suspected that his exhortation for the adult to return to the childlike state, apart form its obvious Biblical references, might have arisen from the fact that a child was in the state of ego-loss necessary for the beholding of phantasms. Anodos' somnambulism was the product of an overworked brain (his excessive studying); Ralph Rinkelmann's phantasms or shadows were the result of mental illness (specifically melancholy); the mad, drug crazed Lord Morven of *Donal Grant* hallucinated freely; [59] and the various sleepwalkers in MacDonald's works exhibited signs of having been influenced by animal magnetism, a form of the hypnotic state.[60] MacDonald's awareness of inner-outer vitalic theory was reflected in the dazed Donal Grant's comment that 'whether these forms (of existence) had relation to things outside him, or whether they belonged only to the world within him, he was unaware.'[61] MacDonald, in a short story called 'The Shadows', featured in Adela Cathcart, made much of the fact that the shadows (internal phantasms which the sick Ralph Rinkelmann had projected on the external world) were living. This highlighted the fact that a living imagination had shaped them.

Owing to the confused state where internal and external sensations were indeterminate, the 'nerves of vision' according to Müller 'which may be excited to sensation by internal as well as external causes' produced 'ocular spectra'. Phantasms and hallucinations fell within this category, which included dream images, sometimes seen with the eyes closed and before sleep. Müller listed three major times for this: a) immediately before sleep, at the time of waking, and when half awake; b) during dreams themselves; and c) during the diseased state. Though he did not refer specifically to the state of animal magnetism, he did observe, as did the mesmerists, that during sleep or the state of sleepiness 'both eyes are turned inward and upwards.'[63] The Greek name ἄνοδος, which MacDonald used for his protagonist of Phantastes, actually referred to an inward and upward journey, specifically of the soul, which MacDonald often linked, as did earlier Romantic poets, with the eyes. Müller also lectured on another feature found in that first novel of MacDonald's, the premise that if the 'ideas which occupy the mind during the waking state have a certain degree of persistence, the same ideas will recur in dreams during sleep.'[64] All of the four-square objects which Jungian critics have identified as mandalas in Phantastes actually come from a replication of the four-legged wooden desk on which Anodos has concentrated, his imagination, twisting the object into varied forms still dependent on the initial shape. And in The Golden Key the idea of the golden key had been implanted by the great-aunt's words when she tells the boy Mossy stories. Since in the state of somnambulism the person 'performs acts determined by his dreams' and 'associates only those ideas which bear some relation to those already in action',[65] an important device linking reality with the dream-frame would consist of the protagonist carrying ideas from the waking state into the dreaming state, albeit in forms treated once again by the imagination. In nearly every instance MacDonald managed to make this link. It is important for critics to be aware of this: instead of linking the dream-images to MacDonald's own psyche, we should analyze the protagonist and his or her relationship with the dream images.

Another complaint against MacDonald has been that his fantasy did not change very much over his career, but if we look at scientific treatises on dreaming published before his final novel we find that science has changed little. Taking the 1891 pamphlet on *Dreaming*, published four years before *Lilith*, we find the Scottish Dr MacFarlane of Edinburgh rehashing theories known to Liebig and Müller in the 1840's, with the addition of another known expert on dreaming: George MacDonald. MacFarlane recognised that there was 'truth in MacDonald's remark, – "I never dream dreams, the dreams dream me".'[66] In fact, Dr MacFarlane delineated three main 'activities' of dreaming found previously in MacDonald's works.

First of all, there was 'Activity instigated by Sensory Stimuli',[67] which worked on the plausible hypothesis that the nervous system reacted to suitable stimuli that were reflected later in the dream. Of great importance was the effect of light, which 'by stimulating the visual centres may excite secondary molecular activity in the psychical area, and so induce dreaming.' The rays of the rising or setting sun marked the entrance into fairy land, so MacFarlane's statement that 'a bright light falling upon the eye may give rise to visual dreams'[68] was shown in MacDonald's science-fantasy. As for the other senses, hearing was the next in importance: 'The Aeolian harp and other monotonous sounds have been employed as aids to sleep'.[69] MacDonald quite plainly stated earlier that fairy tales should act like an Aeolian harp.[70] The great-aunt's words also affected Mossy in creating the image of the golden key, and in a second-hand manner the letter of the female relative affected Anodos when he found it in the writing desk. Oral delivery was conductive to the divine inspiration so highly prized by the Congregationalists, but for MacDonald writing had to play a second-rate but still important place. His written message was made more affecting by the Victorian practice of reading bedtime tales to children (while they are in the drowsy state before sleep). As another instigator, 'cold is sufficient to initiate dreams'[71] and this was of course the main activity found in *At the Back of the North Wind* which relied on Liebig's theories. In passing, however, MacFarlane mentioned that dreams were more frequent for sufferers of asthma, pleurisy, emphysema, and so on,[72] raising the intriguing question of whether MacDonald, who himself was such a sufferer, was more prone to dreaming himself. At any rate, MacDonald did specify the need for sturdy lungs in writing about the ill and somnambulent Diamond.[73] Indeed as his friend the homeopathist Dr Russell noted, the lungs were important in humans, as was the skin, in being the living boundary between the within and without.[74] And MacFarlane did mention that recurring dreams in children – such as Diamond's repeated dreams about the North Wind – indicated approaching illness, specifically that caused the disruption of cold.

As MacDonald was aware, the ancients including Herodotus knew that dreams originated from incidents during the day; medical science confirmed this, for 'When mental work of an arduous and engrossing kind is pursued, certain centres are kept in active function, and in hyperaemic condition for long periods'.[75] MacFarlane listed this activity as *inherent in the Psychical Centres maintained either by Erethistic or Adynamic Conditions*'. Blood flow pooled in the area affected by the external stimulus and was repaired by sleep, but not until the dream had occurred. Thus the scholar Anodos had caused his illness by his repeated studying after graduation, with the events in fairy land reflecting his initial state and the books he had studied. So it was unfair to chide MacDonald for allusions to science and obscure books in *Phantastes*: the scholar was merely releasing tension from the erethistic condition caused by his excessive studying of science and obscure books.

Finally, there was *'Activity Maintained by an Altered Blood-supply'*.[76] This concerned illness proper. And here was revealed a main difference in the cognitive theories of dreaming between the 1840s and the 1890s: 'In dreaming sleep is imperfect, the cerebral textures continue their functions; potential or latent energy is expended instead of being hoarded up and accumulated.' In short, dreaming represented imperfect sleep caused by external stimuli or illness, and thus was vitalistically draining. This must have concerned MacDonald somewhat, as it very nearly undid everything he stood for, prone as he was to urging people to make life a dream. As it was, critics have long noticed that his dream-fantasies grew more apocryphal and cynical toward the end of his life, his Lady Natura of the vegetative vitality was exchanged for the unatural, animalistic, vitality-robbing Lilith. MacDonald still stood by his favourite quotation from Novalis that our life was no dream, but it should and perhaps would become one. But there was a subtle difference in the attitude of the protagonists: Anodos awaited the return of his dream; Vane awaited to escape his by a sounder sleep. MacDonald used the vitalistically-draining yet tension-revealing quality of dreaming, however, to explore the uneasy comparison of death and sleep; just as death was feared and forestalled, yet believed by MacDonald to be good, so was sleep denied by Lilith who needed it most. Critics such as Tolkien were aware that death was MacDonald's greatest subject, but sleep was his greatest analogue for death.[77] So it should be no surprise that, as new theories evolved about sleep, the character of its analogue would be revised. Since the Natura figure was representative of the vegetative vitality in its unconscious state, then in Lilith we may see the animalistic vitality which has volition in consciousness: MacDonald, worried that a religion which downplayed predestination might cause people to act without regard to the hereafter, had to focus on the conscious Will and its effect. There was evidence, he believed, that just as dreams resulted from the events of the day, the afterlife depended on the events of the preceding life; a person literally made heaven or hell with images from life, just as a dreamer brought up images from the memory of his or her own experiences during the day.[78]

In fact, the comparison of the central female character of the early fairy tales with the later ones demonstrates this development very well indeed. Her role has always intrigued MacDonald scholars, for it represented a prominent feature for which many explanations were available, most notable Robert Wolff's assertion that she represented MacDonald's loss of a mother.[79] However, he overlooked the fact that the Habundia or Natura figure was featured in medieval dream visions, providing MacDonald with a ready-made archetype that had literary associations, many of which entered Jungian interpretations of her role as the *anima* or soul.[80] Many Victorian medical textbooks discussed how in sleep the πνεῦμα was loosened, indicating a heightened spiritual state with which the soul was linked. Jung as well as Freud had access to the culmination of these texts. But MacDonald's central female character seemed primarily linked with Liebig's vegetative force seen mostly in females. The Green Lady of *The Golden Key* was the best example, with Victorian fears over survival of the fittest evident in her negative as well as positive aspects. MacDonald took to heart the Biblical statement that nature, whose laws followed God's, clothed as well as cast into the oven (Matthew 6:30); Darwin's view merely rephrased the concept in some new clothes of its own. This ambiguity might well give unease to the older reader as well as to the young. One commentator mentioned in MacDonald's obituary that far from being popular with children, At the Back of the North Wind caused them 'puzzlement'.[81] The ambiguous North Wind (the loosened πνεῦμα was aligned with the wind in many of Mac-Donald's tales) was a wrecker of ships as well as a friend. She in turn was succeeded by Watho the witch, a much darker figure who caused good only by accident, undone in turn by Nature against which she was the antagonist force. Comparing *Phantastes* and *Lilith*, it was also

evident that the female associated with Nature, the sound of which·
caused drowsiness, was supplanted by Lilith, an unnatural female who
denied sleep.

But those who have delighted in the supposed prominence of the
central female should consider that her counterpart in Lilith at the
boundary of dream was not female at all, but male, the raven-man.[82]
MacDonald's continual opposing of the internal and external grafted
sexual characteristics on to both worlds, so that the passive/internal/
vegetative/feminine unconsciousness (the anima as as described by
Jungians) was in vitalic equilibrium with the volitive/external/ani-
mal/masculine consciousness. Certainly, the actual dream-frame of
Phantastes as compared with Lilith was in parallel with this entry of
the protagonists: Anodos by unconsciousness in his somnambulism,
and Vane in his attentive consciousness, heightened by his self-hypnosis state. Therefore we have to be careful in thinking that there was
a great change in MacDonald. We may find a mere change in emphasis from unconsciousness to consciousness. If the men could be in
either a conscious or unconscious state, so could the women; yet it
did seem that once MacDonald fixed a trait in a story, he was consistent throughout. So if we found Richard and Alice entering fairy land
by being awake and asleep respectively, this was counterbalanced by
Mossy sleeping and Tangle leaving her house awake. And if a female
representative of Nature caused drowsiness in Phantastes, then a
raven-man urged sleep in Lilith.

Furthermore, the central figure, male or female, was not alone: the
man-woman equilibrium formed as central a part as Natura which
intermediated between the couple. MacDonald's Natura figure was
therefore a trickster, an enantiodromian reflection of the male and
female balance; her/his aspect would at times separate or join the two
poles, perhaps even both in the same story, but in the end his/her
actions worked to bring them together again. This was clearly seen in
The Golden Key, where the Green Lady had Mossy and Tangle meeting at her hut (but sleeping in different rooms, just as Alice and
Richard slept apart); her aspect was split into three and turned masculine later, for the three Old Men likewise worked to join the two
children.

Here then was the basic pattern of a George MacDonald fairy tale:
a central figure, male or female or split between the two, brings
together, seperates, and then rejoins a male and female couple by the
story's end. This was of course the familiar pattern of the Cupid and
Psyche legend, present in all of MacDonald's science-fantasy as the
most basic myth of all.[83] For he believed, it seemed, that Nature/God

was responsible for the polarity of the sexes and guided the struggle toward balance. Internally we were led by natural images just as externally we were led by original images of Nature, following these visions as surely as Photogen stalked his beasts and Nycteris her moth. In MacDonald's own vitalist psychology the two worlds sought harmony. We cannot dismiss him as unrealistic just because he identified central Natura, whether the internal force of the imagination or the external workings of biological life, with an organising force; today's DNA theory seems equally miraculous to some.

MacDonald did believe that those who placed ascendency on the physical world and focused like Watho on just *scientia* went awry; without the balancing pole of *sapientia* the world turned back on the materialist and taught a lesson through the skin. But those who, like Lord Morven, over-indulged in the interior world, without a grasp of reality, suffered too. For Nature, whether unbalanced on the physical exterior or in the mental interior, ruled by scientific law which worked toward equilibrium: this could be wished away only at the dreamer's peril.

References

1. An account of Wells' appreciation of George MacDonald's *Lilith* may be found in Patrick Parrinder and Robert M. Philmus's H. G. Well's Literary Criticism (Sussex: The Harvester Press, 1980), ch. 6 'On Science Fiction, Utopian Fiction, and Fantasy', pp. 222-31. It seemed that Wells thought *Lilith* went a bit too far, with too litttle consistency in its fantastic suppostion; and like Darko Suvin, Wells deemed it to be 'metaphysical fiction' (223). But he still placed *Lilith* over Jules Verne's assumptions!

2. T. E. Apter, *Fantasy Literature: An Approach to Reality* (Hong Kong: The MacMillan Press, Ltd., 1982), p.132.

3. Ibid., p.25.

4. Kenneth J. Zahorsky and Robert H. Boyer, 'The Secondary Worlds of High Fantasy', in *The Aesthetics of Fantasy Literature and Art*, ed. by Roger C. Schlobin (copublished by the University of Notre Dame Press, Indiana, and the Harvester Press Limited: John Spiers, Brighton, Sussex, 1982). The neo-Platonic element which the two critics attribute to MacDonald was supported by his mentor, the Christian Socialist F. D. Maurice, who thought Plato second only to the Bible in insight. See the letters edited by his son Frederick Maurice in *The Life of F.D. Maurice* (2vols.; London: MacMillan and Co., 1884) for some intersting views on science and medicine which may have rubbed off on MacDonald as well (cf. letters II, 29, 59, and311). MacDonald was a bit more liberal than Maurice, however, as the latter preferred Aristotle to 'modern German works which young men translate' (II, 412).

5. Ibid., p.64.

6. Greville MacDonald, *George MacDonald and his Wife* (London: Allen and Unwin, 1924).

7. Joseph Johnson, *George MacDonald* (London: Sir Isaac Pitman & Sons, Ltd., 1906), p.79. Greville objected strongly to this biography, rushed out

after the death of his father, even though Johnson claimed in the dedica-
tion that Greville had proof-read the manuscript. Certainly the biography
was sloppy in parts (e.g. it listed MacDonald's birthday as 24 Nov. 1824
instead of 24 Dec., but it also showed a certain incisiveness, particularly as
concerned MacDonald's knowledge of the sciences and medicine. In speaking of MacDonald's The Portent (1864), Johnson noted that 'Lady Alice,
the somnambulist, full of great sympathy and remarkable understanding, is
the first of many characters, beset with a form of mental or nervous disease,
that appear in other stories' (p.228). There was, however, the sleepwalking
Miss Cameron in the earlier David Elginbrod (1863).

8. Darko Suvin, The Metamorphosis of Science Fiction (London: Yale University Press, 1979), pp.68-9.

9. Ibid., p.4.

10. MacDonald's training at Highbury College in London was under the
Reverend Ebenezer Henderson, who maintained in Divine Inspiration; or,
the Supernatural Influence exerted in the Communication of Divine Truth; and
its Special Bearing on the Composition of the Sacred Scriptures (London: Jackson and Walford, 1836) that both classes of dreams, normal and supernatural, were produced in sleep and that God 'made use of the instrumentality
of sleep, the various affections of the physical constitution, the action of the
faculty of imagination upon that of memory for the reproduction of previous ideas; and, when the mind was exactly in that state of natural preparation which was necessary for the reception of the supernatural communication . . . such celestial intervention took place' (p.154). This stamped the
character of the dreamer and his circumstances upon the dream. As a liberal Congregationalist, Henderson urged scientific treatment of the Bible as
a valid means of revelation.

11. Casey Fredricks, THE FUTURE OF ETERNITY (Bloomington: Indiana University Press, 1982), 127.

12. Ibid., p.127.

13. Ibid., p.125.

14. Vane noticed a picture of a male ancestor–'my eyes full of the light
reflected from it' (Lilith, ch.3)–which acted as an object normally of a non-
excitatory nature but which proved self-reflective through the male line
and the glass of the picture acting as a mirror. For the hypnotic power of
such non-excitatory objects, see the Scottish researcher James Braid's
Neurypnology; or the Rationale of Nervous Sleep, considered in Relation with
Animal Magnetism (London: John Churchill; Edinburgh: Adam and Chas.
Black, 1843), pp.48-9. I have concentrated on the full sciences in this essay,
but have covered these pseudo-sciences and their import in MacDonald's
work more fully in my unpublished Ph.D thesis, 'The Science-Fantasy of
George MacDonald' (Edinburgh University, 1985).

15. The adult romances Phantastes and Lilith neatly framed MacDonald's
career and fell within Henderson's given categories of the divine dream and
the divine vision, arising out of 'brainular affections' (Henderson, Divine
Inspiration, p.159) with the distinction that in Phantastes a state of
somnolency was involved, making it a divine dream, and in Lilith a state of
consciousness 'which did not exclude the healthy exercise of the mental
faculties' induced in Mr. Vane a divine vision. The emphasis on consciousness might explain why Lilith was taken more seriously than Phantastes,
although we today have to deal with the irony that Lilith had the greater
spiritual intent.

16. Andrew Stewart Granger, The Academic Gregories, in the famous Scots
Series (Edinburgh and London: Oliphant, Anderson, and Ferrier, n.d.).

Gregory the 'mediciner' of King's College during MacDonald's stay there, was apparently addicted to muriate of morphia and had a 'singularly child-like and trustful disposition'.

17. Ibid., p.144.

18. George MacDonald, *David Elginbrod*, 3 vols. (London: Hurst and Blackett, 1863), II, 156. Also the Cassell edition (London: Cassell and Company, Ltd., 1927), p.186.

19. Ibid. II 157; 187.

20. A. W. Hoffman, *The Life Work of Liebig: in Experiment and Philosophic Chemistry; with allusions to his influence on the development of the collateral sciences and of the useful arts*, (London: MacMillan and Co., 1876).

21. Ibid., p.7.

22. Ibid., p.11.

23. Mary Wollstonecraft Shelley, *Frankenstein; or the Modern Prometheus* (London: Thomas Hedgeson, n.d., probably 1868).

24. Ibid., p.v.

25. Ibid., pp.ix-x.

26. See Paul Faber, Surgeon, 3 vols. (London: Hurst and Blackett, 1879), I, 213; and also, 1 vol., 9th ed. (London: Kegan Paul, Trench, Trübner, & Co., Ltd., n.d.), p.123. Here MacDonald registered no complaints with the theory of the 'vitalic machine', only begging to differ with the presumption that it was 'equally void of beneficence and malevolence'. This presumption was in regard to the Darwinian controversy, of course; and MacDonald, familiar with the subject as Greville stated, seemed to have had no qualms about the theory as a whole except, once again, over the question of whether nature was without guidance or plan. Also, in keeping with Liebig's emphasis on the internal reaction to the external environment, MacDonald stressed internal (i.e. mental and moral) improvements over external physical features. MacDonald may have been willing to follow Darwin's theory because it did explore the reaction of the organism to the external environment in line with Liebig.

27. Justus Liebig, *Animal Chemistry, or Organic Chemistry in its Applications to Physiology and Pathology*, ed. by William Gregory (London: Taylor and Walton, 1842). p.xviii.

28. See Justus Liebig, *Animal Chemistry, or Organic Chemistry in its Application to Physiology and Pathology, Third Edition, Revised and Greatly Enlarged, Part 1*, ed. by William Gregory (London: Taylor and Walton, 1846). Here Liebig changed course from his inductive approach and declared physiology a 'deductive science' (p.158). MacDonald's fairy tales worked almost entirely by inductive homologues, so he would have parted from Liebig's view that 'No real insight can be gained by apparent analogies, that is, by images' (p.174). However, MacDonald would have agreed with Liebig's remarks that 'causes . . . can never, in the province of natural science, be ascertained by the power of imagination . . . one and the same effect . . . may be produced by various causes' (p.167). It would be a trap to believe here that MacDonald, just because he placed such a high emphasis on the imagination, disbelieved this; witness his statement in his *Adela Cathcart*, (3 vols., London: Hurst and Blackett, 1867), III, 354: 'Did you ever know anything whatever resulting from the operation of one seperable cause?'. . . Except in physics, we can put nothing to the *experimentum crucis*, and must be content with conjecture and probability.'

29. Liebig, Animal Chemistry, 1st ed., p.1.

30. Ibid., p.209.

31. Ibid., p.233.

32. George MacDonald, *At The Back of the North Wind*, first published in

serial form in the 1869 and 1870 volumes of *Good Words for the Young* (London: Strahan and Company, 1868-1869) with MacDonald as editor. The ratio between sleep and work was important in Liebig's theories; when the equilibrium was disrupted, disease resulted.

33. In *Paul Faber, Surgeon* (1879) MacDonald uses the unusual device of pitting an atheistic against a curate, Thomas Wingfold, with the latter winning the argument over spontaneous generation and with good scientific reasoning. The atheistic Faber, making experiments on his own, finally came to the conclusion that 'no form of life appeared where protection from the air was thorough' (I, 272; 158), a correct conclusion as Pasteur proved.

34. Justus Liebig, *Researches on the Motion of Juices in the Animal Body*, ed. from the manuscript by William Gregory (London: Taylor and Walton, 1848). Here Liebig placed great emphasis on the reaction of internal vitality against the external atmosphere, a view which MacDonald upheld when he granted control of the internal vegetative and animal vitality to the Will; for a man so interested by the unconscious, MacDonald placed great esteem in the consciousness of vitalic control.

35. George MacDonald, 'A Hidden Life', in *The Poetical Works of George MacDonald* (London: Chatto and Windus, 1893), I, 133-68. 'Within and Without' also appeared in I, 1-131.

36. 'A Hidden Life', op. cit., p.154.'

37. Ibid., p.162.

38. Liebig, op. cit., p.27.

39. George MacDonald, *The Flight of the Shadow* (London: Kegan Paul, Trench, Trübner & Co., Ltd., 1891), 12. This strange little book, dealing with doubles, was to have had another volume but MacDonald never wrote it.

40. George MacDonald, 'Cross Purposes', in *Dealing with the Fairies* (London: Strahan, 1867). For more in-depth analysis of this interesting little story, especially in regard to the dream-states involved, see my The Science-Fantasy of George MacDonald, ch.4. The title of 'Cross Purposes' referred to the action of the child's double, the goblin to Richard and the fairy to Alice.

41. J. Müller, *Elements of Physiology*, translated from the German, with notes, by William Baly, 2 vols (London: Taylor and Walton, 1838).

42. Ibid., I,8.

43. Ibid., I,4.

44. Ibid., I,7.

45. 'The Golden Key' was apparently written for special inclusion in *Dealing with the Fairies.*

46. Müller, *Elements*, I,29.

47. George MacDonald, *The History of Photogen and Nycteris*, first published in *The Graphic Christmas Number* 1879, vol. xx. This version is somewhat different from the later version found in Glenn Edward Sadler's *The Gifts of the Child Christ: Fairy Tales and Stories for the Childlike* (Grand Rapids, Michigan: William B. Eerdman's Publishing Company, 1973), a two volume set and a handy collection of MacDonald's short fantasy. Since this specific fairy tale was about science (as fully discussed in chapter six of my thesis), it had particular import in judging MacDonald's views of science. We found the 'backward-undoing' with which MacDonald faulted science in the actions of Watho, yet again Liebig's views of equilibrium and interaction with the environment came through clearly. Just because MacDonald found fault with certain aspects of scientific research does not mean that he

dismissed science altogether.

48. Müller, Elements, I, 71.

49. Ibid., I, 789.

50. Robert Falconer's theory was that the mesmerised Miss Cameron's nerves were more on the surface so that she was more reactive to external influences; he was aware that the mesmerised state was similar to sleep and so felt that she exhibited the externally-caused sleepwalking state at night because it was then that she was most susceptable (*David Elginbrod*, III, 210; 337).

51. Gary Kern, 'The Search for Fantasy', in *Bridges to Fantasy*, ed. by George E. Susser, Eric. Rabkin, and Robert Scholes (Carbondale and Edwardsville: Southern Illinois Press, 1982), p.184. Kern also noted that to the ancient Greeks this was a matter of epistemology, not of literary genre; this seemed to be MacDonald's concern as well.

52. P. F. Fletcher's *The Purple Island Or The Isle of Man* (Amsterdam and New York: Theatrum Orbis Terrerum, Ltd., and Da Capo Press, 1971), a Jacobean poem about nympholepsy which influenced *Phantastes*. Fletcher, as Greville explained in his foreward to the Everymen edition of *Phantastes* (London: J. M. Dent & Sons, Ltd., n. d.), had the mind as a castle with three councillors ruling: Judgement, Imagination, and Memory. Traditionally, the cell Phantastic occupied the front of the brain, but here Fletcher placed it after judgement. MacDonald seems to have used his own particular sequence, alternating Judgement and the Imagination, with the Memory bringing back the result to be subjected anew to both, then repeating. Hence his protagonists, after being stimulated into the mesmerised state, came to full consciousness and analysed their experience, only to be carried further down into the mesmeric state where the imagination worked again. Upon regaining consciousness the process repeated. MacDonald, in *England's Anthipon* (London: MacMillan and Co., n.d. (1874), dismissed *The Purple Island* as not a good poem for it contained 'an incongruous dragon of allegory' (p.156). Fletcher chose anatomy as the allegorical subject, but in *Phantastes* MacDonald worked instead by using various mental staes of (un)consciousness to demonstrate his view; perhaps he hoped to avoid allegory by this indulgence in psychology, but critics accused him of it anyway.

53. Müller, *Elements*, II, 1087.

54. Ibid., II, 1079.

55. Ibid., II, 1061.

56. I believe that MacDonald actually had a colour code which imparted signification to the rainbow spectrum of colours in the fairy tales. His named spectrum in *The Golden Key* followed Newton's delineated order in *Opticks: Or, A Treatise of the Reflextions, Refractions, Inflexions and Colours of Light* (London: Sam. Smith and Benj. Walford, 1704). Newton concerned himself with what Goethe called the physiological colours, although he did speak of those psychological ones, which 'appear sometimes by other causes, as when by the power of phantasy we see Colours in Dream . . . (p.120). In *Goethe's Theory of Colours; Translated from the German: with notes by Charles Lock Eastlake* (London: John Murray, 1840), the philosopher attached philosophical meanings to the spectrum which echo in MacDonald. Since Goethe noted that after-images were negatives (pp.22-3), then the after-image of the red sun on Alice's wall would necessarily be green and the prior sensitizing state to the reversed green fairy world would be red, just as indicated.

57. Müller, *Elements*, II, 1080.

58. Rosemary Jackson, *Fantasy: The Literature of Subversion* (London and New York: Methuen, 1981), p.86.

59. George MacDonald, Donal Grant, 3 vols. (London: Kegan, Paul, Trench, Trübner, and Co., 1883); and the one volume by the same company, 1905. The distressed Lady Arctura, observing how her uncle had drugged Donal's wine, commented with a straight face that 'my uncle is in the habit of taking some horrible drug for the sake of its effects on his brain. There *are* people who do so' (II, 67; 159). The unnamed drug was most likely hashish, which was known to produce a 'mental hallucination, with some degree of control over the train of thought–a sort of half waking dream' according to James Braid's *Observation on Trance: or, Human Hibernation* (London: John Churchill; Edinburgh: Adam and Chas. Black, 1850), p.27. MacDonald did not approve of drugs in general, due to his homeopathic belief in letting 'Nature' work her course without the undue aid of outside chemicals.

60. In *Magic, Witchcraft, Animal Magnetism, Hypnotism, and Electro-biology: being a digest of the latest views of the author on these subjects* (London: John Churchill, Edinburgh: Adam and Chas. Black, 1852), James Braid quoted a Mr J. J. G. Wilkinson (MacDonald's friend James John Garth, who said that 'The atom of sleep is diffusion; the mind and body are dissolved in unconsciousness . . . The unit of hypnotism is intense attention, abstraction–the personal ego pushed to nonetity.' (p.54) So loss of self would be common to the hypnotised states as well as to the young child, the mystic, and the sleeping or drugged person. Also, the unconsciousness of *Phantastes* would produce the same loss of self as the attentive abstraction in *Lilith.*

61. *Donal Grant*, II, 58, 155.

62. Müller, Elements, II, 1125.

63. Ibid., II, 1415.

64. Ibid., 1416.

65. Ibid., 1419.

66. A. W. MacFarlane, *Dreaming* (Edinburgh: Oliver and Boyd, 1891), p.16. MacFarlane took this from *David Elginbrod* (III, 194; 331) and found phantasms and hallucinations common when the consciousness and unconsciousness rapidly alternated. 'When we close our eyes,' the doctor wrote, 'object-consciousness is cut off; subject-consciousness, untrammelled, may be exaggerated' (p.10). MacDonald had already explored this in *Phantastes* in the scene where Anodos had his view of the exterior world–or, in the world where outside and inside were confused,it could be the interior–cut off by the farm woman with a book.

67. MacFarlane, *Dreaming*, p.21.

68. Ibid., p.23.

69. Ibid., p.24.

70. In 'The Fantastic Imagination' in *A Dish of Orts: Chiefly Papers on the Imagination and Shakespear* (London: Edward Dalton, 1908), MacDonald wrote that '. . . where is object is to move by suggestion, to cause to imagine, then let him assail the soul of the reader as the wind assails an aeolian harp' (p.321). Note that the motive was 'to move by suggestion', an act of hypnotism; such sounds of Nature were believed to be sleep-inducing, thus putting the subject in the correct state of receptivity.

71. MacFarlane, *Dreaming*, p.26.

72. Ibid., p.28.

73. 'At all events we could not do without the wind. It all depends on how big our lungs are whether the wind is too strong for us or not.' MacDonald commented in *At the Back of the North Wind*, in *Good Words for the Young.*

1870 volume, 84. The lungs were recognised, following the atmospheric theory of Liebig, to be on the border between the inside and outside, as was the skin. In seeking help for both lung and skin problems, MacDonald would have had it pointed out that these were considered to have psychosomatic causes. His friend Dr John Rutherford Russell, the great homoeopath, acknowledged this thoroughly, for he wrote that 'more than most, the lung requires a full allowance of nervous influence (as is shown by the phenomena of asthma . . .)', another ailment that troubled MacDonald. See John Rutherford Russell, *Pneumonia* (London: Leath and Ross, n.d., probably late 1850's), p.28. Incidentally, William Gregory was a friend of Russell's, and so may have introduced MacDonald to him.

74. Russell's views on homoeopathy permeated much of MacDonald's work. In a memoir of Dr Russell, who died on Dec. 2, 1866, a 'D.M.' wrote that in Leamington, where the Edinburgh native Russell had moved in 1853, there often gathered 'Mr Alexander J. Ellis, the Philologist, M.E.S. Dallas, Signor Saffi, and the poet and novelist, Mr. George MacDonald, one of whose works is dedicated to him'. *D.M., Memoir of the Late Dr. Rutherford Russell* (London: Henry Turner and Co., n.d.), p.13). The unnamed work was *Adela Cathcart*, written in the period of Russell's death. It was not coincidental that MacDonald's theories of writing fairy tales were included in this work devoted to Dr Russell, for the healing powers granted to the tales which were used on the ill Adela worked on many homoeopathic principles (see my Ph.D. thesis, chapter 2). Foremost among these was the fundamental place of 'Nature' in the healing process, which might explain in part the abundant use of the Natura figure in MacDonald's fantasy.

75. MacFarlane, *Dreaming*, p.30.

76. Ibid., p.37.

77. For this statement and a pioneering, though brief, folkloric look at MacDonald's fairy tales, see Tolkien's 'On Fairy Stories', in *Tree and Leaf* (London: Unwin & Allen, 1964). Comparisons of death and sleep go back to Homer, but in MacDonald's day the medical belief was that the vital strength consisted of the actual physical body and a multi-sided spiritual body, a condition of the $\psi v \chi \acute{\eta}$. It would take a loosening of the $\pi v \epsilon \hat{v} \mu a$, such as occurred in sleep or hypnotism, to bring into play the body and soul connection of the $\psi v \chi \acute{\eta}$. A loosened $\pi v \epsilon \hat{v} \mu a$ was a higher spiritual state; thus in death the $\pi v \epsilon \hat{v} \mu a$ would be totally separated. The various states of consciousness therefore dipped downward into higher spirituality, the more unconscious the person the more spiritual state. In my Ph.D. thesis, chapter 2, I have shown how the states of consciousness in MacDonald's dream-frame were also evident in Lewis Carroll, probably due to their association with Dr Hale's group in Ore, where both men were treated for psychosomatic problems, MacDonald with his lung condition and Carroll with his stammering.

78. MacDonald, in his annotation of *The Tragedy of Hamlet, Prince of Denmarke* (London: Longmans, Green, & Co., 1885), took special note of Shakespear's lines 'To die-to sleep.-/-To sleep! perchance to dream!' and commented that Hamlet 'had been thinking of death only as the passing away of the present with its troubles-its own thoughts, its own consciousness: if it be a sleep, it has its dreams . . . but there is the question of the character of the dreams. This consideration is what makes calamity so long-lived!' (p.124).

79. Robert Lee Wolff, *The Golden Key* (New Haven: Yale University Press, 1961).

80. See especially George D. Economou, *The Goddess Natura in Medieval Literature* (Cambridge, Massachussetts: Harvard University Press, 1972). This is a pregnant field of research for the medievalist interested in Mac-Donald's fairy tales. Nature received its prominence from overlapping allusions to not only medieval literature, but theology, medicine, homoeopathy, and biochemistry as well; we cannot therefore attribute the supposed central female figure to any one area: rather, it was a handy focus for the inductive homologues that MacDonald was particularly gifted in using.

81. From an unmarked newspaper clipping made shortly after MacDonald's death and found as one of four obituaries in the *Civica Bibliotica Internationale* of Bordighera, Italy.

82. Adam, the first named man in the Bible, was hybridised with a raven, the first-named animal of the Bible. Edward Wilton's essay 'Two Examples of the Many-sidedness of the Bible: The First Example–The Raven', in *Good Words for 1863*, ed. by Norman MacLeod (London: Alexander Strahan & Co., 1864), pp.790-5, gave some traits of the bird that perhaps influenced MacDonald's portrayal.

83. See Jan-Ojvind Swahn, *The Tale of Cupid and Psyche* (Aarne-Thompson 425 and 428) (Sweeden: Cwk Gleerup-Lund, 1955), in which seven major motifs are listed. MacDonald's shorter fairy tales were variants of these, his earlier works more traditional in having the family relations included in the story, but even in the final short story, the tale of the Day Boy and the Night Girl, the witch took the parent's place (and Swahn lists the killing of a witch as a specific trait found in some of the collected legends). The two adult romances also followed the pattern, but were notable, however, in not concluding with the final motif found in the shorter tales, the reunion of the couple, as neither Anodos nor Vane was reunited with their love interest in fairy land. MacDonald ended his fairy tales for children with easy solutions, but when working for adults he kept the works open-ended, a remarkable display of modern scepticism. We need not infer that MacDonald knew the legend; Greville reported great regret over losing his father's favourite ring, an intaglio of Psyche.

6

Fictions and Metafictions: 'Phantastes', 'Wilhelm Meister', and the Idea of the 'Bildungsroman'

STEPHEN PRICKETT

Ever since it was first published in 1858, *Phantastes* has presented something of a problem to critics who want to classify it in terms of genre. We, of course, in the wake of *Alice* and the *Water Babies*, have the inestimable advantage of hindsight over the first puzzled and contemptuous reviewers who could hardly have been expected to hail it rapturously as the harbinger of the new literary form that we now call 'Victorian Fantasy'.[1] The introduction of a fresh descriptive holdall, however, does not necessarily clarify the original problems – which have, if anything, tended to multiply rather than diminish with the passage of time.

Take, for instance, that subtitle: *A Faerie Romance for Men and Women*. If it is to be read in conjunction with MacDonald's prefatory quotations from Novalis as implying that his story is based on the model of the German *Märchen* (or 'fairy story'), as it is commonly taken to be, we must apparently also assume that the structure is intended to be *essentially* irrational and fragmentary. The passage in question has been translated as follows:

> One can imagine stories which have no coherence, but only association of events, like dreams; poems, which simply sound lovely, and which are full of beautiful words, but which lack sense or coherence, or at most have single verses which can be understood, like fragments of the most varied objects. This true poetry can at most have a general allegorical meaning and an indirect effect like music. For that reason, nature is as purely poetic as a magician's room, or a physicist's, a children's nursery, a padded cell and a larder . . . .
>
> A fairy story is like a disjointed dream-vision, an ensemble of wonderful things and occurences, for example, a musical fantasy, the harmonic sequences of an Aeolian harp, nature itself. . . .
>
> In a real fairy tale everything must be wonderful, secret and coherent; everything must be alive, each in a different way. The whole of nature must be marvellously mixed with the whole of the world of spirits; here the time of the anarchy, lawlessness,

freedom, of nature in its natural state, the time before the world, comes in . . . The world of fairy-tale is a world which is the exact opposite of the world of reality, and for that very reason is as thoroughly lie it as chaos is to completed creation.[2]

Yet to what extent might that loose yet suggestive word 'Romance' of the subtitle be taken to suggest a stronger formal unity? Certainly many, if not all, readers, have found an innate underlying unity in the whole work that belies its superficially fragmented construction. Robert Lee Wolff, in his pioneering study of MacDonald,[3] was one of the first to discuss this tension between the apparently episodic and even picaresque arrangement of incidents and the possibility of an overall allegorical or symbolic structure. As Wolff points out, this problem of intention is compounded by the fact that Novalis had originally written *not* that 'everything must be wonderful, mysterious and coherent' (thereby seeming to contradict the first paragraph) but that it should be '*incoherent*' (*unzusammenhängend*). It was his friends and editors, Tieck and Schlegel, who had made the alteration for purposes of their own. For Wolff's largely Freudian interpretation, any sense of unity overriding the apparently fragmented construction can be attributed more to the degree to which its author reveals his own unconscious needs and fantasies than to any deliberate constructional subtlety,[4] but for others the novel's structural coherence (however achieved) has been its essential feature. C.S. Lewis, for instance, records that a key step in his conversion to Christianity was triggered by the chance finding a copy of *Phantastes* on a railway station bookstall in 1916.

The more one studies Lewis's account of this particular accident of fortune, indeed, the more bizarre does it become. Admittedly, any 'conversion' narrative is likely to be a more than usually edited and subjective version of the facts, but, if Lewis's telling of the story is to be given even suspended credence, it makes the conversions of Augustine, Wesley or Newman seem events of the severest necessitarian logic by comparison. Here is part of his account of that first reading of *Phantastes*:

> Turning to the bookstall, I picked out an Everyman in a dirty jacket, *Phantastes, a faerie Romance*, George MacDonald . . . That evening I began to read my book.
>
> The woodland journeyings in that story, the ghostly enemies, the ladies both good and evil, were close enough to my habitual imagery to lure me on without the perception of change. It is as if I were carried sleeping across the frontier, or as if I had died in the old country and could never remember how I came alive in

the new. For in one sense the new country was exactly like the
old. I met there all that had already charmed me in Malory,
Spenser, Morris and Yeats. But in another sense all was changed.
I did not yet know (and I was long in learning) the name of the
new quality, the bright shadow, that rested on the travels of
Anodos. I do now. It was Holiness. For the first time the song of
the sirens sounded like the voice of my mother or my nurse.
Here were old wives' tales; there was nothing to be proud of in
enjoying them. It was as though the voice which had called to
me from the world's end were now speaking at my sides . . . .[5]

Here is certainly that sense of wonderful and secret coherence that
MacDonald had discovered (however illegitimately) in the Novalis
quotations, but in recollecting that coherence Lewis immediately and
naturally enters into the allegorical imagery of the story he is describing. It was as if, almost like Anodos in the novel, he had been 'carried
sleeping across a frontier' to somewhere where the allurements of the
most exotic literary forms–which clearly included for him the
Arthurian cycle and the Faerie Queen–were one and the same with
the stories of his mother or nurse–and here he slips easily into the
imagery of the 'grandmother' and 'wise-woman' that pervades not
just *Phantastes*, but so many of MacDonald's other stories. Yet the
inversion of the sinister dark 'shadow' of the novel into the 'bright
shadow' of 'holiness' seems nevertheless in context almost wilful. It is
one thing to read the episodic and loosely-strung narrative of *Phantastes*
as some kind of moral allegory; it is surely quite another to find in it a
gateway to the whole doctrinal panoply of institutional Christianity.
Fairy stories, whether German or English, have played a significant
underground role in European cultural history, but they have not
been especially noted in either country for causing religious conversions. Far from it–indeed, so much so that they have more often
been the object of gravest suspicion by guardians of culture and
orthodoxy.[6]

It may be that part of the clue to Lewis's reaction to *Phantastes* is to
be found in the meaning he attached to that word 'holiness'. Though
at that stage he does not seem to have been particularly well-read in
German literature, by the early 1930s, when he came to reflect on
what had happened to him, he was certainly enough of a classically-
trained philologist to know that *hagios*, the New Testament word
most often translated into English as 'holy', like its Hebrew Old Testament counterpart, *quadosh*, came from a root meaning 'seperate' or
'set aside' for a deity or deities[7]–with suggestions of an even earlier
meaning of 'polluted' or 'unclean'.[8] Indeed his final comments on the

unexpected effects of his casual purchase seem to be an implicit reference to such connotations of the word:

> Up till now each visitation of Joy had left the common world momentarily a desert–'The first touch of the earth went nigh to kill'. Even when real clouds or trees had been the material of the vision, they had been so only by reminding me of another world; and I did not like the return to ours. But now I saw the bright shadow coming out of the book into the real world and resting there, transforming all common things and yet itself unchanged . . . That night my imagination was, in a certain sense, baptised; the rest of me, not unnaturally, took longer. I had not the faintest notion what I had let myself in for by buying *Phantastes*.[9]

The language of the Wordsworthian visionary reaches back through a whole literary tradition to the classical world, both pagan and Christian. Thus for Lewis 'holiness' is not so much an attribute of particular characters in the narrative, nor even of plot-structure, but rather the transformation of the mundane world into something new, 'set aside' by divinity, and transcendent. Indeed, the transformation of the 'shadow' from what was originally 'polluted' and destructive into a source of inspiration and joy is precisely the kind of metaphor of redemption that would have appealed to his philological imagination. But, of course, as we have seen from the earlier quotation, Lewis's previous sense of the mundane world (even at the stage, where he then was, of what he was later to call 'popular realism') was already essentially a *literary* one–and a literary one, moreover, of a certain kind. As Lewis himself was to note afterwards, his road to conversion via Philosophical Idealism, Pantheism, and finally Theism, though it seemed a natural enough one to him at the time, was in fact a highly unusual one for the early twentieth century.[10] What he does not add, but which seems very clear in retrospect, is the degree to which his route was influenced by his literary taste. The world of his imagination was, we note, that of Malory, Spenser, Morris and Yeats. None of them, it is true, were notably 'Christian' writers (indeed, two of the four were distinctly hostile to the Christianity they had encountered in their society) but all four were not merely writers of fantasy but also the creators and users of potent literary myths. All four were creators not just of fictions, but of complex meta-fictions–creating from the material of myth and legend highly self-conscious mythopoeic works of art. The 'baptism' of Lewis's imagination was thus, it seems, 'baptism' and a santification not so much of literature a means of approaching the transcendent (a view Lewis was both drawn to and, for that reason, highly sceptical of) but more specifically of the particular kind of literary synthesis such works implied.

In his first popular success, *The Screwtape Letters*, Lewis had made the acute observation that, unlike almost every society of the past, the fragmentation of modern Western society was such that anyone living in it was accustomed at any given moment to having 'a dozen incompatible philosophies dancing about together inside his head.[11]' An earlier work, *The Pilgrim's Regress* (1933), had already given an allegorical form to some of his own personal struggles with those seeming incompatibilities. In particular, it offers what is perhaps the clearest statement of that vision or, as he calls it sometimes, that 'sweet desire' for something glimpsed but unachievable which drove him inescapably forward to what only later he was to recognise as a religious position. For some reason, therefore, what *Phantastes* had given to Lewis above all was a glimpse of the possibility of a developing synthesis in which language, literature, and thus the entire record of human imaginative experience could be brought into a unified whole. It had showed him a way (or, at least, perhaps the possibility of a way) in which the literary or poetic transformation of sense-experience – what in *The Pilgrim's Regress* is symbolised by a magic floating island that seems at once everywhere and nowhere – could be given some kind of objective meaning and validity. In one sense this may seen a very far cry from Novalis's idea of a fairy story, but in another it may also serve to illuminate certain elements in what Mac-Donald was attempting with his new and highly potent fictional form. In any case there were other influences besides Novalis at work on his imagination.

Among the epigraphs in *Phantastes* are quotations from the Arthurian legends, Spenser, Shakespeare, the Metaphysical poets, Coleridge, Wordsworth, and Shelley; and from the Germans: Heine, Jean Paul (Richter), Schiller, Schleiermacher, and Goethe. Though such a heterogeneous selection of writers could hardly be accused of any kind of religious orthodoxy, what they do have in common is that they are all creators of 'Romance' of one kind or another. Certainly, whatever MacDonald was attempting to do in creating the 'adult fairy story', Lewis was clearly right in detecting in him an eclectic literary taste in many ways akin to his own, at once meta-fictional and intertextual in its mode of operation.

Notably absent from this list, interestingly enough, is E.T.A. Hoffmann, whose novella, *The Golden Pot*, has, following Greville MacDonald's suggestion in his biography of his father, regularly been

cited as being the probable model for *Phantastes*[12] Yet, though Mac-
Donald's general enthusiasm for Hoffmann is clearly beyond doubt,
such a statement is, in fact, highly misleading. Though certain incidents in *Phantastes*, such as the whispering voices in the tree that
begin Hoffmann's story and end MacDonald's, are clear examples of
the latter's borrowing (be it said, to good advantage), any structural
resemblence between *The Golden Pot* and *Phantastes* is in fact very
slight. Hoffmann's story, with its tightly-constructed sequential narrative and its plethora of irrelevant magical wonders, offers no development of character or suggestion of hidden allegory. In no way does it
offer the kind of model for a sustained full-length allegorical
'Romance' that MacDonald by his network of epigraphs and quotations seems to be so self-consciously striving to re-create in his new
form.

For this, the influence of Goethe would seem much more important. Though he had, of course, been well-known to the comparatively small circle of German-speakers in Britain from before the end
of the previous century, Goethe was little more than a name to the
British public at large – known chiefly through a bad translation of
Werter – and he had only come to wider prominence with the appearance of Carlyle's classic translation of *Wilhelm Meister* in 1824 – the
year of MacDonald's birth. Though Carlyle had previously contributed translations for serialization in the *London Magazine* (including a
Life of Schiller) and was later, in 1827, to translate *The Golden Pot*,
this was his first independantly published literary work and, as such,
it was undoubtedly chosen with the aim of furthering the reputation
of its translator as well as its original author. In this he was at least
partially successful: if the initial public response was not overwhelm-
ing, demand was strong enough for a second edition in 1839. As Carlyle was well aware, nothing quite like it had appeared in English
before.

From its first publication in 1796, *Wilhelm Meisters Lehrjahre* had
attracted controversy. Goethe had begun his loose and episodic
novel as early as 1777, when he was both a Minister of State in
Weimar and director of the Court Theatre, and he worked on it
spasmodically until 1785, by which time he had completed the fifth
book. He did not resume writing until 1794, in very different circumstances, when he rapidly completed the remaining three books[13]. By
that stage, what had seemingly begun as an autobiographical novel of
theatrical life had turned into the first (and arguably the greatest)
example of the genre later to be known by the word *Bildungsroman*.

The degree to which the novel reflects this chequered writing-history is a matter of controversy. The earlier books tell the story of how the young Wilhelm rejects the middle-class commercial world in which he was brought up, and, under the guise of a business trip financed by his father, joins and eventually runs a group of itinerant actors. While on this extended period of absence from home, he has a series of more or less disastrous and unsuitable love-affairs with women ranging from two actresses to a countess, in the process acquiring a number of dependents including a small child which, as he afterwards learns, is his own – borne by Marianne, his first love who has subsequently died. The loosely-strung episodes of this narrative are given further shape by a second, meta-fictional, plot based on Shakespeare's *Hamlet*. On first being introduced to the play by the mysterious Jarno, Wilhelm undertakes not merely to rewrite in accordance with the needs of the time, but also to direct it, and even to act the part of the prince himself. The parallels with his own life are carefully highlighted. He is haunted by guilt over the neglect of his father (significantly, less so over Marianne – a not-so-innocent but equally tortured Ophelia). His closest friend and confident is even known as 'Horatio' (though we are told that this is not his real name). In the later sections of the book, direct references to the players in Hamlet and his own troupe are stressed, culminating in a scene where Jarno points out, in a passage reminiscent of Act II, sc.ii, the symbolic parallels between the playhouse and the world[14]

In the final books of the *Apprenticeship* and in its sequel, the *Travels*, all semblance of conventional naturalism is set aside. Jarno, along with several other equally enigmatic figures, turns out to belong to a secret society, the Society of the Tower, which takes its name from the tower of the mysterious rambling castle of a nobleman called Lothario. This organisation, it transpires, has been keeping a beneficient watch over Wilhelm almost from the start, limiting the potentially disastrous consequences of his mistakes and, eventually, in a scene echoing the initiation of Tamino in *The Magic Flute*, admitting him to the mysteries of their order. At the end of the novel, he is finally rewarded with the hand of the beautiful lady, the 'Amazon', whose image he has been in love with, for most of the novel, and who conveniently turns out to be the sister of the Countess for who he has long also nourished a hopeless passion.

He is not to be allowed to enjoy his lady at this stage, however. Once safely betrothed, he is immediately sent off again on his travels– the subject of the next volume. In its meta-fictional structure the *Travels* relies less on Shakespeare than on a work by another, no less meta-fictional English writer: Sterne's *Sentimental Journey*: at one point Wilhelm is even casually referred to as 'Yorrick'. Though at the narrative level there are a good many 'Shandian' interludes, at a philosophical level the emphasis is less on the gaining of worldly experience than on the stages of religious awareness.[15]

Any reader of MacDonald cannot fail to be struck by the startlingly familiar imagery from which these complex allegories are created. We have already mentioned the rambling castle, with the secret in the tower (and even, at one point, hobgoblins!), so central to *The Princess and the Goblin*, but these borrowed elements of the *Apprenticeship* pale into insignificance with the flood of ingredients MacDonald appears to have culled from the *Travels*. Miners 'allured by the metallic veins', boring through the rock, are held up by Jarno as types or exempla of the 'enquiring thinker in a thousand ways endeavouring to solve the hardest problems,'[16] there is a golden casket with a (missing) golden key – in connection with which character even has, in the words of Carlyle's translation, to toil 'through moss and tangle';[17] the protagonists are, at another point, led on a pre-ordained route by mysterious arrows; there are even, for those who like to mix MacDonald with Tolkien, dwarves (who, like MacDonald's goblins, have chosen to go underground and shun the light) and dragons.

Such elements, interesting though they may be, are less significant to our understanding of MacDonald than the way in which the episodic plots of both novels are constructed around a sense of the larger whole in which it is suggested that there is a hidden order permeating all existence, and that the growth of the youthful but symbolically-named 'Meister' is achieved both through its guidance and, eventually, by the discovery of it. That this discovery is at the same time a self-discovery is made clear in the ceremony of Wilhelm's admission to the Society of the Tower when he is presented with an already-printed book of his own life. The constant cross-reference to other works of literature, moreover, serves to create the impression that there is, similarly, a hidden meaning and order to be discovered through literature, and that there, too, understanding and self-discovery are but twin aspects of the same process. As a spiritual advisor to the 'fair saint', a noblewoman who comes under the influence of Count Zinzendorf's Moravian sect, says:

> Life lies before us, as a huge quarry lies before the architect: he deserves not the name of architect, except when, out of this fortuitous mass, he can combine, with the greatest economy, and fitness, and durability, some form, the pattern of which originated in his spirit. All things without us, I may add, all things on us, are mere elements: but deep within us lies the creative force,

which out of these can produce what they were meant to be; and which leaves us neither sleep nor rest, till in one way or another, without us or on us, that same has been produced.[18]

What Lewis was to find with such astonishment in MacDonald was a re-deployment not just of individual motifs and elements culled from Goethe, but a whole way of structuring experience, part fantasy, part realism, which go to make up the origins of the German *Bildungsroman*.

The German word *Bildung* is almost untranslateable in English. The most literal meaning would be that of 'formation' or 'growth' with the implication of internal organic self-development rather than merely the acquiring of a skill or training (as in the parallel word, *Ausbildung*). Thus Goethe's contemporary, the philologist Wilhelm von Humboldt, wishing, as he put it, to study 'the faculty of speech in its inward aspect, as a human faculty' insisted that it must be understood in the context of a 'philosophical survey of humanity's capacity for formation (*Bildung*) and with history'.[19] Such connotations of 'inwardness', 'culture', and even introspectiveness have sometimes led to the word *Bildungsroman* being rendered in English as 'the novel of self-cultivation'–a genre which no less a literary figure than Thomas Mann saw as being Germany's most distinctive cultural form.[20]

Though the term seems to have been coined in the early 1820s by Karl Morgenstern,[21] it did not achieve wide currency until the end of the nineteenth century when it was taken up by Wilhelm Dilthey–who at first simply defined it in terms of what he saw as its progenitor: 'I propose to call those novels which make up the school of Wilhelm Meister . . . Bildingsromane.'[22] This he later summarised as a 'regulated development within the life of the individual . . . Each of its stages has its own intrinsic value and is at the same time the basis for a higher stage. The dissonances and conflicts of life appear as the necessary growth points through which the individual must pass on his way to maturity and harmony.'[23] Morgenstern's original definition had, however, been more subtly reflexive. For him the term should apply not merely to the *Bildung* of the hero, but also to that of the *reader*, whose own personal 'formation' and self-development is fostered through involvement with the text.[24] Without plunging into the interesting question of his anticipation of later reader-response theories, it is worth noticing how closely such an idea of the *Bildungsroman* foreshadows the effect of *Phantastes* at least on a reader such as Lewis–not to mention his friend Arthur Greeves, with whom he corresponded at length about his discovery.[25]

Recent English-language discussions of the genre have tended to move away from Dilthey's concentration on the character of the hero and to see such novels much more in terms of self-conscious literary artifacts. Michael Beddow, for instance, following a line of thought begun by Martin Swales, argues that 'despite the implications of the generic name they acquired after they were written, the development of the hero is not the ultimate cononcern . . .' [26] In an echo of Morgenstern's idea of the self-conscious reflexiveness inherent in the genre he continues:

> We are invited to view the entire narrative as a piece of fiction which requires of us a response that includes an awareness of reading an imaginative construction, rather than an empirically accurate representation. At this level of reading, the mimetic claim to be 'about' the hero's development is relativised by the wider claim that the narrative of the hero's experiences, *precisely insofar as we perceive it to be a piece of fiction,* offers insights into human nature which could not be adequately conveyed either in the form of discursive arguments or through a rigorously mimetic, non-self-conscious fictional work. [27]

Such an inherently meta-fictional description applies not merely to Goethe's *Wilhelm Meister* – still for Beddow, as for Dilthey, the supreme example of the genre – but also with extraordinary accuracy to *Phantastes* and to the new form of 'Faerie Romance' in English that we would now see as probably MacDonald's most significant stylish achievement. It also suggests the magnitude of MacDonald's debt to Goethe.

Yet the obvious question persists: what difference does it make to our reading of *Phantastes* if we see it in terms of the organic unity of a *Bildungsroman* rather than the alogical fragmentation of a fairy story? Surely, for instance, we do not need to refer to German literary theory to discover that Anodos' spiritual growth and development is a central theme of the story? Are there in fact elements in the story that we might be led to look for by such a reclassification that we might otherwise be inclined to miss?

I believe there are. The most obvious example is irony – especially irony in that peculiar new sense that we find with Goethe and the German romantics. [28] Though we are familiar enough with it in Augustine, Dante, the Metaphysical poets, and even in Bunyan, irony is not a quality that we are necessarily quick to associate with Victorian religious writing. Yet the moment we formulate the question it is clear that *Phantastes* is in fact a pervasively ironic work at many levels. At the most obvious level is the constant disconfirmation of Anodos' expectations – from his first meeting with his variable sized 'grandmother' in the bureau to his mistakes over the various 'white' and 'marble' ladies he pursues with such energy throughout the narrative. It is clear throughout that this 'fairy land' corresponds neither to his wishes nor his expectations – derived mostly from other literature on the subject. This brings us at the meta-fictional level to the truly Goethean irony in the use of other parallel literary texts – not least, of which, as we have seen, is the one from Novalis stressing the fragmentary and eliptical nature of fairy stories. Not merely must we bear Novalis in mind when reading *Phantastes*, we need also to re-read the Novalis passage itself in the light of that experience.

It is this pervasive sense of literary irony that is the clue to so much of the relationship between MacDonald's novel and the other works on which it draws. For a variety of historical reasons, the novel as a form never came to enjoy the kind of prestige in eighteenth-century Germany that it held in England.[29] A reference book of the 1770s published in Leipzig, for instance, has no entry under 'novel', only 'novelistic', where it comments: 'Thus one describes whatever in content, tone, or expression bears the characteristics which prevailed in earlier novels – such as fondness for adventures, stiltedness in actions, events, feelings. The natural is more or less the exact opposite of the novelistic.'[30] In Martin Swales' memorial phrase, the novel in Germany was born with 'a bad conscience'[31] Thus it was normal for prose works to be judged not on their own terms, but rather for their 'poetic' content. In this connection it is revealing, for instance, that, in MacDonald's quotation from Novalis with which we began, the fairy story is discussed not as narrative (which, it is taken for granted, will have 'no coherence') but as 'poetry' – and the word used in the German is not *dichterish*, which would tend to be employed in connection with actual verse and imaginative writing, but *poetisch*, which has a much more theoretical, abstract, and spiritualised flavour to it.[32]

Thus not least among the reasons for the enormous popularity and prestige of *Wilhelm Meister* in early nineteenth-century Germany was that it served to rehabilitate what had hitherto seemed to many critics a dubious and even illegitimate fictional form. In his introduction to the first edition of his English translation, Carlyle quotes Schlegel on the contrast between it and its predecessors: 'To judge of this book, – new and peculiar as it is, and only to be understood and learned from itself, by our common notion of the novel, a notion pieced together and produced out of custom and belief, out of accidental and arbitrary requisitions, – is as if a child should grasp at the moon and stars, and insist on packing them into its toy-box.'[33] What was felt to be the inwardness and dignity of the way in which Goethe handled the new medium gave the lie to the eighteenth-century English stereotype of German literature summed up by Wordsworth in 1789 in his attack on 'frantic novels, sickly and stupid German Tradgedies'[34] and helped to pave the way for the great re-appraisal that, helped by Carlyle's influence, was to fire the next generation of young Scots (in particular)[35] such as MacDonald with an enthusiasm for German literature, culture and theology.

Yet the general improvement in status of the German novel with Goethe's great *Bildungsroman* served only to highlight a paradox that had always been latent in any literary expression of 'self-development' as an aesthetic form. In his comments on the novel in his *Aesthetics* Hegel puts in general terms what is, in effect, the central problem of *Wilhelm Meister*. The heroes of such novels he writes,

> . . . stand as individuals with their subjective goals of love, honour, ambition, or with their ideals of improving the world, over against the existing order and prose of reality which from all sides places obstacles in their path . . . These struggles are, however, in the modern world nothing but the apprenticeship, the education of the individual at the hands of the given reality . . . For the conclusion of such an apprenticeship usually amounts to the hero getting the corners knocked off him . . . In In the last analysis he usually gets his girl and some kind of job, marries and becomes a philistine just like the others.[36]

In other words, the very process of self-formation and the gaining of worldy wisdom, essential as it is to growth and maturity, is actually towards a goal that is fundamentally less interesting and less morally worthy than the raw immature idealism that preceded it![37] Certainly the ending of *Wilhelm Meister*, where our hero is paired with a beautiful aristocrat and given the job of managing a large estate purchased as an investment by a business syndicate, is highly ambigious.

It is part of the ironic literary structure of MacDonald's *Bildungsroman* that the ending of *Phantastes* can be read not merely in relation to the narrative that precedes it, but also in relation to this problem in its progenitor, *Wilhelm Meister*. Thus Anodos at the end of his experience, instead of being better fitted for accommodation with the real world, is left actually wondering how far he is now un-fitted for it.

> . . . I began the duties of my new position, somewhat instructed, I hoped, by the adventures that had befallen me in Fairy Land. Could I translate the experience of my travels there, into common life? This was the question. Or must I live it all over again, and learn it all over again, in the other forms that belong to the

world of men, whose experience yet runs parallel to that
of Fairy Land? The question I cannot yet answer. But I
fear . . . I have a strange feeling sometimes, that I am a ghost
sent into the world to minister to my fellow-men, or, rather, to
repair the wrongs I have already done . . . Thus I, who set out
to find my ideal, came back rejoicing that I had lost my
shadow . . . What we call evil, is the only and best shape,
which, for the person and his condition at the time, could be
assumed by the best good. And so, *Farewell*.[38]

Whereas Wilhelm Meister, at the end of the *Apprenticeship*, is
compared with Saul the son of *Kish*, 'who went out to seek his
father's asses, and found a kingdom',[39] Anodos can be certain not of
present happiness, like Goethe's hero, but only of future good.
Though he is in some ways a sadder and a wiser man, there is no suggestion that his final condition involves any kind of moral compromise with the values of the world. His 'formation' has, on the contrary, given him a stronger sense of his own ideals – even if he is also
correspondingly more humble about his capacity to attain them or
their applicability here. He notably does not get any of the woman he
has been pursuing so earnestly. This strangely hesitant agnosticism of
MacDonald, the religious believer, similarly also loses something of
its quiet irony if we fail to set it alongside the formulaic certainties of
the 'agnostic' religious instruction of Goethe's ideal community at
the end of the *Travels*:

Two duties we have most rigorously undertaken: first to honour
every species of religious worship, for all of them are compre-
hended more or less directly in the Creed: secondly, in like
manner to respect all forms of government; and since every one
of them induces and promotes a calculated activity, to labour
according to the wish and will of constituted authority, in whatever place it may be our lot to sojourn, and for whatever time.
Finally, we reckon it our duty, without pedantry of rigour, to
practise and forward decorum of manners and morals, as
required by that Reverence for Ourselves . . . All this, in the sol-
emn hour of parting, we have thought good once more to
recount, to unfold, to hear and acknowledge, as also to seal with
a trustful Farewell.[40]

It is at points like this that we sense MacDonald's wisdom in prefer-
ring Novalis's studied incoherence to Goethe's portentousness.

Nevertheless, if the striking parallels between *Phantastes* and *Wilhelm Meister* suggest that MacDonald, in creating his 'fairy romance
for men and women', was in fact transplanting the Goethean

Bildungsroman into the alien but high fertile context of English literature, we need to recognise first of all the inevitable and ironic transformation wrought by that change of air. Whereas the prose romance
in German was scarcely recognised, in England it had a lineage reaching back to Mallory; whereas similarly, the indigenous German theatre was of little account, England had Shakespeare. In this sense the
context of meta-fictional reference available to MacDonald was far
richer and more evocative than was possible for Goethe in his own
literature. It is highly significant that when Goethe, comparing the
demands on the hero of the drama (*Hamlet*, naturally!) with the hero
of the novel, needed to evoke a string of protagonists from novels,
his entire selection was from England: 'Grandison, Clarissa, Pamela,
the Vicar of Wakefield, Tom Jones. . . '.[41] Contrarywise, in returning
the compliment, MacDonald by his references to Novalis, Hoffmann,
Jean Paul, Schleiermacher, Heine, Schiller, and Goethe is in fact
doing something very different: whereas Shakespeare and the English
eighteenth-century novelists were comparatively familiar in Germany,
German writers of the late eighteenth-century literary renaissance
were, in contrast little-known, and even exotic, figures to the more
insular British readership of the 1850s. Whereas Goethe's literary references had the effect of placing his novel in relation to what he saw
as the mainstream development of prose realism, MacDonald's con-
trive to suggest that behind the veil of normality in that tradition was
something marvellous and magical that could not be wholly eradi-
cated from everyday life. In the very literature in which Goethe had
assiduously sought bourgeois reality, MacDonald discovers romance –
awaiting only the mysticism of Novalis and his fellow-Germans to be
awakened into new life.

But the ironies of the change in referential context are minor compared with the consequences of the shift in medium from realism to
fantasy. Though *Wilhelm Meister* is, as we have said, hardly realistic by
the later standards of the nineteenth century, it is certainly no fairy
story either. MacDonald was one of the few nineteenth-century writers to recognise that realism and fantasy are two sides of the same
coin: that realism is as much an arbitrary and literary convention as
fantasy, and that fantasy is as dependant on mundane experience as
realism.[42] By invoking Novalis as his mentor, and moving his own
Bildungsroman boldly into the realm of the fantastic, MacDonald was
able to bring out latent resources of irony in the genre that were
unavailable even to Goethe himself in his more overtly naturalistic
mode. Anodos's adventures in Fairy Land, after all, conclude with his
account of his own death – the acceptance of which, as we know from

Lilith, MacDonald saw as being an essential factor in any kind of spiritual maturity. The irony of Christ's maxim, 'He that would save his life, must lose it', is always present in MacDonald's imagination. Moreover, the structural technique of placing the process of 'self-formation' not in this world but, in a fantastic 'other' world, immediately circumvents what we have seen is the major thematic problem of the Goethean *Bildungsroman*. If there is, as I believe, a sense in which *Phantastes* is the most satisfactory English adaptation of the *Bildungsroman* – much more so than, say, Dickens' *Great Expectations* or Meredith's *Ordeal of Richard Feverell*, which have been more commonly advanced as examples of the genre[43] – it is not so much because it is the most faithful replica of its outward characteristics, but because (to use a very German argument) it is the truest expression of its spirit. More: in adapting and radically changing the original form to suit his particular needs, MacDonald in fact solved the problem that had dogged Goethe and his successors working, however loosely, within the tradition of realism. There is no suggestion that in returning to the 'real' world Anodos has had to compromise with it. The contradiction between moral idealism and worldly accommodation that worried Hegel is ultimately, of course, a theological one, and can in the end only be solved in theological terms. But theological solutions do not necessarily make good novels. To find through Goethean irony an appropriate literary and aesthetic form for such an abstraction is an extraordinary achievement – perhaps in its own way one of the greatest achievements of Victorian fiction.

But important as this metaphysical transformation of the *Bildungsroman* undoubtedly is in terms of literary history, it would hardly explain the impact that *Phantastes* had on the eighteen-year-old Lewis, who, at that stage of his life and in the middle of the First World War, was most unlikely to have known or cared about the problems of the German novel. What seems to have excited Lewis is the manner in which MacDonald had managed to give a new relevance and meaning to the fantastic romances of Malory, Spencer, Morris, and his other heroes. By showing the limitations of conventional realism in its portrayal of vital aspects of human growth and development, MacDonald had not merely helped to legitimize Lewis's own literary taste, he had also obliquely and ironically suggested a profound critique of genre and, incidentally, of contemporary assumptions about 'realism'. To suggest that, for Lewis, Phantastes served as an introduction to what we would now, rather parochially, call postmodernism seems at first sight an unlikely perspective, yet, as we have seen, there is a good argument for such a case. It should also make us look more carefully at our own conventional assumptions about postmodernism.

References

1. See Stephen Prickett, *Victorian Fantasy*, (Hassocks: Harvester Press, 1979). ch.5.

2. Translation from *Phantastes*, Introduction by Derek Brewer, (Woodbridge, Suffolk: Boydell Press, 1982). The passage has altogether had a chequered history, since two further mistakes were made in the transliteration at the initial printing of the novel. (See Wolff, pp. 42-4.) The corrected German text reads as follows: *Es lassen sich Erzählungen ohne Zusammenhang, jedoch mit Association, wie Träume, denken; Gedichte, die bloss wohlklingend und woll schöner Worte sind, aber auch ohne allen Sinn und Zusammenhang, höchstens einzelne Strophen verständlich, wie Bruchstücke aus den verschiedenartigsten Dingen. Diese wahre Poesie kann höchstens einen allegorischen Sinn im Grossen, und eine indirecte Wirkung, wie Musik haben. Darum ist die Natur so rein poetisch, wie die Stube eines Zauberers, eines Physikers, eine Kinderstube, eine Polterund Vorrathskammer. . . Ein Mährchen ist wie ein Traumbild ohne Zusammenhang. Ein Ensemble wunderbarer Dinge und Begabenheiten, z. B. eine Musikalische Phantastie, die harmonischen Folgen einer Aeolsharfe, die Natur selbst. In einem echten Mährchen muss alles wunderbar, geheimnissvoll und zusammenhängend sein; alles belebt, jeders auf eine andere Art. Die ganze natur muss wunderlich mit der hanzen Geisterwelt gemischt sein; hier tritt die Zeit der Anarchie, der Gesetzlosigkeit, Freiheit, der Naturstand der Natur, die Zeit vor der Welt ein . . . Die Welt des Mährchens ist die, der Welt der Wahrheit durchaus entgegengesetzte, und eben darum ihr so durchaus ähnlich, wie das Chaos der vollendeten Schöpfung ähnlich ist.*

3. See Robert Lee Wolff, *The Golden Key*, (New Haven: Yale University Press, 1961), pp.43-5.

4. Ibid., ch.2.

5. C.S. Lewis, *Surprised by Joy*, (London: Geoffrey Bles, 1955),. p.169.

6. See Prickett, *Victorian Fantasy*, pp.4-5.

7. *A Theological Word Book of the Bible*, ed. Alan Richardson, (SCM Press, 1950), p.215.

8. Gabriel Josopivici, *The Book of God*, (New Haven: Yale University Press, 1988), pp.6-7.

9. Lewis, *op. cit.*, pp.70-1.

10. *The Pilgrim's Regress*, (London: Collins, Fount Paperback, 1980), p.9.

11. (London: Geoffrey Bles, 1942), p.11.

12. See Greville MacDonald, *George MacDonald and his Wife*, (Allen & Unwin, 1924), pp.73, 259; Wolff, p.45; C.N. Manlove, *Modern Fantasy*, (London: Cambridge University Press, 1975), p.274; Rolland Hein, *The Harmony Within: The Spiritual Vision of George MacDonald*, Grand Rapids, Michigan: (Christian University Press, Eerdmans Publishing Co., 1982), p.7.

13. W.H. Bruford, *The German Tradition of Self-Cultivation: 'Bildung' from Humboldt to Thomas Mann*, (Cambridge University Press, 1975), pp.31-2.

14. *Wilhelm Meister's Apprenticeship and Travels*, trans. by Thomas Carlyle, 2 vols. (Centenary Edn. Carlyle: *Works*, Chapman & Hall, 1896-1903, Vols, XXIII & XXXIV) London: II,14.

15. For a partial but interesting discussion of some of the religious symbolism of the *Travels*, see Ruth ap Roberts, *The Ancient Dialect: Thomas Carlyle and Comparative Religion*. (Berkeley: University of California Press,

1988), ch.2.
16. II, p.225.
17. Ibid., p.230.
18. Op. cit., I, p.444.
19. Wilhelm von Humboldt, *On Language*, trans. by Peter Heath, Introduction by Hans Aarsleff. (Cambridge University Press, 1988), p.xiv.
20. Bruford, op. cit., p.vii.
21. Martin Swales, *The German Bildungsroman from Wieland to Hesse*, (Princeton University Press, 1978), p.12.
22. *Leben Schleiermachers*, Berlin, 1870, I,282. Cited by Michael Beddow, *The Fiction of Humanity: Studies in the Bildungsroman from Weiland to Thomas Mann*, (Cambridge University Press, 1982) p.1.
23. *Das Erlebnis und die Dichtung*, Leipzig & Berne, 1913, p.394. (Swales, op. cit., p.3.)
24. Swales, op. cit., p.12.
25. See *They Stand Together: The Letters of C.S. Lewis to Arthur Greeves* (1914-1963), ed. Walter Hooper (Collins, 1979), pp.92-3, 94, 96, 106, etc.
26. Op. cit., p.2.
27. Ibid., p.5.
28. For a discussion of this sense see Katherine Wheeler, ed., *German Aesthetic and Literary Criticism: The Romantic Ironists and Goethe*, (Cambridge University Press, 1984), p.viii.
29. For a discussion of one aspect of this imbalance, see Hans Frei, *The Eclipse of Biblical Narrative: A Study in Eighteenth and Nineteenth Century Hermeneutics* (Newhaven: Yale University Press, 1974), p.142; also Stephen Prickett, *Words and the Word: Language, Poetics, and Biblical Interpretation* (Cambridge University Press, 1986), pp.82-3.
30. Johann George Sulzer, *General Theory of the Fine Arts*, Leipzig 1773-5, cited by Swales, op. cit., p.19.
31. Ibid.
32. For a further discussion of the implication of these two terms and their historical significance, see Prickett, *Words and the Word*, p.83.
33. *Wilhelm Meister*, I,7.
34. Preface to the *Lyrical Ballads*, ed. R.L. Brett and A.R. Jones (London: Methuen, revised impression, 1965), p.249.
35. For an account of the impact of German literature in Edinburgh in the 1820s, see Anne-Marie Jordens, *The Stenhouse Circle* (Melbourne University Press, 1979), ch.1.
36. *Vorlesungen über die Ästhetik*, ed. F. Bassenge (Berlin, 1955), pp.557-8. Cited by Swales, op. cit., pp.20-21.
37. Ibid., p.21.
38. *Phantastes*, p.166.
39. II, 189.
40. II, 415-16.
41. I, 345.
42. For an extended discussion oof this point without mentioning MacDonald, see Paul Coates, *The Realist Fantasy: Fiction and Reality Since Clarissa*, (Macmillan, 1983).
43. See, for instance, Jerome Buckley, *Season of Youth: The Bildungsroman from Dickens to Golding*, (Cambridge, Massachusetts: Harvard University Press, 1974).

7

George MacDonald and the Victorian Fairy Tale

GILLIAN AVERY

George MacDonald was born in one of the bleakest periods for children's books, into a milieu in any case that, had the deepest possible distrust of the imagination. Current educational theory, which has always had great influence upon reputable publishing for children (the downright subversive, of course, goes its own way), had decided in the early nineteenth century that children finally had grown out of the absurd and marvellous tales of heroes and giants and dragons and talking animals which in unregenerate days they had shared with adults unsophisticated enough to enjoy such matters. It was felt that a new and more glorious era had begun in which the young would be educated and improved through their reading, reasoned into sensible and upright behaviour through moral tales, and filled with useful information through 'geological catechisms, entomological primers, and tales of political economy – dismal trash, all of them; something half way between stupid story-books and bad school-books,' as an American scholar angrily called them.' (He was writing in a preface to a collection of French fairy stories, and making an impassioned plea for recognition of the genre in the New World, a brave but futile gesture since the American mood was even more antagonistic than the English to fantasy, and fairy stories could not be said to be generally popular in the United States until Frank Baum wrote *The Wonderful Wizard of Oz* in 1900.) In addition to these secular considerations, which blighted juvenile reading until well into the reign of Queen Victoria, the Calvinist religion in which the young George MacDonald was reared regarded all imaginative writing as anathema. The imagination in itself was held to be evil, and all that was not actual fact was a lie and therefore damnably wicked.

The usual date given for the turn of the tide, for the beginnings of children's books in which the imagination was allowed free rein, is 1865 when *Alice's Adventures in Wonderland* was published. F.J. Harvey Darton, possibly the most distinguished of all children's book historians, described Alice as 'the first unapologetic, undocumented appearance in print, for readers who sorely needed it, of liberty of thought in

children's books'.² He also went on to claim that henceforth there
would be 'in hours of pleasure no more dread about the moral value.'
As with all generalizations both statements are open to dispute;
examples of 'liberty of thought' can be found in earlier authors, and
what Darton himself described as the 'creeping paralysis of seriousness' afflicted plenty of subsequent books. The works of A.L.O.E. (A
Lady of England, the pseudonym adopted by Charlotte Maria
Tucker, 1821-93) are far more dreary and notably more severe than
the earlier 'Peter Parley' books of information to which Darton
devoted a chapter of denunciation. 'I'm not going to read any books
now but grown-up ones, unless it is an adventure book. I'm sick of
books for young people, there's so much *stuff* in them' says a ficti-
tious 1880s boy. His sister explains: 'We call it *stuff* when there seems
to going to be a story and it comes to nothing but talk.'³ And though
writers treated the younger child with increasing tenderness as the
century wore on, there was still a tendency to lecture and reprove.
Mrs Molesworth, for instance, doyenne of the nursery tale in the late
Victorian period, portrayed nursery faults such as discontent and
peevishness with a merciless accuracy that must have made many
wriggle with discomfort.

The tide of facts had been retreating, almost imperceptibly at first,
for several decades before *Alice*. The eleven year old Emily Pepys had
recorded in her diary in 1844 her amazement at how few books her
mother had had when she was a child.⁴ No *Child's Own Book*, she
noted incredulously. This compilation, first published in 1830, was an
agreeable mixture of French fairy tales, stories from the *Arabian
Nights*, and retelling of assorted English works such as *Little Goody
Two-Shoes*, *Gulliver's Adventures in Lilliput*, and the *History of Little
Jack*. There had been a moment in the opening years of the century
when it looked as though levity might prevail, when John Harris, who
had taken over the Newbery firm, was issuing, in addition to such
pedagogical titles as *The Juvenile Preceptor or a Course of Moral and
Scientific Instructions*, light-hearted picture books like *The Comic
Adventure of Old Mother Hubbard and her Dog* (one of the few nursery rhymes where the author – in this case one Sarah Martin (1768-
1862) who wrote nothing else that has survived – is actually known),
and versions of traditional rhymes like *Cock Robin* and *The House
That Jack Built*. These are earthy and humorous rather than fantastic,
but there was one brief example of an original piece of fantasy in the
verses written for his children by William Roscoe, Member of Parlia-
ment for Liverpool, *The Butterfly's Ball and the Grasshopper's Feast*,
published by Harris in 1807. It begins:

Come take up your hats, and away let us haste,
To the Butterfly's Ball, and the Grasshopper's Feast.
The trumpeter Gadfly has summoned the crew,
And the revels are now only waiting for you.

William Mulready illustrated it with delicate drawings in which the
insects are represented as fairies, and it stands out among all that had
been written for English children hitherto as having a magical element and being totally without any moral purpose.

Darton, fairly enough, referred to Roscoe's verses as 'a temporary
levity', for they were not typical for the mood of the times, and many
dreary years were to follow. He also conceded the nonsense of
Edward Lear, a first sample of which had appeared in 1846, and
might just as well have claimed, as he had claimed for *Alice*, that
Lear's *A Book of Nonsense* was a 'revolution in its sphere', for its
intention to entertain is advertised right from the start:

There was an old Derry down Derry
Who loved to see little folks merry.
    So he made them a Book,
    And with laughter they shook,
At the fun of that Derry down Derry.

But in truth the highly personal nonsense of Lear, which no one
attempted to imitate, and the very different nonsense of Lewis Carroll, which was repeatedly and ineffectively plagiarized, stand well
apart from the subsequent history of Victorian children's book. Both
were ruthless, violent and anarchic, and Carroll's (although not
Lear's) is extraordinary for its impersonality. 'Lewis Carroll' succeeded in wholly detaching himself from the sentimentality com-
bined with pernickety scruples that was so marked in the Revd
Charles Dodgson. And while the Revd Mr Dodgson would not hesi-
tate to rebuke a person in whom he detected even unwitting irrever-
ence, his *alter ego* mockingly parodied the hymns that for children
like the Liddells would have been an integral part of Sundays. The
levity of Lear and Carroll was unique. From 1850 onwards, increasing
numbers of Victorian writers chose to write fantasy for children but,
with different degrees of obstrusiveness, there was purpose and a
moral code; good would be rewarded, evil punished – this is something that Victorian children would understand, even expect, and it
had always been an integral part of the traditional fairy story.

Versions of stories from the *Arabian Nights* suitable for children had
been published in the last years of the eighteenth century. The fairy
stories of Charles Perrault and Madame d'Aulnoy had been translated
early in the century and reprinted several times. The London

bookseller Benjamin Tabart had issued versions of some of them between 1804 and 1809, together with suitably pruned and edited retellings of English chapbook stories such as *The Seven Champions of Christendom*, *Valentine and Orson* and *Jack the Giant-Killer* between 1804 and 1809 in a series which he called *Popular Stories*. But tales like *Aladdin*, *Little Red Riding-Hood*, *Cinderella* and *The Yellow Dwarf* cannot be said to have played a great part in the ordinary child's upbringing then; the mood of the times was against them. Since their first commercial beginnings in the mid-eighteenth century, books for children had been didactic, though often jollier and rarely so deadeningly technical and scientific as they were to become in the pre-Victorian period. Nor did Perrault's suave sophistication and Madame d'Aulnoy's baroque ramblings make very much literary impact on English writers.

The great impetus behind the golden period of Victorian fantasy came from the German tradition. It is notable how much allusion there is to German literature in books for the earlier Victorian young. In domestic stories there are many references to girls who delight in Goethe and Schiller and the mystical romances of Friedrich de la Motte Fouqué, (particularly *Undine* (1811) and *Sintram and his Companions* (1815)), and there are German names scattered round allegories and tales of fantasy. In Francis Paget's *The Hope of the Katzekopfs* (1844), the first full-length English literary fairy story, the spoiled prince Eigenwillig (Self-will) is enslaved to the wicked imp Selbst (Self-love) and has to be taken in hand by the grave old man, Discipline. Bishop Wilberforce introduced characters with significant names such as Goethe (Lover of God) and Irrgeist (Wanderer) into the religious allegories he told his children, later published as *Agathos* and *The Rocky Island*.

Germanic fairy tales also had a potent impact. Hans Christian Andersen, the first of whose stories had been translated in 1846, was eagerly imitated by many writers – sometimes too closely, so that stories by, say, Oscar Wilde, where nightingales and roses and fireworks provide their bitter-sweet commentaries on human folly and the fleetingness of life, seem like pastiche. George MacDonald himself included one story in the Andersen vein, 'The Shadows', in *Adela Cathcart* (1864) which with its dreamlike journeyings, Nordic landscape, and contemplation of the human condition is clearly inspired by Andersen. Ralph Rinkelmann, hovering between life and death, is caught up in a dream-world that seems to him a supernatural revelation, far more real than life. Here, the shadows round his bed-chamber have their own existence and he listens to them recounting their experiences.

(MacDonald had already given Anodos a shadow as a sinister companion in *Phantastes*: this is more dramatic use).

'I made him confess before a week was over,' said a gloomy old Shadow.

'But what was the good of that?' rejoined a pert young one. 'That could not undo what was done.'

'Yes, it could.'

'What! bring the dead to life?'

'No; but comfort the murderer. I could not bear to see the pitiable misery he was in. He was far happier with the rope round his neck, than he was with the purse in his pocket.'

But the initial stimulus to English fantasy had come a generation before, from the tales collected by the brothers Grimm. The first volume of these had been published in Germany as *Kinder und Hausmärchen* in 1813, a second volume the following year. Despite the 'kinder' in the title, the tales were presented in a sober and scholarly manner with a long introduction and notes, and it was not until Edgar Taylor, a London lawyer, had made the first English translation of a selection of them in 1823, under the title of *German Popular Stories* with illustrations by George Cruikshank, that the brothers saw the possibilities of making their compilations more accessible to German children.

Grimm stories were responsible for two early essays in the same vein by English writers. Ruskin's *The King of the Golden River* (1851) was shrugged off by the author himself as totally valueless, 'a good imitation of Grimm and Dickens, mixed with some true Alpine feeling of my own'.[5] It is a story with a powerful feeling for place, using the traditional theme of two greedy and selfish brothers who meet their just reward, and the warm-hearted youngest who prospers. Nor is it merely derivative as Ruskin suggests. There are two strikingly original characters, though Ruskin (who as he himself admitted was a prentice hand at storytelling) threw them away, so to speak, without making adequate use out of them: the bugle-nosed South West Wind who tries to take shelter in the brothers' house and who on being rebuffed destroys it, and the king of the Golden River himself who emerges from the golden mug that the greedy brothers try to melt down, and tells the youngest how to achieve prosperity. Frances Browne's *Granny's Wonderful Chair* which came four years later in another story in the Grimm tradition, or rather a series of tales told within a frame story. The narrative is more skilfully organized than Ruskin's though it lacks the vitality of his characterization, and again the emphasis is upon the good results of virtue and the punishment of greed.

For it is rare that a fairy story has not some moral point to make. Jack Zipes in *Fairy Tales and the Art of Subversion*[6] and John M. Ellis in *One Fairy Tale Too Many*[7] have both shown how Perrault and Grimm recast and added to their source material to make a satisfying literary shape, giving their stories a morality that fitted the society for whom they were writing. 'By examining the major feature and behaviour of [his] male and female protagonists, it becomes crystal clear that he thought to portray ideal types to reinforce the standards of the civilizing process set by upper-class French society', Zipes says of Perrault.[8] He quotes Ingeborg Weber-Kellermann's comment on how the Grimm brothers fused the heterogeneous elements they had collected 'to bring about a work which was both "bourgeois" and "German" and fully corresponded to the scientific temper and emotional taste of their times. . . . . [The success of their tales] cannot be explained without knowledge of the social history of the nineteenth century.'[9] And the earlier Victorians, seizing on the new licence to write fantasy, used the literary fairy tale as a medium for expressing the moral or religious truths that were closest to their heart.

Charles Kingsley's *The Water Babies* (1863) was the most eccentric example. The core of this muddled and passionate story is the purgation undergone by the little chimney sweep Tom before he can cast off the old Adam and become fit for heaven. It is an ordeal of water rather than of fire, water and washing being one of Kingsley's obsessions,[10] but though Tom is duly punished and cleansed of his sins, the adult world – unusually for a Victorian fairy story – comes in for a good deal of castigation too; Kingsley fires off salvoes at what he considers cruelty to children: at the people who cram young heads with facts, at the doctors who dose and purge, at nursemaids who neglect their charges, at the materials put in cheap sweets, at popular evangelical stories of the day, and at didactic literature generally. Then there were King Charles's heads of his own; Americans and Irish, 'frowzy monks', evolution theories, and people who dined at the new fashionable hour of eight o'clock – all came under fire.

But the punishment and the purification that form the main substance of the book are both characteristic of the Victorian fairy tale. Hans Christian Andersen, ever a stern moralizer, can be said to have set subsequent writers on this path with such stories as 'The Girl Who Stepped on Bread' – a girl who is condemned to stand at the bottom of a bog, her feet locked to the loaf that she has used as a stepping-stone to avoid getting her feet wet. Here she stays through countless ages, racked with hunger and consumed with anger, until she admits her fault and, transformed into a bird, atones for her sins.

'The Red Shoes' punishes with the same inexorability. Vain Karen's obsession with her new shoes takes her mind off holy matters; she thinks of a ball rather than of her dying adopted mother. Her feet dance and will not stop, and when they take her into church an angel bars the way with a shining sword: 'You shall dance,' he said, 'dance in your red shoes until you become pale and thin. Dance till the skin on your face turns yellow and clings to your bones as if you were a skeleton. Dance you shall from door to door, and when you pass a house where proud and vain children live, there you shall knock on the door so that they will see you and fear your fate. Dance, you shall dance . . . Dance!'[11] She screams for mercy but the relentless shoes carry her away, always dancing. At last she begs an executioner to cut off her feet – not her head, 'for then I should not be able to repent', and 'she kissed the hand that had guided the axe'. But penitent thought she is, there is still further expiation to be made before the angel appears with a rose branch instead of a sword and carries her soul to God.

The savageness of this punishment in both these stories has so deeply impressed generations of readers that they have often forgotten the redemption that follows. It is always easier to describe evil than good, sorrow than joy. The Victorian writers of fantasy found this, as did C. S. Lewis in the Narnia books; here many adults who enjoy the White Witch have reservations about the lion Aslan who symbolises Christ. Andersen's English admirers mostly lacked his powerful imagination, and rarely achieved the economy of his narration. Nor had they his supreme confidence in rebuking the whole of human folly; they mainly confined themselves to nursery matters, inventing ingenious ways to punish by fairy means, though to describe redemption convincingly was beyond them. MacDonald and only one other, as will be described later, succeeded in presenting the beauty of holiness; lesser writers who attempted it were only mawkish. But generally they prefered to chastise.

In one such story, Alice Corkran's *Down the Snow Stairs*, a mother tells her child: 'Punishment always follows naughtiness. It comes like the shadow that follows you in the sunshine. It may not be in pain to your body that it will come. It may come in grief for seeing another suffer for your fault; but punishment must follow wrongdoing.'[12] This wilful little girl, who has brought her brother near to death by her thoughtlessness, is sent to Naughty Children Land, where she meets various categories of disagreeable children, and recognizes that Daddy Coax's method of trying to cajole them into good behaviour to keep them out of Punishment Land is useless. In Punishment Land itself the author shows cruel ingenuity: the children who tell lies are entangled in spiders' webs; the disobedient are trapped in a maze; the selfish are turned into lumps of ice who despairingly wail 'We wish we could thaw'; the quarrelsome are set to pinch, bit and scratch themselves; the legs of the lazy have turned to stumps and their fingers are welded together. Christina Rossetti in *Speaking Likenesses* (1874) wreaks the same sort of ferocious retribution upon childish faults. Flora, guilty of behaving badly at her own birthday party, finds herself in a dreamland party where the grotesque physical deformities of the other guests represent their moral failings, and who all close in round her to torment and tease. 'And I think if she lives till she's nine years old and gives another party, she is likely on that occasion to be even less like the birthday queen of her troubled dream than was the Flora of eight years old; who, with dear friends and playmates, and pretty presents, yet scarcely knew how to bear a few trifling disappointments, or how to be obliging and good-humoured under slight annoyance.'[13]

MacDonald himself did not escape the Victorian preoccupation with punishment. Indeed, because of the force of his writing the two children whom he pillories in *The Wise Woman* are among the most disagreeable of their kind, though both, as he admits himself, are the victims of the besotted parents, who have indulged one until she is a loathsome little tyrant, and flattered the other until she is insanely vain: 'What is there to choose' MacDonald asks, contemplating these Frankensteins of his own creation, 'between a face distorted to hideousness by anger, and one distorted to silliness by self-complacency?'. 'This is a harsh, angry tale.' said Maurice Sendak, 'whose magic . . . is black, erratic, and appears finally to be nearly impotent against the force of evil.'[14] But this story seems to spring out of the black despair and rage against human folly that brings out the final desolation of the kingdom of Gwyntystorm in *The Princess and Curdie*. At his best there is a radiance about MacDonald's fantasy for children that makes the work of his contemporaries appear negative and nagging.

Although it is unlikely, given the climate of the 1820s and MacDonald's Congregational background, that he was brought up on traditional fairy tales in youth, he is known to have enjoyed them in later life and indeed organized acting versions of them for his family. Andrew Lang, born twenty years later, was steeped in the legends and fairy tales of the Scottish borders, but if MacDonald heard such stories when he was a child they seemingly made little impression on him, and only in 'The Carasoyn', which is otherwise a quest story, do the 'good folk' who are such a powerful presence in Lang's *The Gold of Faimilee* make any appearance. The romances of De la Motte Fouqué, as has been said, were very popular with early Victorians, especially *Undine* (where a water nymph falls in love with a human), which MacDonald thought the most beautiful of all fairy tales[15] and *Sintram and his Companions,* the story of the progress of a soul struggling with temptation, the companions being Sin and Death. The introduction to a Victorian edition of *Undine* says much of that equally applies to MacDonald's fantasy. Calling it the 'shadowing of high truth in a romantic tale' with 'wild picturesque imagery', it concludes: 'Instead, then, of dwelling upon what might be regarded as faults of construction in these tales, since they have in them a life beyond life, and a fine spirit has here fashioned their romance into tales, not trivial, of Earth and Heaven, let us seek rather to be alive to all their good.'

Much the same could have been said about the German philosopher Friedrich Wilhelm Carové's *The Story Without an End.* This over sweet prose-poem, an allegory of the progress of the human soul towards eternity, was first translated on 1834 and was very popular with Victorians. Frequently reissued in editions for children, its best known illustrator was Eleanor Vere Boyle, whose cloying style overemphasized the same tendency in Carové. A child wanders through the green wood, feeding on dewdrops and violet honey, and conversing with the living creatures that he meets, frightened just occasionally, as when the lizard talks enviously and sneeringly of the birds, but mostly experiencing mounting rapture. The final chapter begins:

> And the child was become happy and joyful, and breathed freely again, and thought no more of returning to his hut; for he saw that nothing returned inwards, but rather that all strove outwards into the free air ... And as the butterflies came forth from their chrysalids in all their gaiety and splendour, so did every humbled and suppressed aspiration and hope free itself and boldly launch into the broad and flowing sea of spring.

Rather too high flown for English taste now perhaps. It was MacDonald's great strength that when he wrote for children he could incorporate this vein of German romanticism into something far more solid, but still keep the poetry, the sense of awe at a mystery too great to be defined.

There had been plenty of early Victorian religious allegory for children. Bishop Wilberforce's *Agathos* (1840) had made the genre popular. Allegory was ideal, he said in his preface, for attracting children's attention and stretching their faculties as 'glimpses of the under-meaning continually flash into their minds.' The title story is about a soldier who, alone among his fellows, obeys his king's command to wear his armour. He is thus able to withstand the attack of the terrible dragon who catches the rest of the troops off their guard. And in case the young reader misses the point, each story is followed by questions and answers about its purpose.

Norman MacLeod's *The Golden Thread* (1861) has the same uncomplicated message; Dr MacLeod takes the precaution of spelling it out first in his preface: 'We should always trust God and do what is right, and thus hold fast our golden thread in spite of every temptation and danger, being certain that in this way only will God lead us in safety and peace to His home.' The young prince in his story who is beguiled from his proper path eventually has the thread restored to him with a scolding and a warning:

'It was your duty to have held it fast; but instead of doing your duty, trusting and obeying your father, and keeping hold of the thread, you let it go to chase butterflies, and gather wild-berries, and to amuse yourself. This you did more than once. You neglected yous father's counsels and warnings, and because of your self-confidence and self-pleasing, you lost your thread, and then you lost your way . . . . Had you only followed your father's directions, the gold thread would have brought you to his beautiful castle, where there is to be a happy meeting with your friends, with all your brothers and sisters.'[17]

MacDonald would not have been this explicit. An adult perceives that *The Princess and the Goblin* is partly at any rate, about the vision of childhood or the eye of faith. Where the princess sees her fairy grandmother spinning gossamer in a room lit by its own moon and warmed by a fire of roses, the little miner Curdie, who is not so far along the spiritual road, can see only 'a tub, a heap of musty straw, and a withered apple'. But there are other elements less obvious, and MacDonald is content that there should be a veil of mystery. 'It cannot help having some meaning.' he said of the fairy tale; 'if it has proportion and harmony it has vitality, and vitality is truth'[18] Further than this he was not prepared to go. 'If you do not what it means, what is easier than to say so?' he says in answer to those who press for more. 'If you do see a meaning in it there it is for you to give [the child].' Unlike the allegorists he was far more concerned with imagery and invention than with a consistent didactic line, sometimes perhaps bewilderingly so.

Where it is outstanding among children's writers is in his power to make holiness vital, natural and desirable, and to show a spiritual progress. All children's writers had found it difficult to personify the spirit of Good, and most settled to show it as a mother-figure representing Love, as in Kingsley's Mrs Doasyouwouldbedoneby, 'the most nice, smooth, pussy, cuddly delicious creature who ever nursed a baby', or Love in *Down the Snow Stairs* whom the heroine at first thinks is her own mother. One of the most bizarre representations comes in *The Wind in the Willows* where Mole and Rat find the missing baby otter safe in the everlasting arms of Pan; Grahame's unique achievement being, as Neil Philip dourly remarks, 'to reduce the savage god to a sort of woodland nanny'.[19] MacDonald's North Wind, 'Grandmother' in 'The Golden Key', and the elusive and beautiful 'mother of grandmothers' in *The Princess and the Goblin* would appear to be at various moments aspects of death, eternal life, the will of God, heavenly love, but MacDonald invests them with mystery and their exact role is never stated, though even the youngest reader is aware of the love that radiates from them. The literary character who most resembles them is perhaps the venerable fairy Potentilla in Sara Coleridge's *Phantasmion* (1837) who first appears to the prince Phantasmion when he is a child, but who is invisible to everyone else, even to his mother. The fairy tale wanderings of Anodos in *Phantastes* indeed have a flavour of those of Phantasmion, and though in the latter the landscape is literary–oriental, both derive fom German romantic tradition.

MacDonald also excelled at making virtue in children both credible and attractive. Plenty, of course, had attempted it, beginning with James Janeway in *A Token for Children: in being an exact account of the conversion, holy and exemplary lives and joyful deaths of several young children*, which was probably first published in 1672 and remained a classic for many decades. Though the Puritan concept of a child ripe for heaven differed in many respects from what would later be found acceptable (for one thing, the godly child then was expected to be 'putting children, play-fellows, servants, neighbours, upon minding their poor souls'[20] in fact these factual accounts are far more convincing than the literary creations of later generations. The Georgian good child was merely a cardboard personification of some particular virtue and no sentiment was wasted on him. The Victorians expended plenty but few of their exemplary heroes and heroines, whether they be ringletted darlings in black velvet suits, sunny-faced evangelists, ministering children, or street urchins who have found salvation, really convince us–'those consequential. priggish little monsters', MacDonald called them. 'When a child like that dies, instead of having a silly book written about him, he should be stuffed like one of those awful big-headed fishes you see in museums.'[21] But the natural goodness of both Diamond and the Princess Irene shines out, so that the authorial comment, that 'it seemed to me, somehow as if little Diamond possessed the secret life, and was himself what he was so ready to think the lowest living thing living – an angel of God with something special to say or do' is superfluous.

Diamond is a very rare example among storybook heroes of the child who is 'touched': 'he has been to the back of the north wind' says MacDonald.

> He never took any notice of [the cabmen's rough words], and his face shone pure and good in the middle of them, like a primrose in a hailstorm. at first, because his face was so quiet and sweet, with a smile either awake or asleep in his eyes, and because he never heeded their ugly words and rough jokes, they said he wasn't all there, meaning that he was half an idiot, whereas he was a great deal more than they had the sense to see.[22]

The American author-illustrator, Howard Pyle (1853-1911) was clearly deeply affected by the character of Diamond, and used it in his only full-length fairy story. *The Garden Behind the Moon* (1895), is in effect a development of MacDonald's chapter 'Nanny's Dream', in which the street waif adopted by Diamond's parents describes how in her dreams she looks out from the moon down at the earth. In Pyle's story the central character David, the 'moon-calf' is a version of Diamond, 'God's baby'. The north wind is replaced by the Moon Angel, who is the angel of death. Though the book is obviously derivative, it is a poignant tribute to one of Pyle's own children who had just died, and he did some of his best illustrations for it, including one of the child David, vacant-eyed, walking beside his moon-struck friend the cobbler who has the wild eyes of a visionary. But the reader feels in this book that Pyle's talent was visual rather than literary and that the pictures have a strength that the text lacks.

MacDonald was difficult to imitate. few had his fertile imagination or could draw on such a wealth of imagery; the Narnia fantasies of C. S. Lewis, who took his inspiration from MacDonald, seem earthbound and their moral laboured beside, say, 'The Golden Key'. The American Horace Scudder (1837-1902), a great admirer of the European fairy tale at a time when the genre was suspect in his own country, wrote several stories in the Andersen vein, and one, 'The Pot of Gold', that is based on 'The Golden Key'. It is also a quest story, though the young hero sets out alone to pursue the gold that is buried at the foot of the rainbow leaving his childhood sweetheart behind at home. But whereas in a MacDonald quest the protagonists shake off earthly ties, in the Scudder story it is the thought of home, always such an emotive force in American literature, that halts the hero when he is at last about to achieve his goal. The pot of gold in this American version of MacDonald is revealed to be home itself.

As has been said, there was one writer other than MacDonald who succeeded in showing children the beauty of holiness, of making spiritual values seem real and living. This was Mrs Craik (best known for *John Halifax, Gentleman*) in *The Little Lame Prince* (1875). She subtitled it 'a parable for young and old', but the meaning is not immediately obvious, certainly not as Bishop Wilberforce and Norman MacLeod had made theirs. The story is of Prince Dolor, rightful ruler of Nomansland, but crippled from an injury in infancy, and imprisoned in a remote tower by the uncle who has usurped the throne. His only companion is a woman who knows that she will be put to death if any harm comes to the prince, but he has his books and toys and accepts his disability and isolation with a gentle fortitude that is genuinely moving. His fairy godmother brings him a magical cloak in which he can travel and see a world from which he is totally excluded. Eventually, when the usurping uncle is dead and Nomansland is torn apart by revolution, he is discovered in his prison and restored to the throne, where he proves a beneficent ruler. But the time comes when he feels he must hand over to the heir.

'Yes, I must go. It is time for me to go. Remember me sometimes, my people, for I have loved you well. And I am going a long way, and I do not think I shall come back any more.'

He drew a little bundle out of his breast pocket – a bundle that nobody had ever seen before. It was small and shabby-looking, and tied up with many knots, which untied themselves in an instant. With a joyful countenance, he muttered over it a few half-intelligible words. Then, so suddenly that even those nearest to his Majesty could not tell how it came about, the King was away – away – floating right up in the air – upon something, they knew not what, except that it appeared to be as safe and pleasant as the wings of a bird . . . King Dolor was never again beheld or heard of in his own country. But the good he had done there lasted for years and years; he was long missed and deeply mourned – at least, so far as anybody could mourn one who was gone on such a happy journey.[23]

This is not an imitation of MacDonald, but rather an extension. It lacks the extraordinary richness of his imagination, the complexity of his imagery; but in its quiet way it showed both what could be done with religious allegory, and, by the absence of anything comparable, how difficult a genre it was.

References

1. *The Fairy Book* (New York; Harper, 1836), v.
2. F. J. Harvey Darton, *Children's Books in England*, 3rd ed., revd. by Brian Alderson. (Cambridge University Press, 1982), p.260.
3. Juliana Horatia Ewing, *Mary's Meadow and other tales* (Society for Promoting Christian Knowledge, 1896), p.29.
4. *The Journey of Emily Pepys*, ed. Gillian Avery (London: Prospect Books, 1984). p.44.
5. John Ruskin, *Praeterita* (London: Rupert Hart-Davis, 1949), II, 275.
6. Jack Zipes, *Fairy Tales and the Art of Subversion* (New York: Wildman Press, 1983).
7. John M. Ellis, *One Fairy Tale Too Many* (University of Chicago Press, 1983).
8. Zipes, op. cit., p.26.
9. Ibid., p.48.
10. See Humphrey Carpenter, *Secret Gardens* (London: Allen and Unwin, 1985), pp.30,31.
11. Hans Christian Andersen, *The Complete Fairy Tales and Stories*, trans. by Erik Christian Haugaard (London: Gollancz, 1979), p.292.
12. Alice Corkran, *Down the Snow Stairs* (London: Blackie, 1887), p.33.
13. Christiana Rossetti, *Speaking Likenesses* (London: Macmillan, 1874), p.48.
14. Maurice Sendak, 'George MacDonald' in *Caldecott & Co.* (London: Reinhardt Books, 1988), p.46.
15. George MacDonald: 'The Fantastic Imagination' in *A Dish of Orts* (London: Sampson, Low and Marston, 1893), p.313.
16. Preface to Friedrich de la Motte Fouqué, *Sintram and his Companions* (London: Cassell, 1887).
17. Norman MacLeod, *The Gold Thread* (Edinburgh: Strahan, 1861), p.25.
18. 'The Fantastic Imagination', op. cit., p.316.
19. Neil Philip, 'The Wind in the Willows' In *Children and their Books*, ed. Gillian Avery and Julia Briggs (Oxford University Press, 1989).
20. James Janeway: *A Token for Children, the Second Part* (London: Dorman Newman, 1676), p.79.
21. *At the Back of the North Wind*, ch.38.
22. Ibid., ch.17.
23. Dinah Mulock (Mrs Craik) *The Little Lame Prince* (Isbister, Daldy, 1875), p.167.

8

MacDonald and Kingsley: A Victorian Contrast

COLIN MANLOVE

There are arguably only two significant writers of Christian fantasy in the Victorian period: George MacDonald and Charles Kingsley. That officially Christian age, in which fantasy was extensively written for children at least, tended to produce moral rather than religious or mystical works of this kind.[1] Part of the reason for this was doubtless an Arnoldian hostility to the notion of mixing fairy tales with religious insights;[2] part, too, perhaps was a reluctance in that naturalistic and 'this-worldly' period, to write narratives about the believed supernatural.[3] MacDonald and Kingsley were both in their ways eccentrics in relation to their age, the one often isolated from or at odds with it, the other full of bursts of odd thoughts. Both felt the need to describe and demonstrate the presence of God and miracle in the world. It was natural therefore that they should write supernaturalist and Christian fiction. What was unusual, in relation to the past history of such works, was that rather than retell the basic pattern of Christian life and history, as did Spenser, Milton or Bunyan, they should have invented wholly new and non-biblical narratives through which to render Christian truth. This we should perhaps understand in relation to an unspoken 'Broad Church' desire to relate God's doings to the actual world and to the human mind and heart rather than to the increasingly questioned confines of a book of doctrinaire narratives; and, actually, Kingsley's *The Water-Babies*, in contrast to MacDonald's fantasy, contains scarcely any biblical references.

What we will be considering here are first, and more briefly, the similarities betweeen MacDonald and Kingsley; and then at greater length their many sheer differences, differences heightened all the more by what they strikingly have in common. Not only are they alone as writers of Christian fantasy, but they wrote at roughly the same time. MacDonald's *Phantastes* appeared in 1858, Kingsley's *The Water-Babies* in 1863, MacDonald's *Dealings with the Fairies*, *At the Back of the North Wind* and *The Princess and the Goblin* in 1867, 1871 and 1872 respectively. Both writers shared a number of near-heterodox ideas, in part derived from their common debt to the thinking of

F. D. Maurice. These include a readiness to doubt the existence of a final hell for sinners and a tendency towards universalism, the belief that all people might eventually be redeemed. Kingsley adhered to, and in *The Water-Babies* dramatised, the notion of an 'intermediate state' within nature which might provide second chances to all eternity; and like Kingsley, MacDonald gave credence to the notion of spiritual evolution, by which a person's sins might determine that person's outward shape in another life, and thus punish and so better the offending soul until it recovered primal purity. Believing as they both did that Hell was not final, they neither of them accepted that man's will was wholly free to choose evil: all such choices were either nugatory or would be resisted by the character of the universe. Even when she is desiring Hell, MacDonald's Lilith in his fantasy of that name (1895) is told that "there is no slave but the creature that wills against its creator",[4] and Kingsley, who gave more scope to the will, declared, 'Evil, as such, has no existence; but men can and do resist God's will, and break the law, which is appointed for them, and so punish themselves by getting into disharmony with their own constitution and that of the universe; just as a wheel in a piece of machinery punishes itself when it gets out of gear.'[5] The stress in both is on a loving rather than a judging God, though that love can be experienced very painfully.

To these similarities we may add the preference of both writers in their fantasies for destructured and often chaotic-seeming narratives. *The Water-Babies* is crammed with continual digressions, abrupt shifts of context, and authorial intrusions of a frequently idiosyncratic type. *Phantastes* is a dream-like sequence of images and often little-connected experiences, with interpolated narratives, metaphysical and moral discourses, and transitions between worlds. To some extent it must be said there was a tendency towards dislocated or dream-like narratives in other fantasies or near-fantasies of the time – in Carlyle's *Sartor Resartus* (1836), in some of the 'Spasmodic' poets of the forties and fifties,[6] in Browning's 'Childe Roland' (1855), William Morris's early romances (1856-8) and Lewis Carroll's *Alice in Wonderland* (1865).

MacDonald and Kingsley were in fact quite well acquainted. Kingsley was one of the few who at the appearance of MacDonald's first work, *Within and Without* (1855), wrote to its author to praise the poem, before he and MacDonald had met. He and MacDonald later met quite frequently, though their friendship was not on terms of such intimacy as that between MacDonald and that other great contemporary writer of fantasy, C. L. Dodgson ('Lewis Carroll'). Kingsley

wrote in support of MacDonald's application for the Regius chair of
Rhetoric and Belles-Lettres at the University of Edinburgh in 1865.

It is hard to believe that Kingsley, who had noticed MacDonald's
first and relatively little-known work, and who had subsequently
become on terms of friendship with him, would not have been in
some way acquainted with *Phantastes*. Certainly it and *The Water-
Babies* have several features in common, even if some of those features may be traced back to works of the Romantics, such as Novalis's
Heinrich von Ofterdingen (1802), E. T. A. Hoffmann's *Der Goldne
Topf* (1814) or Shelley's *Alastor* (1816) or even to that work for
which Kingsley and MacDonald showed a partiality exceptional even
among Victorians, Bunyan's *The Pilgrim's Progress*.[7] The object of
both *Phantastes* and *The Water-Babies* is to reveal the divine presence
in the world, whether within nature or the mind. Both works deal
with a single protagonist who must enter into and journey through a
strange realm, while experiencing a process of spiritual education on
the way. The narratives are largely episodic, a series of adventures and
meetings; but there is also a growing purpose, which involves searching for an elusive goal – in *Phantastes*, the hero Anodos' quest for a
'white lady' who has escaped him after he re-animated her statue, and
in *The Water-Babies*, Tom's search for other water-babies, and later
for his own 'white lady' whom he too once woke up, in the form of
Ellie. In both works another purpose later develops, involving self-
denial by the hero: Anodos must yield up the white lady to another,
and Tom must help someone he does not like. In both stories there
is much in the way of a watery medium: Anodos follows a stream
through Fairy Land, or travels down a river, or voyages across an
ocean; and while more continuously immersed, Tom also follows a
journey from steam to river to ocean. In *Phantastes* the supernatural
helpers of Anodos are female – his fairy grandmother, a beech tree, a
farmer's wife in a cottage, an old lady in a cottage in the midst of
the sea; and in *The Water-Babies* all the great fairies are women, from
the Irishwoman who watches Tom go into the stream and the Queen
of Fairies she then reveals herself to be, to the educational fairies Mrs
Bedonebyasyoudid and Mrs Doasyouwouldbedoneby, and to the creative principle of nature itself embodied in Mother Carey, sitting on
her iceberg in the Peacepool at the North Pole, making the creatures
'make themselves'. And there are other possible parallels. The fairy
palace Anodos reaches in the midst of his adventures, and wherein
he momentarily rediscovers the white lady, is matched by the fairy
palace at St. Brandan's Isle beneath the sea in *The Water-Babies*. In
the early stage of his journey, Anodos is in danger of being

devoured by an evil Ash-tree, just as Tom is in danger of being eaten while he is in the stream, particularly by a family of marauding otters. An evil shadow Anodos acquires despite being warned against it makes him unable to see the wonder of Fairy Land and fills him with the lust to possess things. More humorously, in *The Water-Babies* we have a Professor Ptthmllnsprts, who, finding Tom in the water, refuses to admit that he is a water-baby and insists on making him a new variety of marine species discovered by himself; and later, on the serious side, we have Tom's greedy desire to be the centre of the fairies' love, and his theft of Mrs Bedonebyasyoudid's sweets for all good water-babies from her cupboard. Both stories have as their end a form of heaven, though in the case of *Phantastes* Anodos is returned to his own world to await the coming of some 'great good'.

If the partial debt of *The Water-Babies* to *Phantastes* may thus be argued, that in turn of MacDonald's *At the Back of the North Wind* (1871) to *The Water-Babies* seems still more evident, even while less pervasive. The idea of the poor boy being able to escape his fairly miserable social environment to visit some fantastic place or realm is present in both books. The North Wind herself, who says she cannot help what she does, and looks to a far-off song as a guarantee that all will eventually come right is clearly based on Kingsley's Mrs Bedonebyasyoudid, who says the same and who, as she looks up and away, through sea and sky, to something very far off, gives 'such a quiet, tender, patient, hopeful smile . . . that Tom thought for the moment that she did not look ugly at all'.[8] And when Little Diamond in MacDonald's book finds North Wind sitting frozen at her door near the North Pole, her image comes directly from that of Mother Carey sitting on her block of ice in the midst of the Arctic Peacepool in *The Water-Babies* – even if the one is in a state of extreme depletion and the one in the fullness of energetic creativity.

So much for the many points of contact between MacDonald and Kingsley. All the more striking, then, must be the fact that in nearly every aspect of their art and outlook the two are in fact radically different, so much that together they could be said to form nothing short of a dualism. The prime reason for this can be clearly stated at the outset. MacDonald is a latter-day Romantic where Kingsley is a Victorian.[9] Although they both lived at the same time and were born within five years of one another, MacDonald's spiritual roots are with the Romantics and the mystics – with Blake, Shelley, Dante, Boehme and Swedenborg – while Kingsley is much more concerned to grapple with the movements and issues of this day in a literary mode that will do justice to their novelty. Writing of the fragmentary and unconnected form of his *Yeast* (1850) he said, 'Do not young men think, speak, act, just now, in this very incoherent, fragmentary way; without methodic education or habits of thought; with the various stereotyped systems which they have received by tradition, breaking up under them like ice in a thaw; with a thousand facts and notions, which they know not how to classify, pouring in on them like a flood?–a very Yeasty state of mind altogether . . .'[10] In many ways the opposition between MacDonald's and Kingsley's ways of seeing might be put equally as that perennial one between the Platonist and the Aristotelian, the one with a spiritual and inward gaze, believing in innate ideas, the other directed outwards to the senses and the world, and to science.[11] But dualism was also in the very fabric of the Victorian period: as one writer has put it, 'The Cartesian divorce of mind and matter that increasingly characterised . . . the Victorian sensibility results from a growing inability to accommodate personally perceived, experiential knowledge that the Romantics claimed as the only validly human truth, as opposed to that sought by the 'Man of Science . . . as a remote and unknown benefactor.'[12]

The enormous progress of science, accompanied by the urbanisation of man in the Victorian period, posed a special challenge to that Romantic synthesis accomplished by Wordsworth through his imagination between the human mind and the external world. The two poles of naturalism and idealism, in which the former held the dominant place, came to divide the Victorian intellectual and spiritual landscape. Kingsley, as both a Christian supernaturalist and a scientist, registered the divide and its tensions in himself: 'I am the strangest jumble of superstition and of a reverence for scientific induction . . . What is a poor wretch to do . . . ? A mystic in theory, and an ultra-materialist in practice . . . What shall I do? I fear sometimes that I shall end by a desperate lunge into one extreme or the other.'[13] Kingsley's answer was an attempt to unite both sides: but whether he succeeded is another matter.

The differences between MacDonald and Kingsley can be seen at a personal level also. In character, MacDonald was unconventional, courageous in his beliefs to the point of plain stubborness, proud, passionate, caring not greatly for high or literary society, loving, and yet with his gaze always part-directed beyond the walls of this life. For most of his life he had no church because of some of his beliefs, and had to support himself and a large family by his writing and any other honest means available. As a Scot living in England he was never fully at home; as a sufferer from several painful illnesses, particularly a form of tuberculosis, all of them steadfastly borne through his life, his tendency to disengagement from the world could only have been increased; and the ties to this life were further cut by the deaths over the years of a number of his children, including his favourite, Lilia Scott MacDonald, in 1891. Kingsley, by contrast, held the living at Eversley in Hampshire most of his short life, supported the establishment and the status quo, had the health and the desire to pursue throughout his life all manner of hobbies from naturalism to fishing, could speak of heaven as a continuation of the pleasures (including the sexual ones) of this world, and offered his more unconventional theological and other views not in his sermons but in a book for children. Kingsley, unlike MacDonald, secured a professorship, that of modern history at Cambridge in 1860, and reached a pinnacle of acceptance when Queen Victoria sent the young prince of Wales to be tutored by him. Quite what the two men made of one another when they met one can only guess. Given MacDonald's close friendship with Dodgson one cannot suppose that he would have disliked any light-heartedness or even whimsicality on Kingsley's part, but it may be that he found it less easy to accept Kingsley's accommodations, both natural and at times political, to the standards of his day, not to mention his veneration for royalty, his jingoism and his often racist views. What is certain is that while it was a friendship of fellow-Christians with some shared ideas, it was also a conjunction of unlikes. Two cultures, two nations, two relations to life itself, seem here to collide.

These differences of personality determine much of the contrasting character of the works of both writers. But, for our purposes, it will be better to start with a more 'abstract' distinction between the two. In terms of 'faculty psychology', we find that MacDonald most looks to the imagination, Kingsley to the intellect and senses. For MacDonald, the imagination is 'that faculty in man which is likest to the prime operation of God, and has, therefore, been called the *creative* faculty, and its exercise *creation.*' And he goes further. For him the human imagination is not only *like* God, it *is* God working in man. For 'God sits in that chamber of our being in which the candle of our consciousness goes out in darkness and sends forth from thence wonderful gifts into the light of that understanding which is His candle.'[14] MacDonald's belief in God's presence in the human imagination leads him to assert that the normal filters and controls on the imagination – in particular, reason and the ordering and interpreting human intellect – should be suspended, so that the divine voice may be clearly heard. MacDonald's extremist Romantic affinities are thus with Novalis rather than with Coleridge, but with a Novalis

Christianised. The products of this diving unconscious imagination, whether they be worlds or fictional narratives, MacDonald calls fairy stories. These works will be disconnected, chaotic-seeming, mysterious, full of strange and haunting imagery; or, in the words of Novalis, which MacDonald made the epigraph to *Phantastes*, 'Erzählungen ohne Zusammenhang, jedoch mit Association, wie Träume . . . Ein Märchen ist wie ein Traumbild ohne Zusammenhang. Ein Ensemble wunderbarer Dinge und Begebenheiten, z.B. eine Musikalische Phantasie, die harmonischen Folgen einer Aeolsharfe, die Natur selbst.' And that is why MacDonald writes so continually in the fairy-tale mode, and why his tales have a mystery and frequent incomprehensibility which in his comments on them he is at pains to insist they should retain: 'The greatest forces lie in the region of the uncomprehended.'[15] With this view of the fairy tale as the direct expression of the unconscious imagination, which is in turn the expression of God, MacDonald implies that a proper reading of his fairy tales may approximate to a mystical experience.

Kingsley has little to say about the imagination. Indeed, his literary criticism is scant beside MacDonald's. His only essay on the Romantics, on Shelley and Byron, is condemnatory, particularly of the former; and in a piece on the poet Alexander Smith he attacks the use by the 'metaphysical' poets of conceits on almost the same empiricist grounds as Hobbes or Dryden.[16] He shows a hearty contempt for 'Art'–'What's "Art"? I never saw a little beast flying about with "Art" labelled on its back'–as against 'the transcendental variety of life and fact'.[17] As for the fairy tale, in his view the making by nature of a valley by the force of glacial ice is a much more amazing fairy tale than any man could invent: the phenomena and workings of the world are far more wonderful than any fiction: nature is 'the Tale of all Tales, the true "Märchen allen Märchen"', and 'novels and story-books are scarcely worth your reading, as long as you can read the great green book, of which every bud is a letter, and every tree a page.'[18] Needless to say, this did not hinder Kingsley from writing his own novels. But unlike MacDonald he wrote just one fairy tale, and that intended supposedly for children alone. His interest is always empirical–the imitation of the variety of physical nature and the demonstration of the hidden and ultimately God-derived laws by which nature operates. In *The Water-Babies* that is one main reason for his continual interruption of any 'fictional microcosm': he will not leave us with his character Tom without continually putting himself or a whole series of digressions forward, lest the fiction take on an imaginative independence of its own, isolating it from life. For him the idea of 'self-evolution' in a story is inadequate to the manifold nature of reality, and the use of apparent irrelevances is 'to connect the subject with the rest of the universe . . . and show that it does not stand alone, that it is not a world of itself'. In his view, 'the modern novel ought to have all this, if it is to be a picture of actual life'.[19] When Kingsley wrote in 1849, 'we want something yet, in the telling of a Christian fairy-tale, and know not what we want',[20] the eventual empiricist tale he gives us in *The Water-Babies* is of a far different character from the directly supernatural tales recounted in the book he was reviewing, Anna Jameson's *Sacred and Legendary Art* (1848).

These differences between MacDonald and Kingsley are further evident in their contrastive attitudes to science and scientific knowledge. MacDonald read Chemistry and Natural Philosophy (Physics) at King's College, Aberdeen from 1840-45, but soon after entered the ministry. Kingsley, while reading Classics and Mathematics at Cambridge from 1839-42, was all along 'intended' for the Church. MacDonald became in large part hostile to science, which he felt gave only a reductive and schematic view of life: 'human science', he came to write, 'is but the backward undoing of the tapestry-web of God's science, works with its back to him, and is always leaving him – his intent, that is, his perfected work – behind it, always going farther and farther away from the point where his work culminates in revelation'.[21] Kingsley, however, found precisely the scientific investigation of nature to be the only true route to a sense of the wonder of divine workmanship: 'below all natural phenomena we come to a transcendental – in plain English, a miraculous ground . . . This belief was first forced on me by investigating the generation of certain polypes of a very low order. I found absolute Divine miracle at the bottom of all.'[22]

It was to show this that he wrote *The Water-Babies*: 'I have tried in all sorts of queer ways, to make children and grown folks understand that there is quite a miraculous and divine element underlying all physical nature.'[23] Certainly *The Water-Babies* may be conceived of as a scientific exploration, in whole and in part. Tom the hero is transformed into a newt-like creature so that he may observe directly some of the wonders of miniature marine life which would otherwise have to be remotely apprehended by magnifying glass or other apparatus. Further, his whole journey, from stream to river to sea, might be taken as a metaphor for deepening scientific analysis into the essential nature of the world: it is when he reaches the ocean that he finally encounters some of those essences or principles of existence in the forms of the great fairies Bedonebyasyoudid and Doasyouwouldbedoneby. MacDonald's Anodos in *Phantastes*, how-

ever, is discouraged from close analysis, which is associated with an
evil shadow he acquires during his travels through Fairy Land. Its
effect is to reduce, not to enhance, being:

> Once, as I passed by a cottage, there came out a lovely child,
> with two wondrous toys, one in each hand. The one was the
> tube through which the fairy-gifted poet looks when he beholds
> the same thing everywhere; the other that through which he
> looks when he combines into new forms of loveliness those
> images of beauty which his own choice has gathered from all
> regions wherein he has travelled. Round the child's head was an
> aureole of emanating rays. As I looked at him in wonder and
> delight, round crept from behind me the something dark, and
> the child stood in my shadow. Straightaway he was a common-
> place boy, with a rough broad-brimmed straw hat, through
> which brim the sun stole from behind. The toys he carried were
> a multiplying glass and kaleidoscope. I sighed and departed.[24]

MacDonald's view that 'The greatest forces lie in the region of the
uncomprehended', is seen in the preference here for the vague, the
emotively apprehended, rather than the starkly or objectively seen.
Anodos describes the region of fantasy as one where 'all is intensely
vivid, but nothing clearly defined.'[25] The emphasis is not on what is
seen but on how it is seen; not on the sight but on insight, and the
imagination. In *The Water-Babies* the mysteries of life are explored
and in part understood; in *Phantastes* the world becomes steadily
more and more mysterious and opaque. The movement in *Phantastes*
is not further and further out into this world, as in *The Water-Babies*,
but inwards into a Fairy Land which in part figures the mind. The
movement is away from sense-data and the empirical, symbolised in
the way Anodos' adventure begins as he wakens to find the furnish-
ings of his familiar bedroom transforming themselves before his eyes
into the landscape of Fairy Land.

The relative commitments of both authors to this world can be
seen in the different contexts of their fairy tales. In the first part of
The Water-Babies Tom is portrayed living in this world as a chimney-
sweep, apprenticed to the cruel Grimes. We have vivid portrayals of
his life as a sweep, of his journey one day with Grimes out of the
town to Harthover House; and then a more particular account of
how, mistaken for a thief when he accidentally enters and runs from a
beautiful little girl's bedroom, he is pursued out of the grounds, runs
across the moor and climbs down a huge cliff until, worn out, he falls
into a stream and is turned into a water-baby. Even when Tom is a
water-baby, he is still in this world, as he lives in the Yorkshire stream

and eventually travels down it to the river and the sea at Hull, paus-
ing at a resort meant to be Scarborough, before meeting the other
water-babies, and then, later, setting off northwards across the Atlantic to Jan Mayen's Land and then to the North pole. In *Phantastes*, by
contrast, there is little account of Anodos' life in this world, and no
social setting. We meet Anodos alone, he having just awakened 'with
the usual perplexity of mind which accompanies the return of consciousness'. Clearly, flight from the perplexities of mind endemic to
awareness of this world is to be preferred. We learn that one of the
'ceremonies' relating to Anodos' twenty-first birthday on the day
before involved the handing over to him of the key to an old secretary of his father's. When he opens the secretary he finds in it a secret
drawer from which emerges a tiny fairy, who tells him that she is his
great-grandmother, and that he will find his way into Fairy Land the
next day–as indeed he does. All this is over within the first few
pages: MacDonald's urge is clearly to get his hero out of 'this' world
as quickly as possible. As for Anodos' 'worldly' self, we do not know
who he is, where he lives, or what friends and relations he has
(except at the end, where some mention is made of sisters). Again, in
contrast to Tom in *The Water-Babies*, Anodos is throughout in an
'other' world full of devouring trees, ogresses, fairies, giants,
enchanted statues, magic books and dragons. He starts in a forested
landscape; then, pursuing a roughly eastward direction, he travels
down a river to a fairy palace, thence via an underground realm to a
bleak ocean which he crosses to first bare and then once again forested land. A similarly indefinite topography is seen in the 'region of
the seven dimensions' in *Lilith* (1895). Also involving an 'other'
world are the two 'Curdie' books, *The Princess and the Goblin* (1872)
and *The Princess and Curdie* (1883), not to mention *The Lost Princess*
(1875) and the shorter fairy-tales in *Dealings with the Fairies* (1867).

The apparent exception to this difference between Kingsley and
MacDonald is the latter's *At the Back of the North Wind*, which as we
have seen is in part indebted to *The Water-Babies*, and which is set
largely in this world. Having started with many trips by the boy hero
Diamond within and beyond the world with North Wind, we are
eventually set down squarely in London with Diamond's family struggling to make a living after their previous employer has turned the
father away. Here something of the character of life in a Victorian city
comes out – the hard work of a cab-man or a crossing sweeper, the
wretched condition of the poor girl Nanny in Old Sal's cellar, the desperate struggle for respectability of the money-obsessed Mr Coleman.
Yet as the book proceeds, these things, and the world in which they

are set, become thinner and more insubstantial, as Diamond turns towards the final meetings with North Wind that prelude his death: his family take less notice of him, Nanny regards him as having "a tile loose", the problem of sustaining the family vanishes with their rescue by the benificent Mr Raymond. Further, in contrast to Kingsley, Mac-Donald does not show a liking for this world or a love of its variety for its own sake; for him, people are to be loved rather for their souls than for their personalities, and the world not for itself but to the extent that it figures forth the things of God. Unlike in *The Water-Babies* no programme of social reform is implied, apart from a temperance homily read by Diamond to one drunken cab-man. The emphasis is on individual evil. And this world is considered less for itself than as a jumping-off place for the next, for which Diamond longs throughout. We will find the same even in MacDonald's novels of real life, such as *Robert Falconer* (1868), *The Vicar's Daughter* (1872) or *Sir Gibbie* (1879).

Not surprisingly, then, Kingsley's work is much more responsive to the outside world and its opinions than is MacDonald's. *The Water-Babies* is crammed with references to contemporary issues, among them the American Civil War, Robert Lowe's Revised Education Code of 1862, positivism, the fountains in Trafalgar Square, the setting up of Broadmoor Criminal Lunatic Asylum on Easthampstead Plain in 1863, American 'greenbacks', Napoleon III's annexation of Nice, the Acclimatization Society, the 'hippocampus minor' controversy between Richard Owen and T. H. Huxley, and the rejection of Monckton Milne's Bill (March, 1862) to permit marriage with the sibling of a deceased spouse.[26] There are scarcely any such references in MacDonald's fantasy. Kingsley is acutely conscious of the scientific discoveries of Darwin and Huxley and of the need to square them with his Christian faith. MacDonald's reaction to contemporary scientific discovery is, as we saw, simply to dismiss it as irrelevant to true insight into the world. This makes Kingsley an apologist and a proselytizer in a way that MacDonald is not. When Kingsley states his aim in *The Water-Babies* of showing the miraculous element that lies beneath physical nature, he goes on, 'And if I have wrapped up my parable in seeming Tom-fooleries, it is because so only could I get the pill swallowed by a generation who are not believing with anything like their whole heart, in the Living God.'[27] One of Kingsley's objects was also to answer people's fears concerning Darwin's theory of natural selection: Kingsley constructed a theory of spiritual evolution, dramatized in *The Water-Babies*, whereby the form of every creature, rather than being the product of random brutish forces, expressed the spiritual condition to which the creature had arrived. Thus an ape's form expressed a stupid ape soul (and we might take any animal form in subsequent reincarnations), while man at his best portrayed the spiritual summit of creation .[28] All this would not only help overcome doubts, it would fit with Victorian progressivism and give it meaning. The sense of engagement with an audience is furthered by the way that the whole of *The Water-Babies* is permeated by the presence of its author, whether Kingsley or a metaphor of God, organizing the whole, pointing out lessons, commenting on stray facts or wonders, worrying bones of contention, and generally turning a highly public and suasive face to the reader: 'You must not say that this cannot be, or that it is contrary to nature'; 'Or was it such a salmon stream as I trust you will see along the Hampshire water-meadows before your hairs are grey, under the wise new fishing laws?'; 'just think – what is more cheap and plentiful than sea-rock? Then why should there not be sea-toffee as well? And every-one can find sea-lemons (ready quartered too, if you look for them at low tide . . . '[29]

MacDonald, while not averse to moralizing, generally lets the reader follow as he may. He never acknowledges the problem of doubt in the face of scientific discovery. His answer, as we saw, is simply to dismiss science as an irrelevance. Indeed, he tends as it were to amputate from himself those faculties which are most conscious and outward-looking. Where Kingsley tries to square his intellectual awareness with his faith, MacDonald rather does away with it: 'No wisdom of the wise can find out God . . . The simplicity of the natural relation is too deep for the philosopher . . . the child alone can understand (God).'[30] Perceptual experience is put above thought: 'To know a primrose is a higher thing than to know all the botany of it– just as to know Christ is an infinitely higher thing than to know all theology, all that is said about his person, or babbled about his work.'[31] And as for the human will, that obstreperous thing that may choose evil rather than good, faith-less science rather than child-like belief, that too, seen from a true 'spiritual' perspective, becomes a mere illusion in a universe where God's power is supreme, 'a stream that cuts itself off from its source and thinks to run on without it'.[32] Where Kingsley could entertain a dialogue between science and religion, and consider God Himself as a scientist, for MacDonald there is no real debate, for only one side of the 'debate' is real. Ultimately MacDonald's universe is non-dialectical. Like MacDonald, Kingsley could maintain that evil is finally unreal, but there is a peculiar immediacy in the stress on this concept in MacDonald. Kingsley may be theologically adventurous in maintaining that the universe is so constituted

and that will collide with and correct acts of evil; but MacDonald seems
at quite a further stage in telling us through Anodos in *Phantastes* that
'What we call evil, is the only and best shape, which, for the person and
his condition at the time, could be assumed by the best good'.[33]

This dislocation of the self from the world in MacDonald is also seen in
the way that in his fantasies the characters are moved from the real to the
faërian world when they are in some form of unconsciousness – whether
asleep (Anodos), ill (Diamond), confused (Vane) or lost (Irene in *The
Princess and the Goblin* and the children in the story 'The Carasoyn'). In
The Water-Babies Kingsley refuses to allow any such mystery or loss of connection. He will not tell us that Tom died when he fell into the stream;
rather, he makes it an apparently physical process of metamorphosis,
whereby Tom sloughed off his old body like a husk and swam out in the
form of a water-baby 'about 3.87902 inches long, and having round the
parotid region of his fauces a set of external gills (I hope you understand all
the big words) just like those of a sucking eft'.[34] MacDonald never
'explains' the supernatural or fantastic event. It simply happens, and the
protagonist is left to account for it as best he may. Anodos learns in Fairy
Land to accept what happens without question, 'like a child, who being in
a chronic condition of wonder, is surprised at nothing'.[35] As a trusting
child, Diamond in *At the Back of the North Wind* soon comes to accept
North Wind and her powers as a new part of his 'normal life'. Like Diamond with North Wind, so Princess Irene in *The Princess and the Goblin*
accepts her strange grandmother because she loves her. Love, indeed,
becomes reason enough. Kingsley, however, is at pains to prove that fairies
exist, or that a child may turn into a water-baby; he wants to prove the
process 'natural', in the belief that nature is far more various and wonderful
than we can guess.

While Kingsley tries to subsume the supernatural within nature, Mac-
Donald's purpose is always rather to put nature within supernature. That is
why MacDonald so often shows our real world fading before the 'other' of
Fairy Land. His concept of 'bi-local existing'[36] enables him to show this
world invisibly dipped in a 'bath' of wonder: in *Lilith*, Vane is told how
faërian flowers from another dimension grow through a piano a lady is
playing in our world, '"and give that peculiar sweetness to her
playing "'. The difference comes out also in the ways that MacDonald
and Kingsley present great natural forces. MacDonald's North Wind
is obviously paralleled by Kingsley's great fairies Bedonebyasyoudid,
Doasyouwouldbedoneby and the creative principle embodied in
Mother Carey, though it is typical of MacDonald that his figure
should have the romantic image of the wind. North Wind is too
mobile for any one name: '"I don't think I am just what

you fancy me to be. I have to shape myself various ways to various people. But the heart of me is true. People call me dreadful names, and think they know all about me. But they don't. Sometimes they call me Bad Fortune, sometimes Evil Chance, sometimes Ruin, and they have another name for me which they think the most dreadful of all. '''[37] People see North Wind in their own selfish terms; the truth about her is that she is part of a far larger reality than they can conceive, in which such names as they give her must fall away. But Kingsley's fairies are precisely described by their names. They are all natural forces acting as (delegated) sub-vicars of God, one the law of action, the other of reaction, the third the *élan vital*. Mrs Bedonebyasyoudid tells Tom that ''' I work by machinery, just like an engine; and am full of wheels and springs inside; and am wound up very carefully, so that I cannot help going. '''[38] It is only at brief moments that we get any direct sense of anything beyond them, as when Mrs Bedonebyasyoudid looks 'up and away, as if she were gazing through the sea, and through the sky, at something far, far off', or when all the fairies come interchangeably together in a vision at the end and bid the children read the blazing name in their eyes, which they cannot yet do.[39] But MacDonald's North Wind continually acts within both a natural and a supernatural context. She is the wind; she is the harshness and yet the chilling invigoration which the wind represents; she is the architect of much human suffering; she is the divine breath itself, waking us to spiritual consciousness. Most of all, North Wind is the doorway to the country at the back. When Diamond has reached the North Pole he finds that he must go through her frozen self to reach that realm. What he reaches, aching delight though it is to remember, is, since he is still alive, only a poor version of the reality he will find after death: '''The real country at my back is ever so much more beautiful than that.'''[40] As Diamond experienced it, it could not be put into any but the most glancing words, because it at once transcended our world and was far more fully what it ought to be. But we understand most about the differences between MacDonald and Kingsley when we realise that MacDonald's fantasy all looks to that far-off world which is yet in some ways here with us, while Kingsley's looks to this world primarily. MacDonald writes about 'otherness', Kingsley about 'thisness'; the one about a Fairy Land or an approach to Heaven, the other about earth or heaven on earth. When Tom has done his duty and won his moral spurs, he goes to a heaven that certainly does not defy description and is steeped in the things of the earth: 'So Tom went home with Ellie on Sundays, and sometimes on weekdays, too; and he is now a great man of science, and can plan railroads, and steam engines, and electric telegraphs, and rifled guns, and so forth;

and knows everything about everything . . . '[41]

The difference also expresses itself the way the two writers regard God's relation to nature. Kingsley, while believing that God worked immanently within nature, tended rather to infer rather than feel the fact. He called himself 'A mystic in theory, and an ultra-materialist in practice': and that does indeed precisely describe him. His investigations as a naturalist led him to the discovery that 'below all natural phenomena we come to a transcendental – in plain English, a miraculous ground': but he did not experience this, he only intuited it from his wonder at physical nature.[42] MacDonald, who saw God as 'on top of', rather than beneath, nature, does come nearer to a mystical apprehension. We feel that the symbols he uses let light in from some distant source.[43] We feel that the Fairy Land that Anodos enters is more than just some bizarre place his subconscious has wandered into: the place is shot through, as C. S. Lewis himself felt, with holiness.[44] It is partly a matter of the themes in *Phantastes*, particularly those of self-denial and of 'good death': it is clear that Anodos must lose in a worldly sense to gain and feel the 'great good' coming of another. But it is also the Fairy Land of the soul. And one way MacDonald makes it come over, in *Phantastes* at least, is by writing a dream-like, fragmented narrative, which undermines the very habits of questioning that go into Kingsley's natural theology. (Kingsley's narrative is itself chaotic in form, but it is a chaos in which each item is made to collide energetically and contrastively with the rest, and thus keep us continually awake and alert.[45])

The Water-Babies does, however, maintain more consistent contact with divine significance at another level. For in part it is an allegory of life under grace and the 'infinite network of special providences' that make up nature,[46] moving from an unregenerate, heathen state, through baptism, and to eventual confirmation in Tom's joining the water-baby community, sustained throughout by the changing waters in which he lives, and watched over the by the fairies.[47] Nevertheless, this process is still felt very much as a plain allegory, where we read the faërian narrative and its significance with two acts of mind. Kingsley says as much when he describes to Maurice how he has 'wrapped up' his parable of divine truth in 'seeming Tom-fooleries' in order to make it more acceptable. In the case of MacDonald, the story has a much more intimate, 'incarnational' relation with the 'spiritual' – and the latter element is felt not so much as a pattern of significance as another form of being. MacDonald disliked allegory and definite meanings imposed on fairy tales, saying that such tales, dealing as they do directly with the things of God, should rather be allowed to move, or cause to imagine.[48] His own son Greville has written of the sacramentalist character of MacDonald's symbolism: 'To him a symbol was far more than an arbitrary outward and visible sign of an abstract conception: its high virtue lay in a common *substance* with the idea presented'.[49] And C.S. Lewis speaks of the mythic power of MacDonald's faërian narratives: 'The meaning, the suggestion, the radiance, is incarnate in the whole story': 'There [is]. . . no question of getting through to the kernel and throwing away the shell: no question of a gilded pill. The pill [is] . . . gold all through'.[50]

The whole orientation of MacDonald's fantasy is towards the spiritual and metaphysical, which subsumes the physical; that of Kingsley is much more immediately towards the physical and moral. Though Kingsley says that the soul makes the body, just as a snail makes its shell,[51] his picture of this differs from MacDonald's. For Kingsley it is not so evidently the 'soul' as *acts* of good or bad that determine physical appearance. Thus when Tom steals the sweets, the prickles he grows express the deed itself and its consequent emotions, rather than the spirit itself: 'therefore, when Tom's soul grew all prickly with naughty tempers, his body could not help growing prickly too'.[52] It is the initial *act* which has led to this. And the same goes for the History of the Doasyoulikes, who did nothing, and therefore were unable to adapt to changing circumstances.[53] But in MacDonald one feels that the soul itself is the immediate source of bodily appearance. In *The Princess and Curdie* the forty-nine strange creatures who follow Curdie to Gwyntystorm are purgatorial expressions of formerly grotesque or hideous states of the soul; thus when we read of the dog Lina, we hear of

> the ludicrousness of her horrible mass of incongruities. She had a very short body, and very long legs made like an elephant's, so that in lying down she kneeled with both pairs. Her tail, which dragged on the floor behind her, was twice as long and quite as thick as her body. Her head was something between that of polar bear and a snake. Her eyes were dark green, with a yellow light in them. Her under teeth came up like a fringe of icicles, only very white, outside of her upper lip. Her throat looked as if the hair had been plucked off. It showed a skin white and smooth.[54]

We know from this that all these features which so defy any zoology (unlike the changes in Kingsley which keep to the natural order), must result from a supernatural and spiritual cause.[55] The difference in MacDonald's case is that the soul *presently* inhabiting this grotesque body is that of a child: the 'body' into which it is locked has helped it back to its innocence. For MacDonald, 'body' is not just physical but metaphysical too, for both soul and body partake in a supernatural source. For one thing, the 'body' one sees is not objective–what we see depends on what we are. Curdie is told by the magic lady he meets in the mines, '" if a thief were to come in here just now, he would think he saw the demon of the mine, all in green flames, come to protect her treasure, and would run like a hunted wild goat. I shall be all the same, but his evil eyes would see me as I was not "'.[56] This is a different form of the soul 'making' the body: the perceiving soul alters what it sees according to its nature. For MacDonald, then, there is really only one final category, that of the spirit, where for Kingsley soul and body have almost equal status, like pearl and oyster. '" Shapes are only dresses, Curdie, and dresses are only names. That which is inside is the same all the time "'.[57] This is also the position of North Wind, who may appear under hideous aspect to the evil, just as to Diamond she appears as a loving if capricious woman: '" But the heart of me is true "'.[58]

Kingsley's emphasis, it might be said, is on life; that of MacDonald on dying out of life. Kingsley gets Tom's 'death' out of the way early, refusing as we saw to admit it as death: he portrays it as a physical transformation by which Tom is able to see more of life, not less. His notion of moral evolution involves Tom developing into his true form throughout, quitting his isolated life as a sweep for that of a productive scientist. In a real sense Tom grows more vital through the story; certainly, when he meets the tide of the sea, 'He felt as strong, and light, and fresh, as if his veins had run champagne.'[59] His being seems to dilate as he travels; and indeed one could follow a pattern of expansion from his narrow life as a chimney-sweep to his escape to the wide country and even from this life, to the stream, river, sea, and then ocean. He is almost like one of the caddis-flies in the stream that goes on adding more things to itself; and, in parallel, the form and style of The Water-Babies itself is fundamentally accretive. But for MacDonald the object is not to get more 'being', to become more and more a 'self', but rather to lose the self, share it with others, or give it away. All his protagonists are either children, or have to drop the 'adult' for the child-like to see alright. For him the way forwards is by going 'backwards': his vision is fundamentally paradoxical; of the divine mysteries of nature he could say, for example, 'The deepest of these are far too simple for us to understand as yet'.[60] In many of his fantasies death is the terminus. Anodos dies in Fairy Land, and then in a different way 'dies back' into this world. Diamond dies, and probably goes to the real country at the back of the North Wind. Vane lies down in a house of the dead at the end of

Lilith. These deaths are often the end-point of a learned passivity, a yielding of the self: Anodos must learn not to want to possess the white lady, and Vane must accept his need to lie down with the others. Rather than a process of expansion, there is often one of contraction. The figures met are not so frequently multiple, as in Kingsley, but single; and where in *The Water-Babies* we feel that in a sense Tom is but one individual creature among many, in MacDonald's fantasies, perhaps fitting their mental character, the focus of the characters in the story is on a central figure around whom events and settings revolve–the Chamber of Sir Anodos in the fairy palace, the goblins tunnelling to seize Irene, North Wind visiting Diamond. Anodos ends his adventures in Fairy Land in the confined circle of the sinister forest church; ends his life there in a grave, though he emerges from it and floats with a cloud above the world; and finally ends his story by 'sinking from such a state of ideal bliss, into the world of shadows which again closed around and infolded me'.[61] Diamond dies in a coffin-like room he has found in the attic. Mossy and Tangle in 'The Golden Key' end up shut in a mountain before the golden key gives them the way into a pillar and upwards. Vane has to enter the cottage and lie down on his death-bed. But if there is confinement relative to this world, death is for MacDonald the sole gateway to a vitality, a freedom, an expansion of being, beyond anything that mortal life can give. This is what Mossy and Tangle seek in 'the country whence the shadows fall'; that is the 'great good' that Anodos awaits; that is the recovered paradise of which Diamond has faint intuitions in his vision of the country at the back of the North Wind; that is the transfigured life that awaits Vane when the dead are raised in *Lilith.*

In *The Water-Babies* there are a few night scenes. Really the only one of significance is that in which Grimes and two other men come to poach salmon when Tom is near; when they are set upon by keepers, Grimes falls into the river and drowns. To this we could perhaps add the time when Tom steals Mrs Bedonebyasyoudid's sweets from her larder, for that is at night too. Night is the time of concealment, for Kingsley; only in the clarity of daylight are things most truly themselves. But for MacDonald night and darkness do not necessarily suggest evil. For him the greatest truths come from the imagination, which is rooted in darkness: 'From darkness to the sun the water bubbles up';[62] 'God sits in that chamber of our being in which the candle of our consciousness goes out in darkness, and sends forth from thence wonderful gifts into the light of that understanding which is His candle'.[63] It is by night that North Wind visits Diamond and takes him with her. Anodos finds

his way to Fairy Land by the night of this world. *Phantastes* is full of
night scenes. Anodos is pursued by the Ash at night, but he also finds
the fairy palace at night. Night is the womb of the unconscious, which
may produce the things of God or horrors of our own making. In *The
Princess and the Goblin*, Irene usually finds her grandmother by night;
and in *The Princess and Curdie*, she always appears then. Night is also
the time of sleep and passivity, which for MacDonald are analogues
for 'good' death; it is that passivity and darkness to which Vane is
directed in *Lilith*, though he for long clings to the frail light of consciousness. Night for MacDonald is much less the place of concealment it is for Kingsley, than it is the medium of the mysterious, of
those dark sayings which alone are truth.

Further emphasising the involvement with the world of the one,
and the continual transcending of it by the other, is the fact that the
action in Kingsley's *The Water-Babies* takes place in a horizontal
plane, where MacDonald often introduces the vertical, which cuts
through life. Tom goes over the surface of the earth, from moor to
stream to river to ocean–though there is a certain amount of
descent, in his climb down Vendale or his journey through the sea
floor to the Other-end-of-Nowhere. But MacDonald's Diamond
travels above the world with the North Wind; and the arrangement
of the castle on the mountain in *The Princess and the Goblin*, with its
cellars and attics, and the mines beneath, suggests the three layers of
mind. In 'The Golden Key', Mossy and Tangle seek to ascend to the
land whence the shadows fall, and do so eventually by entering and
travelling up a pillar within a mountain. In all of MacDonald's fantasy
there is emphasis on the sky and on its celestial bodies, particularly
the moon and stars. No such dimension appears in *The Water-Babies*:
a vista may spread, but it does not ascend. Throughout MacDonald's
fantasy there is imagery of mountains and of stairways, all of a piece
with that upward vision.[64] MacDonald once said 'it is the upward-
reaching that meets the downstretched hand'.[65] Old Sir Upward was
master of the castle before Vane, in *Lilith*.

It can be said in general that where Kingsley goes for nature first,
MacDonald goes for 'supernature'. Much of Kingsley's writing shows
an emphasis on the portrayal of nature and its workings from which
we may infer, by argument or through wonder, the existence of a present creator of them: even when he would lead us, as he does
through the deepening waters of *The Water-Babies*, to the final vision
of the divine source that works through the great fairies or natural
principles, that source is still the end point of an investigation, an
'unknown x' or a 'something nameless' as he put it,[66] not altogether

unlike the 'Unknowable' that Herbert Spencer and other Victorian scientists predicated as a refuge from their own materialism.[67] In place of an 'interfering God' Kingsley substituted an 'immanent, ever-working God'[68] who is so identified with the physical workings of His creation as to be indistinguishable from them save by faith. Kingsley is both a naturalist and a Platonist, both a scientist and a Christian, but what shows under the polarising influence of his adherence to scientific method, is mainly the former side.[69] But because MacDonald turns away from science, because he looks constantly beyond the world and within the imagination to find the things of God, the sense of the supernatural and the mystical in him is much stronger. His God is almost always a person, a father, where Kingsley's is a force. (We find that personal relationships are profoundly important in MacDonald's work – Irene with her 'Grandmother' or Curdie, Diamond with North Wind, Anodos with the white lady, Vane with Adam or with Lilith.) And in part it is the difference in their approach to science that explains the contrast between the two authors. In part only: for beyond this the difference is as wide as that, more characteristic of their age, between the idealist and the realist, and as 'narrow' as between almost every aspect of their individual personalities.

What must remain remarkable, almost like some metaphysical conceit, is the way that for all these polar differences the two writers are yet bound together by apparent likenesses in their work and theological views, and in particular by the fact that they chose, alone and at almost the same time in the nineteenth century, to put what they could of the divine presence in the fairy tale. MacDonald once wrote a story called 'The History of Photogen and Nycteris', otherwise entitled 'The Day Boy and the Night Girl' (1879): in a sense he might have been portraying what we see here. For MacDonald's fantasy is of the night, and of the feminine, the mysterious, the interior and the relatively passive; Kingsley's of the day, of the masculine, the clear, the outdoor, and the active. Perhaps in the coming together of the two at the end of the story MacDonald prefigured that transcendence of his own 'partial' view of the truth which might come at some far or near time: "" But who knows, " Nycteris would say to Photogen, "that when we go out, we shall not go into a day as much greater than your day as your day is greater than my night? ""

References

1. Gillian Avery, with Angela Bull, 'Fairy Tales with a Purpose', *Nineteenth Century Children: Heroes and Heroines in English Children's Stories 1780-1900* (London: Hodder and Stoughton, 1965), ch.2, pp.41-63.
2. Stephen Prickett, *Romanticism and Religion: The Tradition of Wordsworth and Coleridge in the Victorian Church* (Cambridge University Press, 1976),

pp.213-17.

3. At least on the evidence of Margaret M. Maison, *Search your soul, Eustace: A Survey of the Religious Novel in the Victorian Age* (London: Sheed and Ward, 1961) and of Robert Lee Wolff *Gains and Losses: Novels of Faith and Doubt in Victorian England* (London: John Murray 1977).

4. MacDonald, *Lilith: A Romance* (London: Chatto and Windus, 1895), p.278.

5. Frances E. Kingsley, ed., *Charles Kingsley: His Letters and Memories of his Life*, 2 vols. (London: Kegan Paul, 1876), II, 28; see also I, 317.

6. On which see Jerome H. Buckley, *The Victorian Temper: A Study in Literary Culture* (London: George Allen and Unwin, 1952), pp.41-65.

7. Kingsley wrote the introduction to an edition of *The Pilgrim's Progress* in 1860, and MacDonald and his family regularly went on tour enacting the story from 1877 to 1889.

8. Kingsley, *The Water-Babies: A Fairy Tale for a Land-Baby* (London: Macmillan, 1863), p.221.

9. On the Victorian opposition to Romanticism, see Buckley, pp.14-40.

10. Kingsley, *Yeast: A Problem*, in *The Works of Charles Kingsley*, 28 vols. (London: Macmillan, 1879-83), II, 312.

11. David Newsome, *Two Classes of Men: Platonism and English Romantic Thought* (London: John Murray, 1974), esp. pp.1-7.

12. R.A. Forsyth, *The Lost Pattern: Essays on the Emergent City Sensibility in Victorian England* (Nedlands, W.A. : University of Western Australia Press, 1976), pp.54-5. Cf. also Tony Tanner, 'Mountains of Depths–An Approach to Nineteenth-Century Dualism', *Review of English Literature*, 3,4 (Oct., 1962), 60: 'The Cartesian dichotomy of mind and matter [is] . . . part of the landscape of the nineteenth-century mind'.

13. Kingsley, *Letters and Memories*, II, 18-19.

14. MacDonald, *A Dish of Orts, Chiefly Papers on the Imagination, and on Shakspere* (London: Sampson, Low, Marston & Co., 1893), pp.2, 25.

15. Ibid., p.319.

16. Both first appeared in 1853, and were reprinted in his *Literary and General Essays*, *Works*, XX (1880).

17. Kingsley, *Letters and Memories*, II, 40, 39.

18. Kingsley, *Madam How and Lady Why, or, First Lessons in Earth Lore for Children*, *Works*, XXII (1880), pp.125, 145.

19. *Letters and Memories*, II, 39.

20. In *Fraser's Magazine*, 39 (March, 1849), pp.289-90.

21. MacDonald, *Unspoken Sermons: Third Series* (London: Longmans, Green, 1889), pp.62-3. See also pp.48, 63-9; and *A Dish of Orts*, pp.257-8.

22. *Letters and Memories*, II, 66; cf. I, 413.

23. Ibid., II, 137 (Letter to Maurice of summer, 1862).

24. MacDonald, *Phantastes: A Faerie Romance for Men and Women* (London: Smith, Elder, 1858), pp.101-2.

25. Ibid., pp.203-4.

26. Arthur Johnston, 'The Water Babies: Kingsley's Debt to Darwin', *English*, XII (1958-9), 216. See also Valentine Cunningham, 'Soiled Fairy: The Water-Babies in its Time', *Essays in Criticism*, 35 (1985), 121-48.

27. *Letters and Memories*, II, 137-8.

28. See the spiritual-evolutionary ladder from madrepore to man that is followed in a fever-vision by the hero of Kingsley's *Alton Locke, Tailor and Poet* (1850), ch. 36.

29. *The Water-Babies*, pp.77, 128, 217.

30. MacDonald, *The Hope of the Gospel* (London: Ward, Lock, Bowden, 1892), p.163.

31. MacDonald, *Unspoken Sermons: Second Series* (London: Longmans, Green, 1885), p.236.

32. MacDonald, *Unspoken Sermons: Third Series*, p.262.

33. *Phantastes* p.323; see also *Lilith*, p.113, 'I began to learn that . . . evil was only through good! selfishness but a parasite on the tree of life!'

34. *The Water-Babies*, pp. 74-5. In a sense, with his belief in an 'intermediate state' in which men would, in forms expressing their spiritual condition, have fresh chances 'to all eternity' *(Letters and Memories*, I, 483), Kingsley could be said 'really to have believed' in the possibility of water-babies: certainly Tom's newt-form is close to that of the foetus in the womb; and he is set in the little-explored marine world, which Kingsley always felt was full of boundless natural possibility. On the relations between Darwin's and Kingsley's transformationist theories, see Gillian Beer, 'Darwinian Myths', in *Darwin's Plots: Evolutionary Narrative in Darwin, George Eliot and Nineteenth-Century Fiction* (London: Routledge and Kegan Paul, 1983), pp.123-39.

35. *Phantastes*, p.37.

36. See Greville MacDonald, *George MacDonald and His Wife* (London: Allen and Unwin, 1924), p.298.

37. MacDonald, *At the Back of the North Wind*, 2nd ed. (London: Blackie & Son, 1886), pp.363-4.

38. *The Water-Babies*, p.220.

39. Ibid., pp.221, 373.

40. *At the Back of the North Wind*, p.364.

41. *The Water-Babies*, p.374.

42. This is discussed in C.N. Manlove, *Modern Fantasy: Five Studies* (Cambridge: Cambridge University Press, 1975), pp.32-8.

43. See also Manlove, pp.94-8.

44. C.S. Lewis, *Surprised by Joy: The Shape of my Early Life* (London: Geoffrey Bles, 1955), pp.169-71.

45. See also Manlove, pp.20-3, 28-31.

46. Kingsley, *Glaucus: or, The Wonders of the Shore* (1855), *Works*, V (1879), p.100. Cf. Kingsley, *Letters and Memories*, II, 338, 'I believe not only in "special providences", but in the whole universe as one infinite complex of special providences'.

47. Manlove, pp.51-3.

48. MacDonald, 'The Fantastic Imagination' (1893), *A Dish of Orts*, pp.313-22, esp. p.321.

49. Greville MacDonald, *George MacDonald and his Wife*, pp.481-2.

50. Lewis, *George MacDonald: An Anthology* (London: Geoffrey Bles, 1946), pp.17, 21.

51. *The Water-Babies*, pp.94, 244-5; *Letters and Memories*, II. 143-4, 172.

52. *The Water-Babies*, p.245. For a fuller account of Kingsley's treatment of this theme in *The Water-Babies*, see Manlove, pp.38-51.

53. *The Water-Babies*, pp.259-70.

54. MacDonald, *The Princess and Curdie*, 2nd ed. (London: Chatto and Windus, 1888), p.76.

55. See also Manlove, pp.74-5.

56. *The Princess and Curdie*, p. 56.

57. Ibid.; Stephen Prickett, *Victorian Fantasy* (Brighton: Harvester Press, 1979), p.168, mistakenly identifies Kingsley's position with Blake's belief that 'man has no body as district from his soul'. Prickett's tendency to link Kingsley with MacDonald and both with the Romantics leads him to a more mystical view of *The Water-Babies* than the facts warrant.

58. *At the Back of the North Wind*, p.363.
59. *The Water-Babies*, p.149.
60. MacDonald, *A Dish of Orts*, p.18.
61. *Phantastes*, p.318.
62. MacDonald, 'A Cry', *The Poetical Works of George MacDonald*, 2 vols. (London: Chatto and Windus, 1893), I, 394.
63. *A Dish of Orts*, p.25.
64. On MacDonald's fascination for these particular symbols, see Manlove, pp.57, 72, 96-7, 274 n.38, 277 n.89.
65. *A Dish of Orts*, p.72.
66. Kingsley, *Westminster Sermons, Works*, XXVIII (1881), pp. xxxviii, xxvii; cf. p.195.
67. Spencer in *First Principles* (1862).
68. Letter of mid-1863 to Maurice, in *Letters and Memories*, II, 171.
69. For the more widespread occurrence of this process among Victorian Christians from the 1860s onwards, see Owen Chadwick, *The Victorian Church, Part II 1860-1901*, 2nd ed. (London: A. and C. Black, 1972), pp.30-3.

9

George MacDonald

CATHERINE DURIE

At first sight, the relationship between MacDonald and Lewis seems obvious; we have Lewis's own account of it, placing at the centre of his spiritual development a chance reading of *Phantastes*, which baptized his imagination and set him on the road to Christianity. In later life the grateful convert responded by nominating MacDonald as his master and recommending him to other seekers after truth, so introducing MacDonald to a wider reading public than one might expect. If MacDonald were to be judged by his impact on popular religious thought, then his greatest achievement would be the creation of C.S. Lewis, Christian apologist. In turn, the popularity of Lewis's writings has revitalized interest in MacDonald, especially in America. Since 1982, at least twenty-four of MacDonald's novels have been republished in the U.S.A., although some appear in strange guises. Most are considerably abbreviated, many are retitled, and, where necessary, the intransigent Scots tongue has been removed. The situation is not without its ironies; as a result of Lewis's championship, works of MacDonald are reissued of which Lewis actively disapproved. *The Seaboard Parish* is one such; Lewis saw it as uncompromisingly bad, disliking its flat moralising, and never finished reading it. Equally, novels in which Lewis exhibited no interest, such as *Mary Marston*, *Heather and Snow*, and *There and Back* are part of the list; the market for them is inexplicable except in terms of the continuing appetite for anything connected with Lewis, however remotely.

If we examine this relationship in a little more detail the picture becomes more complex; part of the difficulty is that Lewis wrote so little in his professional role about MacDonald. The introduction to *George MacDonald: An Anthology* is the nearest approach to literary criticism; the only other substantial sources are the comments to be found in his autobiography, *Surprised By Joy*, and his letters to Arthur Greeves, a fellow-enthusiast and lifelong friend. The bulk of these letters date from early in his life, but we have no reason to suppose Lewis modified his views; all of the letters demonstrate his real relish for MacDonald. This enjoyment, though, co-exists with a refusal to rate MacDonald in purely literary terms, because of reservations about his prose style and his success as a novelist. 'If we define Literature as an art whose medium is words, then certainly MacDonald has no place in its first rank–perhaps not even in its second.' (Lewis 1946, p. 14) Lewis is primarily interested in MacDonald as a purveyor of Christian truth; literary value, or the lack of it, is hence irrelevant. So if we want to use Lewis as a means of approaching MacDonald, we have to be clear about the kind of guidance we can expect from him. The purpose of this essay is to argue that Lewis draws a great deal from MacDonald and can illuminate whole areas of his work. Equally, his comments on a book like *Wilfrid Cumbermede* (1872), to which we shall return, can help us to read not only MacDonald but Lewis himself. However, Lewis is also an unreliable guide because of the highly individualistic ways in which he uses MacDonald and because of a vested interest in seeing the Victorian writer as reinforcement for his own beliefs.

If Lewis's judgements seem suspect, we must remember that their context is spiritual, not literary. Lewis's personal use of MacDonald was devotional; this is how he recommends him to others. But this leads to a whole set of conclusions that are staggering unless one recollects that the literary critic is off the record, speaking; we are apt to forget this, given that Lewis's whole context of reference is literary. So when he tells Greeves,

> The more I read his novels the more I rage at the tragedy of his being forced to write for money and thus diverted from his true sphere, so that we get only as much of the real MacDonald as he can smuggle in *by the way*. It is, I really think, a loss as irreparable as the early death of Keats. (10 Jan. 1931)

several things are striking. There is the assumption that the 'real' MacDonald is not expressed, indeed is frustrated by the realistic novels; but we may ask is the real MacDonald located in the fantasies or in the straightforward Christian teaching? Lewis seems to be equally happy to discover within a conventional novel either fairy tale or preaching. There is also the appreciation of a smuggled message, with its connotations of excitement and daring, which was how Lewis came to view his own science fiction and children's stories; and there is the breathtaking assertion that the loss is as significant as the death of Keats. We are not clear whether Lewis is speaking personally here, of how acutely he feels that loss, or whether he would be prepared to defend that judgement in a wider sphere. The latter seems likely. Similar examples are easy to find; he contrasts *Annals of a Quiet*

Neighbourhood favourably with Trollope's *Belton Estate*, which he sees
as morally deficient because of its lack of charity and its worldliness
(24 Dec. 1930). The superiority of the MacDonald is such that he is
ashamed to have wasted time on the other. There is also an easy slip-
page from literary judgements to moral and spiritual ones; he is most
comfortable with a devotional use of MacDonald, which compels his
admiration and gratitude. In 1929 he speaks of reading a daily verse
of *Diary of an Old Soul* before bedtime, with cocoa, as a means of
washing off the day; he praises MacDonald's insight, which helps him
to understand his own life: 'He seems to know everything and I find
my own experience in it constantly: as regards the literary quality, I
am coming to like even his clumsiness. There is a delicious home-
spun, earthy flavour about it, as in George Herbert. Indeed *for me* he
is better than Herbert.' (10 Oct. 1929) Lewis's italics are telling, and
here is no confusion about the kind of values adopted. He does not
seriously claim that MacDonald can be ranked above Herbert as poet,
but if a devotional book is to be assessed by the profoundity of its
impact on the individual, then only he is in a position to evaluate
their respective merits. In addition, Lewis indulges in some special
pleading; as a critic he is always partisan, and here, where 'homeliness'
is a key term in the private code of values constructed by himself and
Greeves, he has no difficulty in vindicating his judgement.

The same kind of thinking underlies his ranking of MacDonald's
works; Lewis always rated *Phantastes* and *Lilith* most highly, and usually in that order, following them with the fairy tales. Hitherto there
are no surprises; but next he places *Diary of an Old Soul*, and, as the
best of the novels, *What's Mine's Mine* (17 Jan. 1931). It appears from
other comments that *Sir Gibbie*, in which he loved the 'homeliness'
and the central Christ-like character, would come next followed by
Wilfrid Cumbermede. Lewis has no real affection for the Scottish novels like *Robert Falconer* or *Alec Forbes of Howglen*; he describes the
latter as 'good things in it, but not by any means a good book' (10
Jan. 1931). This makes more sense if a 'good book' means 'a book
which promotes my spiritual development' rather than 'a well-written
book'. Ultimately Lewis is prepared to jettison the criteria he
observes as a literary critic in order to defend what he finds most valuable. He likes *What's Mine's Mine* (17 Jan. 1931) not in spite of its
preaching but because of it. Characters succeed precisely because
they are idealised; they do not have to be convincing, only to make
Lewis wish they were real and so create a longing for goodness. So
the very quality which is a major literary flaw, the novel's obvious-
ness, becomes a devotional asset; the conversations, which Lewis par-

ticularly enjoyed, are little more than passages of *Unspoken Sermons* broken down into dialogue (Like the discussion between Ian and his mother in Chapter 15 on faith and atonement). Incidents carry the freight of a Biblical message. When Alister carries not only the usurper's gamebag but also his gun (Ch.6) we can barely miss the echo of the Sermon on the Mount on going the second mile; when he explains the duty of teaching his oxen to bear the yoke (Ch.10), we all overhear the lesson, and know it echoes 'Take my yoke upon you'.

When in the introduction to the *Anthology* (Lewis 1946) Lewis produces his fullest critical appraisal of MacDonald, he plays all these cards, asserting the magnificence of the preaching, whilst decrying the novels, 'as I think they would appear if judged by any reasonably objective standard. But it is, no doubt, true that my reader who loves holiness and loves MacDonald – yet perhaps he will need to love Scotland too – can find even in the worst of them something that disarms criticism and will come to feel a queer awkward charm in their very faults.' (Lewis 1946, p.18). Charm, of course, is a totally subjective standard; as Lewis recognises, what he is doing is expressing his own love of MacDonald and inviting his readers to share in that response by suspending their critical faculties. The problem is that he moves from this to an apparently objective literary judgement with no sign of transition. He tells us that MacDonald's unique quality lies in his presentation of goodness; 'The 'good' characters are always the best and most convincing. His saints live; his villains are stagey' (Lewis 1946, p.18). What kind of judgement is this? Lewis is right about the weakness of the villains, although characteristically he identifies this as a moral weakness, an indulgence in the pleasure of anger, rather than a literary one: 'I wonder did he indulge (day dreamily) an otherwise repressed fund of indignation by putting into his novels bogeys to whom his heroes could make the stunning retorts and deliver the stunning blows, which he himself neither could nor would deliver in real life.' (17 Jan. 1931). The same letter is the one which accepts that the good characters are convincing in that he wishes reality were like that, rather than in the sense in which 'convincing' would normally be used. So when sixteen years later he claims the saints to be the 'best and most convincing' characters, is he abandoning his earlier position? If they 'live', does that make them lifelike? If that is Lewis's claim, I believe he is wrong; Sir Gibbie, or David Elginbrod, provides us with a model of perfection. Sanctity does not make for a lifelike character, and we are more likely to be convinced of the truthfulness of divided, imperfect characters, like Mr Cupples or Mrs Falconer. But in practice, Lewis is more likely to be engaged in special pleading again; in the guise of a literary argument, he produces a theological one. MacDonald's saints 'live' because they point to ultimate, not present, reality. Hence they are to be weighed against the standards not of Huntly or Aberdeen or London, but against those of the New Jerusalem shining dimly through these unreal cities.

Lewis treats the fantasies with the same highly individualistic sensitivity to the moral and spiritual value of a text. *Phantastes* above all becomes a kind of code-word to summon up his own past and to determine a standard for his emotional and ethical response. Two accounts, from the *Anthology* introduction and from Lewis's autobiography, are important in helping us see how Lewis came to understand the unique impact of that novel on his life. We should remember that these accounts, dating from a later period, demonstrate the inevitable fictionalization of the past, the way in which we all select and heighten in order to extract meaning from randomness. The letters contemporary with his first reading of *Phantastes* show his delight; he asserts that the book is as good as Malory or Morris, but makes no allusion to its spiritual impact. A quarter-century later, *Surprised by Joy*, offers a memorable set piece. In the chapter, 'Check', Lewis recalls that until that point his search for Joy had been fruitless; he had been diverted from the pure, unbidden longing it represents into thrill-seeking, the yen to possess, the Occult. But when he casually picked up *Phantastes* on a railway bookstall, everything changed.

His account itself resembles fairy tale. It suggests the allure and mystery of a new world; his one action, the taking of the book, has unforeseeable consequences, out of all apparent proportion to the act. From that point, he is acted upon, rather than acting: 'The woodland journeyings in that story, the ghostly enemies, the ladies both ood and evil, were close enough to my habitual imagery to lure me on without the perception of a change. It is as if I were carried sleeping across the frontier, or as if I had died in the old country and could never remember how I came alive in the new.' (Lewis 1955, p.169).

Phantastes becomes a metaphor for Lewis's own experience; the 'journeyings' reflect the physical journey he is making, and the psychological transit into Christianity. The 'ghostly enemies' loom large in his pilgrimage; *Phantastes* rescues him, as Anodos needs to be rescued, from the destructive and corrupting elements in his own nature, especially from his own sexuality. The demons of a false Romanticism are driven out: 'I had already been waist-deep in Romanticism; and likely enough, at any moment, to flounder into its

darker and more evil forms, slithering down the steep descent that
leads from the love of strangeness to that of eccentricity and thence to
that of perversity.' (Lewis 1946, pp.20-1).

MacDonald purifies desire by pointing him towards true Romanticism, the hallmarks of which are that it is located in the homely and
humble; that it encourages alertness and innocence; and that it centres
on good death. *Phantastes* heals the division Lewis senses in himself
between imagination and reason; it reunites the real and the imaginary,
fact and ideal, by transfiguring the mundane conditions of his life and
showing all of these – the bread, the coals, even the empiricist teacher–
to be transmitters of mystery: 'Thus, when the great moments came I
did not break away from the woods and cottages that I read of to seek
some bodiless light shining beyond them . . . I found the light shining
on those woods and cottages, and then on my own past life, and on the
quiet room where I sat and on my old teacher where he nodded above
his little *Tacitus.'* (Lewis 1955, p.170).

The transforming power is Holiness; it unlocks the true nature of
reality and it draws him home. 'For the first time the song of the
sirens sounded like the voice of my mother or my nurse' (Lewis
1955, p.169). MacDonald's faery emphasizes the feminine; it is an
attraction to which Lewis dare respond precisely because it is safely
rooted in the maternal and non-sexual, offering intimacy without
danger. And as *Phantastes* ends with the real work for Anodos of
translating his experience into common life, so Lewis is careful to
remind us that the book effected only the baptism of his imagination;
neither conscience nor intellect was moved at this stage, but both
would eventually submit themselves to the shaping power of Mac-
Donald's influence.

In later years, Lewis consistently read the fantasies as determinants
of his moral vision. Curiously, his *imaginative* response to *Lilith* seems
limited; he assumes a clearly discernible moral message, and proceeds
to unpack this for Greeves: 'The main lesson of the book is against
secular philanthropy–against the belief that you can effectively obey
the second command about loving your neighbour without first trying to love God.' (1 Sept. 1933). He seeks lessons; typically, he uses a
phrase or incident of MacDonald's as a way of exploring a moral or
spiritual problem. So he quarries the passage in *The Princess and the
Goblin* (1872) where Curdie dreams he has woken, but wakes to find
he is still in bed (ch.27) for spiritual direction:

> This has a terrible meaning, specially for imaginative people. We
> read of spiritual efforts, and our imagination makes us believe
> that, because we enjoy the idea of doing them, we have done

them. I am appalled to see how much of the change wh. (sic) I thought I had undergone lately was only imaginary. It is so fatally easy to confuse an aesthetic appreciation of the spiritual life with the life itself – to dream that you have waked, washed and dressed & then to find yourself still in bed. (15 June 1930).

Given that this letter, like so many of those referring to MacDonald, dates from the early years of Lewis's religious experience, in fact from the period between his conversion to Theism and his conversion to Christianity, it demonstrates that, whether or not the initial impact on Lewis's spiritual life of *Phantastes* was as he later recollected it, MacDonald's book played a substantial part in the process by which he hammered out how he should live.

Nor was the fiction alone significant for Lewis; *Unspoken Sermons* held a central place in the structuring of his theology. In the *Anthology*, almost three-quarters of the quotations are drawn from their pages, and Lewis justifies his choice thus: 'My own debt to this book is almost as great as one man can owe to another: and nearly all serious enquirers to whom I have introduced it acknowledge that it has given them great help – sometimes indispensible help towards the very acceptance of the Christian faith.' (Lewis 1946, p.18). It rather sounds as if Lewis used the book as a touchstone in determining the seriousness of inquirers. But what help did Lewis himself get from these three volumes? He followed MacDonald in avoiding systems, formulae, creeds, and in choosing to concentrate on practice rather than doctrine. The passages Lewis quotes focus on prayer, anxiety, moral bankruptcy, the use of possessions; but the subject of obedience dominates them all, and provides the central point of reference in Lewis's moral vision: 'And in MacDonald it is always the voice of conscience that speaks. He addresses the will: the demand for obedience, for 'something to be neither more nor less nor other than *done*' is incessant.' (Lewis 1946, p.18). MacDonald teaches that obedience is the only path to understanding; we must obey in order to understand, rather than insist on understanding as a preface to obedience. 'He who does that which he sees, shall understand; he who is set on understanding rather than doing, shall go on stumbling' (MacDonald 1876, pp.98-9). Lewis takes the point wholeheartedly; in *The Abolition of Man* (Lewis 1943, ch.2) he argues similarly that obedience must never be postponed whilst a precept is rationally examined, for true comprehension will only come through practice. His fiction, especially the Narnian books, reiterates the principle almost to the point of monotony; the characteristic test to be faced in these is that of acting faithfully when there is no corroborative evidence, as for instance in *Prince Caspian* (1951, ch.9-11) where Lucy is the only one of the children to see Aslan, and has to follow him obediently when all the others disbelieve her. But as they are persuaded to follow, he also becomes visible to them, because it is only the practical exercise of faith that leads to sight. Equally, Lewis followed MacDonald in viewing obedience as the way of escape from the tyranny of feelings; so MacDonald exhorts those who are perturbed to disregard their feelings, to wait patiently and to continue to undertake the duties close at hand: 'Troubled soul, thou art not bound to feel but thou art bound to arise. God loves thee whether thou feelest it or not . . . bethink thee of something that thou oughtest to do, and go to do it . . . Heed not thy feeling: Do thy work.' (MacDonald 1876, pp.177-8). Lewis, who acknowledged his own deep distrust of feelings, fearing and hating emotion, was much attracted by this emphasis; so when he counsels others, like the lady with whom he corresponded, he reproduces the advice: 'Obedience is the key to all doors; *feelings* come (or don't come) and go as God pleases. We can't produce them at will, and mustn't try.' (7 Dec. 1950). Or in *Mere Christianity* he advises his readers not to worry about whether they love their neighbour or not, but simply to act as if this were the case. Feelings are transformed by the steady and active pursuit of duty.

From obedience, Lewis is led into other areas of understanding; he learns that trust in God's constancy is essential. He quotes extensively from the sermon 'The Cause of Spiritual Stupidity', which stresses that anxiety is only dealt with by recognition of the 'holy Present', and that care is an usurpation 'of something that is required of you this moment! . . . Trust in the living God' (MacDonald 1885, p.50). Lewis saw this underscored by MacDonald's own life history; his own teaching on anxiety in *The Screwtape Letters* picks up, like MacDonald, both the danger of dwelling in the future and the need to bear the cross patiently in this moment. The sufferer should 'accept with patience the tribulation which has actually been handed out to him – the present anxiety and suspense. It is about *this* that he is to say 'Thy will be done', and for the daily task of bearing *this* that the daily bread will be provided.' (Lewis 1942, p.34).

Lewis teases out another strand from this sermon to describe the nature of the God who is to be thus obeyed. MacDonald states that God will force no door to enter the human life, but will send suffering and difficulty to induce, even terrify, the soul into response: 'Every tempest is but an assault in the siege of love. The terror of God is but the other side of his love; it is love outside the house, that would be inside–love, that knows the house is no house, only a place, until it enter.' (MacDonald 1885, p.57). The appeal of this passage, quoted by Lewis in the *Anthology*, is important; he points out that the title by which he prefaces several extracts, 'Inexorable Love', could stand for the whole collection, and he praises MacDonald's yoking together the tender and the severe in God: 'nowhere else outside the New Testament have I found terror and comfort so intertwined' (Lewis 1947, p.19). This Lewis finds wholesome, both as instruction about man, a being whose only right is to be compelled to repent, and about God. As Lewis puts it, 'God is the only comfort, He is also the supreme terror: the thing we most need and the thing we most want to hide from '(Lewis 1952, p.24). But at this point we may begin to suspect that Lewis perhaps over-emphasises one side of the equation, that he underlines inexorability rather than love, divine hardness rather than compassion; when he does so, he is realigning MacDonald to match his own temperament and taste. The difference between the two men can be summed up in the images they choose for divine compulsion. MacDonald speaks of sufferings as 'the strong, sharp-toothed sheep-dogs of the Great Shepherd' (MacDonald 1885, p.194). Pursuit, pain and demand are there, but only to bring the wandering sheep back to the fold; throughout, God remains the Shepherd, an image with all its biblical associations of devoted caring, and he controls the dogs to ensure they inflict no real damage. Yet when Lewis reflects on his own history, he sees God as a divine Angler, playing a fish, and himself as hooked through the tongue (Lewis 1955, p.199); or God as a cat pursuing himself, a mouse. MacDonald could never have used these images of God, with their undertow of sheer power and even cruelty; there may be less affinity than appears between the two men.

This raises the more interesting question of how far Lewis departs from MacDonald; what is significant is not what he quotes but his exclusions. For instance, Lewis does follow MacDonald on the self-abnegating God revealed in the process of Creation, so when he writes 'But perhaps there is an anguish, an alienation, a crucifixion involved in the creative act' (Lewis 1946, p.65), he is echoing points MacDonald makes in 'Life' (MacDonald 1885, pp.140-45). But the nearer MacDonald comes to speaking of a self-sacrificial God, a God who actually suffers himself on Calvary, the less closely Lewis follows him. Lewis chooses to quote a passage such as, 'The worst heresy, next to that of dividing religion and righteousness, is to divide the Father from the Son; . . . to represent the Son as doing that which the Father does not Himself do.' (Lewis 1946, p.58). Removed from its context, we might well miss the force of the original point, which spells out that MacDonald's God the Father is a suffering, self-sacrificial God; what precedes Lewis's quotation is: 'What Jesus did was what the Father is always doing; the suffering he endured was that of the Father from the foundation of the world, reaching its climax in the person of his Son. God provides the sacrifice; the sacrifice is himself.' (MacDonald 1885, pp.142-3). When MacDonald addresses himself to the Atonement (with which, like many a Broad Churchman of his era, he had moral difficulty), Lewis quietly marks his dissent by fixing his gaze elsewhere. If we look to see from which sermons Lewis quotes little, the results are suggestive, given that his normal practice is to quote sufficiently fully to give the reader a reasonable idea, almost an outline, of the piece. 'The Truth in Jesus' (MacDonald 1885) is quoted three times (Lewis 1946, nos.165-7), but all of these come from a brief section on obedience, whereas the ten pages that precede it, and the twenty that follow are unquoted. These pages contain a violent attack on the doctrine of original sin and on any understanding of atonement as propitiation or substitution. MacDonald assails such theories as no better than paganism, claiming he would rather be agnostic than believe them. It is by no means clear from Lewis's writings exactly what he believed about the atonement; his fullest exploration, in *The Lion, The Witch and The Wardrobe*, in which Aslan offers himself in place of Edmund to meet the witch's claim, fits the classic ransom theory (Taliaferro 1988). Alternatively, Lewis tells his readers all explanations can be left aside as long as the *fact* of Christ's saving death is accepted: 'We are told that Christ was killed for us, that His death has washed out our sins, and that by dying he disabled death itself. That is the formula. That is Christianity. That is what has to be believed. Any theories we build up as to how Christ's death did all this are, in my view, quite secondary'. (Lewis 1952, p.45). But it may be that MacDonald does not state this fact with enough assurance for Lewis; he argues (MacDonald 1885, p.240) that he will not believe in atonement but in the atoner, for trusting in formulations about the work, or death, or merits, or blood of Christ is to repudiate the living lord in *whom* we must believe. Any theory of the atonement is immoral; a faith which must rest on such a foundation would be nothing short of damnable: 'A faith for instance, that God does not forgive me because he loves me, but because he loves Jesus Christ, cannot save me, because it is a falsehood against God: if the thing were true, such a gospel would be the preaching of a God that was not love, therefore in whom was no salvation . . . Such a faith would damn, not save a man; for it would bind him to a God who was anything but perfect.' (MacDonald 1885 p.251). Lewis sometimes appeals to a subjective theory of the atonement, sometimes to an objective; mostly he skirts the issue, but he cannot argue as MacDonald argues here.

There is another area of MacDonald's belief that Lewis quietly drops; 'The Child in the Midst' sets out distinctively the childlikeness of God, 'the God-known truth, that the Lord has the heart of a child.' (MacDonald 1867, p.12). Lewis quotes this essay only once, and that a few lines on spiritual dryness. We cannot be certain that it is disapproval that leads to these omissions; it could be that it is not a very good sermon–it does meander at first–or not quotable. All the same, a lack of sympathy seems likely; although Lewis enjoys reading and writing children's books, one would be hard-pressed to find him recommending childlikeness in any other context. Indeed, far from seeing God as childlike, Lewis does not even place much weight on man as a child of God; whereas MacDonald rejects the idea of adoption because all people are already children of God, Lewis suggests a distant notion of sonship as a kind of divinely sanctioned legal fiction (Lewis 1952, ch.7, Book 4). To say 'Our Father' is not to claim our childhood, but to pretend, or dress up as a son of God, a pretence in which God connives and which Christ eventually makes real. Unsurprisingly, then, when, MacDonald moves to the essential childlikeness of God Lewis does not follow. MacDonald consistently claims that theology misrepresents God when it portrays him as the great king; 'All his divine rights rest upon his love. Ah, he is not the great monarch' (MacDonald 1889, p.9). Yet Lewis delights in imagining God as the hunter, king, husband, in terms which underline power, majesty and government. For MacDonald the childlike God is the necessary obverse of the compelling God; so the terror of God serves only to make his child flee to, not from, a God who can 'alone be perfectly, abandonedly simple and devoted'. (MacDonald 1867, p.24) Although Lewis speaks warmly of the union of tenderness and severity in MacDonald, he seems to distrust images of tenderness applied to God; he can scarcely be comfortable with a statement like 'In this, then, is God like the child; that he is simply and altogether our friend, our father–more than friend, father and mother–our infinite love-perfect God.' (MacDonald 1867, p.21). This is a long way from the hierarchial and authoritative images that move Lewis, who always fears that tenderness may be understood as softness; hence his caricature in *The Problem of Pain* of a soft view of God as a 'senile benevolence' or a 'grandfather in heaven'. (Lewis 1940, p.28). It is worth noting that although Lewis identifies in MacDonald

the vision of Fatherhood at the core of the universe, Lewis does not
even really echo him in this. God as creator, author, angered majesty, basic Fact, Omnipotence, and perfect goodness–all of these
loom much larger than Fatherhood in his thinking, and his assent to
such a concept, although unquestioning, is also unmoved and
unmoving.

Do these divergences matter? They would not, were it not for the
extraordinarily high claims Lewis makes for MacDonald's status, and
influence upon himself; 'I know hardly any other writer who seems to
be closer, or more continually close, to the Spirit of Christ Himself'
(Lewis 1946, p.19). But less unanimity than one would expect is to
be found; and in one area at least Lewis seems to set out consciously
to correct MacDonald's stance.

In *The Great Divorce* the figure of MacDonald is introduced to
guide Lewis through his perplexities about heaven and hell, and it is
on the subject of hell that Lewis wants to reclaim his master from an
untenable theological position. What Lewis feared in MacDonald was
the taint of universalism; not that MacDonald was in any way a facile
universalist. His son believed that *Lilith* was written because
universalists were taking hell too lightly (Greville MacDonald 1924,
p.523). Nevertheless, MacDonald's writings show all the horror at the
doctrine of eternal punishment that one might expect of a follower of
Maurice; MacDonald does accept hell-fire, but he can tolerate neither its everlasting nature nor its punitory function. Lewis believes in
punishment as a moral response to evil, and hence is prepared to
argue in favour of both capital punishment and hell. He is passion-
ately committed to the idea that right must be asserted; he asks us to
imagine a totally self-satisfied evil-doer. What should be his fate?
'You are moved not by a desire for the wretched creature's pain as
such, but by a truly ethical demand that, soon or late, the right
should be asserted, the flag planted in this horribly rebellious soul,
even if fuller and better conquest is to follow.' (Lewis 1940, p.110).
For such a one, refusing repentance, hell would be the only appropriate response from a morally good God, claims Lewis; MacDonald
sees things differently, for 'God is not bound to *punish* sin; he is
bound to *destroy* sin.' (MacDonald 1889, p.122). For him, the Christian who loves his neighbour would rather venture into hell, forfeiting his own heaven, than allow one soul to remain lost. Consequently the function of hell is to induce repentance; it is the expe-
dient which brings about self-repudiation. To propose anything else
would be to make God less moral and less loving than man; but
God's nature decrees that he must bring all his children home; 'God

himself must be held in divine disquiet until every one of his family be brought home to his heart'. ('MacDonald 1885, p.263). But this is not how Lewis's MacDonald speaks; in the novel, the narrator is the troubled, questioning one, and MacDonald the guide gives the hard answers:

'What some people say on earth is that the final loss of one soul gives the lie to all the joy of those who are saved.'

'Ye see it does not.'

'I feel in a way that it ought to.'

'That sounds very merciful: but see what lurks behind it . . . The demand of the loveless and the self-imprisoned that they should be allowed to blackmail the universe: that till they consent to be happy (on their own terms) no one else shall taste joy: that Hell should be able to *veto* Heaven.' (Lewis 1945, pp.110-11).

Lewis and MacDonald are here made to change places; but the MacDonald who makes such forceful points is a ventriloquist's dummy. It is Lewis's voice which subverts the real MacDonald's belief in hell as a temporary, purifying force, and heaven as the home of every one of God's children.

Human will and choice cause much of the difficulty here. Lewis stresses that the lifelong choices of the rebels reinforce themselves so that change becomes impossible; in phrases reminiscent of Lilith's predicament, he says of the demand: 'Their fists are clenched, their teeth are clenched, their eyes fast shut. First they will not, in the end they cannot, open their hands for gifts, or their mouths for food, or their eyes to see'. (Lewis 1945, p.113). He leaves the possibility open that some may yet be redeemed from this state, but he has little doubt that some will not. Contrast this with Lilith whose clenched fist is an agony to her, and who begs Adam to sever it with his sword; Lilith is the incarnate principle of rebellion, yet MacDonald not only states her desire to be saved, but suggests that finally the Shadow, Satan himself, will choose to repent. For MacDonald, the more miserable a soul, the more likely is the emergence of a self-disgust which may be the first movings of repentance; hence a suicide, even one like Judas, will be saved: 'I think when Judas fled from his hanged and fallen body, he fled to the tender help of Jesus, and found it–I say not how. He was in a more hopeful condition now than during any moment of his past life, for he had never repented before.' (MacDonald 1867, p.95).

Suicides are usually treated sympathetically by MacDonald; he is sensitive to despair and self-disgust, encouraged by mental instability, in Kate Fraser in *Alec Forbes of Howglen* or Charley Osborne in

Wilfrid Cumbermede. In *The Great Divorce* the suicide is the Tousle-Headed poet, self-obsessed and inflated with pride, who jumped under a train because he was insufficiently appreciated; little hope, if any, is held out for his redemption. This is part of a larger pattern in the novel; set against MacDonald's demand that every one shall be saved, Lewis's story shows plainly that most are not. Of the damned who visit heaven and are given the chance to stay, only one, the lustful man, is shown to make that choice; most refuse, and would presumably go on refusing. Lewis, as he explains in *The Problem of Pain*, dislikes this conclusion about human nature, but cannot reconcile human freedom with anything less than a full doctrine of hell. He remarks almost wistfully, 'I believe that if a million chances were likely to do good, they would be given.' (Lewis 1940, p.112) Yet he cannot believe that they would do good: it is a long way from MacDonald's impassioned plea: 'For then our poor brothers and sisters, every one – O God, we trust thee, the Consuming Fire – shall have been burnt clean and brought home. For if their moans, myriads of ages away, would turn heaven for us into hell – shall a man be more merciful than God?' (MacDonald 1867, pp.48-9). As *The Great Divorce* ends, Lewis can only have his MacDonald abjure universalism by explaining the limitations of earthly knowledge, and suggesting that all formulations distort; the important choice is the one to be made now. It is a device which allows the book to close, but it does not resolve the differences between Lewis and his master.

Much of this account has tried to suggest limitations in Lewis as an interpreter of MacDonald; it is only fair to turn the subject round and consider a case where Lewis's response to a rather neglected novel, *Wilfrid Cumbermede*, casts some light on both writers and on their relation to one another. Lewis rated *Wilfrid Cumbermede* relatively highly, especially the first few chapters; it is a strange uneven book, but in it many key MacDonald themes and techniques appear, and it reveals some of the things that fascinated Lewis. Most noteable among these is MacDonald's use of symbolism; Lewis told Greeves, 'His only real form is the symbolical fantasy like *Phantastes* or *Lilith*. This is what he always writes; but unfortunately, for financial reasons, he sometimes has to *disguise* it as ordinary Victorian fiction. Hence what you get is a certain amount of the real MacDonald linked . . . onto a mass of quite worthless 'plot'.' (31 Aug. 1930). This helps us to see *Wilfrid Cumbermede* as the novel which spans the worlds of the fantasies and the realistic novels. Lewis draws a distinction in it between the creaky and spasmodic mechanism of the plot and 'pure vision', the moments of insight or mystery which beckon us into a different realm. The failings of the plot, 'improbable, obscure and melodramatic' (31 Aug. 1930) need no illustration, although Lewis suggests a rather more exciting and incident-filled story than is the case. Often the plot surprises the reader precisely because nothing happens. Neither the reader's expectations nor Wilfrid's ambitions are realized; unless the reader learns to scan the book with the author's priorities, like his hero shunning the world to profit his soul, he is unlikely to be satisfied by the outworkings of the plot. 'Pure vision' is defined by Lewis's discussion of the incident in which Wilfrid wakes from the dream of Athanasia to find Mary and the sword by his side. For Lewis this episode, somewhat marred by the frantic and unconvincing explanation of how these things came about, is alluring because it reflects the archetype of the empty castle and the mysterious bedfellow which he recognises variously in Norse myth, in *Phantastes* and in his own poem, *Dymer*. This does not indicate literary indebtedness so much as a Platonic awareness of universal truth, waiting to be perceived: 'Don't you get the feeling of something waiting there and slowly being recovered in fragments by different human minds according to their abilities, and partially spoiled in each writer by the admixture of his own mere individual invention?' (31 Aug. 1930).

Much of this quality of vision is transmitted through the dreams which permeate the novel, and which provide the major way of exploring Wilfrid's consciousness and enhancing his spiritual awareness. It is worth remarking in this context how convincing they are as dreams; the dream of Athanasia occurs at a time when Wilfrid is brooding over his friend's unbelief and his own sense of 'several broken links' (MacDonald 1872, II, 288) tying the Moat and the Hall. The content of his dream, with his grief and experience of loss, his moment of joy, the invitation from Death, offers no pat solutions to the problem that troubled his waking hours, and yet hints at how all these things will be resolved as he learns truly to die by forfeiting all the rights he could claim. All the dreams in the novel are effective; in a book often otherwise tightly controlled emotionally, they contain violent and extreme switches of emotion, so that much of the intensity is enclosed in these passages. Liberated from the confines of realistic demands, they can delineate dimensions of personality otherwise unexplored, through extravagant juxtapositions, through the evocation of fear and horror, and through apparently irreconcilable elements in experience. Lewis praises the dream in which Wilfrid and Charley are dead (I, 314-19); it offers all the dissonant and disturbing qualities of dreaming, from the point where the youths verify their

deaths by discovering the rosebushes do not bend under their weight
to the sudden change of focus on Charley's home, and the final
bizarre twist of Wilfrid, deprived of his friend, finding himself with
the rather less congenial mysterious bedfellow, Mr Osborne. Mac-
Donald implies that all dreams offer us images and patterns by which
we can redefine death, in all its allure and terror; they are thus a consistent part of spiritual revelation, and have a truth-telling function
which is God-derived. Through his narrator he tells us;

> I believe that, if there be a living, conscious love at the heart of
> the universe, the mind, in the quiescence of its consciousness in
> sleep, comes into a less disturbed contact with its origin, the
> heart of the creation; . . . makes it possible, as it were, for the
> occupant of an outlying station in the wilderness to return to his
> father's house for fresh supplies of all that is needful for life and
> energy. (III, 73-4)

So sleep is itself a part of divine activity, and dreams bear the fin-
gerprint of God precisely because they lie outwith the control of
mind; in his helplessness a man is, to use MacDonald's phrase, being
thought rather than thinking.

For Lewis 'pure vision' must also express myth, and it is to this
claim that Lewis turns when he wishes to make the case for MacDonald's greatness. Here MacDonald's clumsiness with words is
unimportant because myth exists independently of words, and form
and content can readily be separated. Lewis argues that what matters
is simply a pattern of events which embody mystery; we define myth
not by its attributes but by its impact: 'It gets under our skin, hits us
at a level deeper than our thoughts or even our passions, troubles
oldest certainties till all questions are re-opened, and in general
shocks us more fully awake than we are for the rest of our lives.'
(Lewis 1947, p.16). Lewis does not in this argument stress the univer-
sality of myth; his contention is as individualistic and private as any of
his devotional readings of MacDonald. A further comment must be
made; for Lewis, myth is dependent on moments rather than the sustained whole, so tending to undercut the part story plays in all this.
The myth of Balder, which he cites, works as an integral unit in a way
that the plotless *Phantastes* does not. But assuming that Lewis is
largely right in what he asserts, what is intriguing is his own dissimilar-
ity in practice from MacDonald. One might expect Lewis to emulate
his master; for instance, Hein states that MacDonald 'taught Lewis
many valuable lessons in the art of writing fantasy, for MacDonald was
a master of this literary type. He wrote fantasies not merely for enter-
tainment – and not for direct instruction, either. Rather MacDonald's

intention was by symbolic suggestion to penetrate eternal reality.'
(Hein 1982, p.x).

Lewis is undoubtedly drawn to MacDonald's use of symbolism; but
in his own writings the effect is quite different. Whereas MacDonald's symbols are attractive precisely because of their open-endedness
and ambiguity, Lewis's attempts are logical and crystalline. For Mac-
Donald a symbol always contained more than he knew; in 'The Fantastic Imagination' (MacDonald 1893, p.321) he surmises that its
larger origin is a function of divine shaping. Naturally, therefore, it
will be only dimly perceived by the writer himself, whose task is to be
receptive to such inspiration and communicate it to his reader. Lewis,
however, controls everything; when he uses symbols they have none
of the elusive, haunting quality of MacDonald's. The Narnian books
are flooded with Lewis's almost intrusive clarity; if the children are
given gifts – a sword, horn or vial – despite romantic associations we
can rely on a straightforward practical application. If Eustace in *The
Voyage of the Dawn Treader* is turned into a dragon, we are swiftly led
to understand the 'greedy dragonish thoughts' which made this inevitable; when the children in the same book are invited to share in
Aslan's table, it might be possible for a child not to see the
Eucharistic reference, but it would surely be impossible for an adult
to suggest an alternative meaning. In the science fiction, *Perelandra*
unfolds the enactment of a myth, but there is no doubt which myth
Ransom is enacting; *That Hideous Strength* attempts a broader framework of symbolism, but fails because the two worlds of myth and the
mundane are so incongruously married.

None of this bears much resemblance to the qualities Lewis
enjoyed in *Wilfrid Cumbermede*, with its densely patterned, possibly
even over-loaded, symbolism. The ice-cave, for example, is used as a
means of defining the relationship of Wilfrid and Charley by high-
lighting the difference between them, so that Wilfrid's instant delight
is complemented by his friend's cry of dismay. But it is more than
that:

> All down the smooth white walls evermore was stealing a thin
> veil of dissolution; while here and there little runnels of the
> purest water were tumbling in tiny cataracts from top to bottom.
> It was one of the thousand birthplaces of streams, ever creeping
> into the day of vision from the unlike and unknown, unrolling
> themselves like the fronds of a fern out of the infinite of God.
> Ice was all around, hard and cold and dead and white; but out
> of it and away went the water babbling and singing in the sun-
> light. (MacDonald 1872, I, 254-5)

In a few sentences MacDonald draws the ice-cave into the meta-
phorical heart of the book. Thus the novel's centre is encapsulated in
its unification of dissolution-as-death, and dissolving-as-new-birth.
The vitality of the water, its sound, light and motion, depends on the
dead absence of these in the ice. In the same way Wilfrid's spiritual
vitality hangs upon his self-denial and daily dying to ambition,
whereas Charley, who fears in it the horror of the sepulchre, experiences only the ice cave's threat and not its liberation. Moreover
through extensive cross-referencing within the book the ice cave is
connected with all the imagery of mountains and water (as in the
dream of Mary in the ice-cave set free by the stream of tears in III,
195-200). Equally, many readers will make connections with familiar
MacDonald motifs, such as the intense cold at Eve's door and the
iciness of her couches in Lilith, or the part played by water in
Phantastes.

But if this kind of symbolism resonates with a sense of mystery that
reminds us of the fantasies, we can also find examples which are
much closer to the heritage of realistic fiction. When a white horse
named Lilith is introduced, one anticipates symbolism; but it is carefully integrated into plot and characterisation, and its meaning is only
uncovered through these. Wilfrid explains that the horse is called
after a beautiful demon, 'And what does it matter what the woman
was, so long as she was beautiful?' (II, 101). The mare is thus immediately associated with Wilfrid's blind sexual attraction to Clara; it is
Clara who rides her, leaving her rightful owner poorly mounted; who
jumps her over a high fence when Wilfrid has never dared to do so;
who insists on having the locked small gate in the hall opened for the
mare. But the mare also functions as a more general touchstone of
Wilfrid's spiritual progress; the horse is sold to his arch-enemy
because of Wilfrid's guilt over Charley's death and his possessive love
for Mary and then regained at the instant when Wilfrid relinquishes
Mary and forgives her father. When he is tempted to revenge himself
on the hated Brotherton, Wilfrid is saved by the patient Christ-like
suffering of the animal: 'Was it the whiteness–was it the calmness of
the creature–I cannot pretend to account for the fact, but the same
instant before my mind's eye rose the vision of one standing speech-
less before his accusers' (III, 270).

This is an unusually obvious reference and it might mislead in
describing how Lilith is used; the horse, without in any way violating
the realistic relationship of beast and master, becomes a way of
exploring the Lilith-in-Wilfrid, his spiritual potential for good or
evil. That potential is inhibited by his attraction to Clara, his

possessiveness and his ambition; it is released by self-control, generosity and compassion. The network of suggestion and connection gathers throughout the book; any one instance sets off fresh reverberations. When Wilfrid learns of his inheritance, which would dispossess his enemy, he feels a thrill of pure revenge and in that moment jumps the horse out of the narrow way (III, 88). This echoes through the novel's many references to the narrow way (and the biblical references can scarcely be unintentional); the pack-horse bridge, the wicket gate (alluding to Bunyan perhaps), and the narrowness of the lane to the churchyard are all emphasised. All the threads are woven together; in order to unravel their significance we have merely to guess, and work and connect. There are constant hints and glimpses, but MacDonald does not spell things out for us. His own contrast between the writer who aims for clarity and the writer who aims for suggestion is as good an analysis as any of the distinction between Lewis and himself: 'If a writer's aim to be logical conviction, he must spare no logical pains, not merely to be understood, but to escape being misunderstood; where his object is to move by suggestion, to cause to imagine, then let him assail the soul of his reader as the wind assails an aeolian harp.' (MacDonald 1893, p.321).

Apart from symbolism as such, Lewis mentions several parts of *Wilfrid Cumbermede* he particularly enjoyed. These merit a brief consideration because they tell us the things that did move Lewis, that got 'under our skin'. He praises the fairy tale quality of the opening chapters, and especially 'the grass plain round the old farm (I don't know why this gives such a magical air)'. In fact the passages describing this all reassert the value and presence of mystery, locating it in the homely, so that nothing is as it appears. The house is a rock, or the shell for a crustaceous creature, or an island. The grassy plain is like a lake, level and hollow, yet it contains a dairy invisible to the child; it is a relic of a moat, so the house itself is named for another, vanished world and points to that. The furniture in the house is animal like; the table is a spider or a beast roused from its lair. So the inanimate becomes animate; Wilfrid inhabits a world of shifting changes, of strange transformations, where humans become still and silent–the unseen grandmother up the winding stair, the unspeaking aunt and taciturn uncle. Through his environment Wilfrid is taught to appreciate paradox; it is only when he leaves home that he really discovers it for the first time. Equally, this place of refuge is also the place most fit for dying and self-deprivation (II, 29). Given Lewis's pleasure in both magic and homeliness, the appeal is clear. He similarly liked the scene with the pendulum, where the child believes he has raised the storm and caused the appearance of the mysterious horseman. The episode affirms dramatically the worth of the child's insight and spiritual experience. Rationally he is mistaken; the trees which terrify him do not 'churn' the wind, nor does his action with the pendulum create the storm, nor is the horseman an emissary of the Prince of the Power of the Air. But because every life is a fairy tale and the child is more aware of this – for 'Why should not the individual life have its misty legends as well as that of nations? . . . Every boy has his own fables' – truth is to be discerned more in these naive perceptions than in reason. The helpless child, demonstrated later by the loss of watch and sword, grasps at the chance of power, of using magic to make the world in his image, but he knows he is mor-ally wrong to do so, and rightly senses the seriousness of what he has done. So, too, his childish judgement of the horseman, Mr Coningham, whose ape-face he dislikes, is ultimately vindicated: 'The old ape-face, which has lurked in my memory ever since the time I first saw him, came out so plainly that I started: the child had read his face alright!' (III, 258-9).

The real driving force of the incident, however, is guilt, and this underscores how pervasive and powerful an emotion this is in the novel: Wilfrid's guilt at picking the apple; Charley's at shooting the bird, Wilfrid's at Charley's death, all hinge on this. Guilt is often accompanied by sheer terror; perhaps the darkness and intensity of these states draws Lewis's imagination as strongly as any other stimu-lus. This would be true also of two individual chapters he singles out for praise, 'The Leads' and 'Among the Mountains'. In the first, Wilfrid and Clara are shut out on the roof of the hall; in the course of their adventure Wilfrid has to face his own worst nightmares, as he is compelled to cross with Clara, and recross alone, a narrow flying buttress. Images of height, insecurity, and horror predominate; yet this is only a rehearsal for the more terrifying precipice Wilfrid must encounter when lost in the Alps a few chapters later. Here he discov-ers absolute loneliness and vacancy; but in the isolation of the self, in silence and despair, divine consolation reaches out to him. What attracts Lewis here? These two chapters are held together less by con-solation than by the power of fear, exacerbated by loneliness. Lewis's own writings show a similar fascination with guilt and fear; in *Out of the Silent Planet* Ransom is moved almost entirely by these forces, and both this novel and *Perelandra* focus on a protagonist isolated for much of the time. Lewis does not deal largely in communities, but in the self alone, facing horror and experiencing shame as part of the condition of being human; it is to this he responds most fervently in

MacDonald.

In all these–home as the place of mystery and death; the child's vision and guilty knowledge; the self consoled and yet essentially and fearfully alone–there is a darkness which is as significant in Lewis as it is in MacDonald. Raeper (1987) claims that 'Under MacDonald's shining optimism there was always an ingrained seam of the darkest pessimism, and doubt and despair hung about him'. The pessimism in *Wilfrid Cumbermede* is striking; the note on which the book opens is of a sombre sunset, immediately identified with the close of the narrator's life. Shadows and dying are welcomed as a prophecy of dawn; but the book keeps its focus on the former. No reader is misled; failure is announced at the outset as the central value of the story: 'the saving of my life has been my utter failure' (I, 4). It is a saga of renunciation and loss; the inheritance plot is undermined by the hero's refusal to claim his rights, and love and friendship alike are frustrated by obedience, duty and death. The characteristic novel ending where identity is affirmed through marriage, status, success, a home, is subverted by the Christian ethic; Wilfrid chooses nothing except openness to the will of God. He will not defend his rights to the sword, or book, or family home; the wicked, not the meek inherit the earth, and, moreover, evil appears to seduce the good. Wilfrid loses not just possessions but also the ideal woman, Mary. In *Phantastes*, Anodos loses the white lady to the worthier knight, but in *Wilfrid Cumbermede*, as in *Alec Forbes of Howglen*, the woman is forfeited to a worthless blackguard. This may generate an awareness of the nature of unpossessive devotion, but it also shows a disturbing ambivalence towards women. Why Mary marries Brotherton is not altogether clear; after his death, Wilfrid is unsure whether he should marry her, and leaves the question unanswered at the end: 'I would rather meet her then first, when she is clothed in that new garment called by St. Paul the spiritual body. That, Geoffrey has never touched; over that he has no claim. But if the loveliness of her character should have purified his, and drawn and bound his soul to hers?' (III, 289-90). So, whilst her spiritual beauty survives the marriage, her body is tainted by it; the sense of degradation is not unlike the chilling moment in *Alec Forbes* when, after Kate Fraser's madness and grisly suicide, the narrator comments that anything was better than marrying Beauchamp. Add to this Clara as another of the siren figures, like Kate Fraser, Christine Palmer and Euphrasia Cameron, who must be punished and humbled; and the troubled, thwarted sexuality that runs through the book, with the symbolism of the rusted sword, and the episode of the mysterious bedfellow, or the scene where Wilfrid, rescued from the mountain, is dressed in girl's clothing and is mistaken for a girl by Clara. Meanwhile there is the failure of all other relationships; Wilfrid is left almost friendless, and the Fatherhood so admired by Lewis as part of MacDonald's theology is not incarnate in any of the characters. Wilfrid's uncle is a source of spiritual wisdom and strength, but is cold and remote; Charley's father is a savage tyrant whose religious dogmatism ruins the lives of both his children. All of these are undergirded by a luxuriating in the gothic, with the imagery of the charnel house never far away.

Did Lewis in fact relish these things more than he realised? I suspect he did; there is a deep vein of pessimism in Lewis also, and when he presents the case for a tortured and torturing world at the beginning of *The Problem of Pain*, he does so with great conviction. There is a part of him, sustained and nourished by Norse myths, that would like to go out and die with Father Odin. Sirens are as much a source of fear and fascination as they are for MacDonald; and women and fathers alike arouse powerfully ambivalent feelings. Even gothic horror can be found echoed in his terror of ghosts and corpses just as in MacDonald (as in his letter to Greeves of 15 Sept. 1930). It may be that what he found in MacDonald was the evidence he craved and the imaginative stimulus he needed for optimistic resolution, but also the surreptitious feeding of the doubts he denied.

References

Rolland Hein, *The Harmony Within: The Spiritual Vision of George MacDonald* (Grand Rapids: Eerdmans, 1982).

Walter Hooper, ed., *They Stand Together: the Letters of C.S. Lewis to Arthur Greeves* (London: Collins, 1979).
The following letters are cited:
10 Oct. 1929, p.313.
15 June 1930, p.361.
31 Aug. 1930, p.388.
15 Sept. 1930, p.392.
24 Dec. 1930, p.398.
10 Jan. 1931, p.402.
17 Jan. 1931, p.403.
1 Sept. 1933, pp.460-1.

C.S. Lewis, *The Problem of Pain*, (London: Geoffrey Bles, 1940).

C.S. Lewis, *The Screwtape Letters*, (London: Geoffrey Bles, 1942).

C.S. Lewis, *The Abolition of Man*, (London: Oxford University Press, 1943).

C.S. Lewis, *The Great Divorce: A Dream*, (London: Geoffrey Bles, 1945).

C.S. Lewis, *George MacDonald: An Anthology*, (London: Geoffrey Bles, 1946).

C.S. Lewis, *Prince Caspian: The Return of Narnia*, (London: Geoffrey Bles, 1951).

C.S. Lewis, *Mere Christianity*, (London: Geoffrey Bles, 1952).

C.S. Lewis, *Surprised by Joy: the shape of my early life*, (London: Geoffrey

Bles, 1955).
C.S. Lewis, *Letters to Malcolm: Chiefly on Prayer*, (London: Geoffrey Bles, 1964).
W.H. Lewis, ed., *Letters to C.S. Lewis*, (London: Geoffrey Bles, 1966).
7 Dec. 1950 p.225.
George MacDonald, *Unspoken Sermons*, (London: Strahan, 1867).
George MacDonald, *Wilfrid Cumbermede*, (London: Hurst and Blackett, 1872).
George MacDonald, Unspoken Sermons, Second Series, (London: Longmans, Green, 1885:page reference to new edition 1889).
George MacDonald, *What's Mine's Mine*, (London: Kegan Paul, 1896).
George MacDonald, *Unspoken Sermons, Third Series*, (London: Longmans, Green 1889).
George MacDonald, *A Dish of Orts, Chiefly Papers on the Imagination, And on Shakespear*, (London: Sampson, Low, 1893).
Greville MacDonald, *George MacDonald and his Wife*, (London: Allen and Unwin, 1924).
William Raeper, *George MacDonald*, (Tring: Lion, 1987).
Charles Taliaferro, A Narnian Theory of the Atonement, *Scottish Journal of Theology* 41, (1988) 75-92.

10

Select Bibliography

In the list of MacDonald's own works, only first editions are cited and, where possible, the location of the MS has been shown. My thanks to Roderick F. McGillis for his invaluable help in compiling this bibliography. W.R.

MacDonald's Works

MacDonald's Works
Within and Without. Longmans, Brown, Green, 1855. Brander Library, Huntly.
Poems. Longmans, Brown, Green, 1857. Manchester Public Libraries.
Phantastes. Smith, Elder, 1858.
David Elginbrod. 3 vols. Hurst and Blackett, 1863. Brander Library, Huntly.
Adela Cathcart. 3 vols. Hurst and Blackett, 1864.
The Portent. Smith, Elder, 1864.
Alec Forbes of Howglen. 3 vols. Hurst and Blackett, 1865. Margaret Troup, Huntly.
Annals of a Quiet Neighbourhood. 3 vols. Hurst and Blackett, 1867. Brander Library, Huntly.
Dealings with the Fairies. Strahan, 1867.
The Disciple and other Poems. Strahan, 1867. Brander Library, Huntly.
Unspoken Sermons. 1st Series. Strahan, 1867. National Library of Scotland.
        2nd Series. Longmans, Green, 1885.
        3rd Series. Longmans, Green, 1889.
Guild Court. 3 vols. Hurst and Blackett, 1868. Mitchell Library Glasgow.
Robert Falconer. 3 vols. Hurst amd Blackett, 1868. King's College, Aberdeen.
The Seaboard Parish. 3 vols. Tinsley Bros, 1868. Houghton Library, Havard.
The Miracles of Our Lord. Strahan, 1870.
At the Back of the North Wind. Strahan, 1871. Brander Library, Huntly; five chapters at King's College, Aberdeen.
Ranald Bannerman's Boyhood. Strahan, 1871. Brander Library, Huntly.
Works of Fancy and Imagination. 10 vols. Chatto and Windus, 1871.
The Princess and the Goblin. Strahan, 1872. Brander Library, Huntly.
The Vicar's Daughter. 3 vols. Tinsley Bros., 1872. King's College, Aberdeen.
Wilfrid Cumbermede. 3 vols. Hurst and Blackett, 1872. Houghton Library, Havard.
Gutta Percha Willie. Henry S. King, 1873.
England's Antiphon. Macmillan, 1874.

Malcolm. 3 vols. Henry S. King, 1875. National Library of Scotland.
The Wise Woman. Strahan, 1875. Also published as *A Double Story* (n.d)
and *The Lost Princess* (n.d.)
Thomas Wingfold. Curate. 3 vols. Hurst and Blackett, 1876. Brander
Library, Huntly. Chapter 93 to the end.
St. George and St. Michael. 3 vols. Henry S. King, 1876. Manchester
Public Libraries.
Exotics. Strahan, 1876.
The Marquis of Lossie. 3 vols. Hurst and Blackett, 1877.
Sir Gibbie. 3 vols. Hurst and Blackett, 1879. Gordon Schools, Huntly.
Paul Faber, Surgeon. 3 vols. Hurst and Blackett, 1879. Fitzwilliam College,
Cambridge.
Diary of an Old Soul. Printed privately, 1880. Balliol College, Oxford.
Mary Marston. 3 vols. Sampson Low, 1881. Brander Library, Huntly.
Castle Warlock. 3 vols. Sampson Low, 1882.
Weighed and Wanting. 3 vols. Sampson Low, 1882.
The Gifts of the Child Christ and Other Tales, 2 vols. Sampson Low,
1882.
Orts. Sampson Low, 1882.
A Dish of Orts. Enlarged version. Sampson Low, 1893.
Donal Grant. 3 vols. Kegan Paul, 1883.
A Threefold Cord. Printed privately, 1883. There is a copy with the
poems identified at the Beinecke Library, Yale.
The Princess and Curdie. Chatto and Windus, 1883. The Shakespeare
Centre, Stratford-on-Avon.
What's Mine's Mine. 3 vols. Kegan Paul, 1886.
Home Again. Kegan Paul, 1888. Brander Library, Huntly.
Cross Purposes and *The Shadows.* Reprinted. Blackie and Sons, 1890.
The Light Princess and other Fairy Stories. Reprint. Blackie and Sons, 1890;
   The MS of *The Light Princess* is in the Houghton Library Havard, as is
   the MS of *The Giant's Heart.*
There and Back. 3 vols. Kegan Paul, 1891. Central Library, Edinburgh.
The Flight of the Shadow. Kegan Paul, 1891.
The Cabinet of Gems. Anthology of Sir Philip Sidney, Elliot Stock, 1891.
The Hope of the Gospel. Ward, Lock, Bowden, 1892.
Heather and Snow. 2 vols. Chatto and Windus, 1893. Brander Library,
Huntly.
Lilith. Chatto and Windus, 1895. British Library.
Rampolli. Translations. Longmans, Green, 1897.
Salted with Fire. Hurst and Blackett, 1897.
Poetical Works of George MacDonald. 2 vols. Chatto and Windus, 1893.
Scotch Songs and Ballads. Reprints. Aberdeen: John Roe Smith, 1893.

In addition to the novel MSS there is a copy of *A Sketch of Individual
Development* at the Brander Library, Huntly, as well as an incomplete
draft of the short story *The Snow Fight.* There is a copy of Shakespeare's
Timon of Athens annotated by MacDonald at the National Library of
Scotland, and another Shakespearian production, *Notes on King Lear,* at
the University of California and Los Angeles.

Works Related To MacDonald

Bulloch, John M. *A Centennial Bibliography of George MacDonald.* Aberdeen, Aberdeen University, 1925.

Carpenter, Humphrey. 'George MacDonald and the Tender Grandmother'. In *Secret Gardens: A Study of the Golden Age of Children's Literature* by Humphrey Carpenter. London, Allen and Unwin, 1985.

Franzos, Karl Emil. *For the Right.* Translated by Julie Sutter. Preface by George MacDonald. London: J. Clarke, 1887.

Fraser, Morris. *The Death of Narcissus.* London: Martin Secker and Warburg Ltd., 1976.

Fremantle, Anne. ed. *The Visionary Novels of George MacDonald.* Introduction by W.H. Auden, New York: Noonday, 1954.

Gifford, D. 'Myth, Parody and Dissociation: Scottish Fiction 1814-1914'. *The History of Scottish Literature, vol. 3, Nineteenth Century,* edited by D. Gifford, Aberdeen: Aberdeen University Press, 1988.

Gray, George. *Recollections of Huntly.* Locally printed in Banff 1892; reprinted 1952.

Hart, Francis Russell. *The Scottish Novel.* London: J. Murray, 1978.

Hearnshaw, F.J.C. *The Centenary History of King's College, London.* London: Harrap, 1929.

Hein, Holland. *The Harmony Within.* Michigan: Eerdmans, 1982.

Johnson, Joseph. *George MacDonald: A Biographical and Critical Appreciation.* London: Pitman and Sons, 1906.

Landow, George P. 'And the World Became Strange: Realms of Literary Fantasy'. In *The Aesthetics of Fantasy Literature and Art,* edited by Notre Dame, IN: University of Notre Dame Press, 1982, 105-42.

Letley E. *From Galt to Douglas Brown: Nineteenth Century Fiction and Scots Language.* Edinburgh, Scottish Academic Press: 1988.

Lewis, C.S. *George MacDonald: An Anthology.* London: Geoffrey Bles, 1946.

Lochhead, Marion. *Renaissance of Wonders.* Edinburgh: Cannongate, 1977.

McCrie, G. *The Religion of Our Literature* London, Hodder and Stoughton, 1875.

MacDonald, Greville. *George MacDonald and his Wife.* London: Allen and Unwin, 1924.

MacDonald, Greville. *Reminiscences of a Specialist.* London: Allen and Unwin, 1932.

MacDonald, Ronald. *From a Northern Window.* Edinburgh: James Nisbit and Co., 1911.

McGillis, Roderick. 'George MacDonald's *Princess* Books: High Seriousness'. In *Touchstone: Reflections on the Best in Children's Literature,* West Lafayette, IN: ChLA Publications, 1985, 146-162.

McGillis, Roderick. 'Lilith: A Romance'. In *Survey of Modern Fantasy Literature, Vol.2,* edited by Frank N. Magill. La Canada, CA: Salem Press, 1983, 880-86.

MacNeice, Louis 'The Victorians' in Louis MacNeice *Varieties of Parable.* Cambridge, Cambridge University Press, 1965, 76-101.

Manlove, C.N. 'George MacDonald' Early Scottish Novels' in Ian Campbell ed. *Nineteenth Century Scottish Fiction* Manchester, Carcanet New Press Ltd., 1979.

Manlove C.N. 'Circularity in Fantasy: George MacDonald' in C.N. Manlove *The Impulse of Fantasy Literature* Kent, Chic: Kent State University Press, 1983.

Manlove, C.N. 'George MacDonald, 1824-1905' in C.N. Manlove *Modern*

Fantasy. Cambridge, Cambridge University Press, 1975.

Murray, David Christie. *My Contemporaries in Fiction*. London, Chatto and Windus, 1897.

Phillips, Michael R. *George MacDonald: Scotland's Beloved Storyteller* Minneapolis, Bethany House, 1987.

Prickett, Stephen. *Romanticism and Religion* Cambridge, Cambridge University Press, 1976.

Prickett, Stephen. *Victorian Fantasy*. Sussex, Harvester Press, 1979.

Rabkin, Eric S. 'The Fantastic and Perspective' in Eric S. Rabkin. *The Fantastic in Literature* Princeton, N.J.: Princeton University Press, 1976, 98-108.

Raeper, William. *George MacDonald*. Tring, Herts., Lion Publishing, 1987.

Reis, Richard. *George MacDonald*. New York, Twayne Books, 1972.

Robb, David S. 'Realism and Fantasy in the Fiction of George MacDonald' in Gifford, D. ed., *The History of Scottish Literature, Vol 3, Nineteenth Century*. Aberdeen, Aberdeen University Press, 1988.

Robb, David S. *George MacDonald* Edinburgh, Scottish Academic Press, 1987.

Robinson, Henry Crabb. *The Diary of Henry Crabb Robinson*. An abridgement, ed., Derek Hudson. Oxford, Oxford University Press. 1967.

Sadler, Glenn Edward. 'George MacDonald' in D.L. Kirkpatricfk ed.

Sadler, Glenn Edward. 'The Fantastic Imagination in George MacDonald' in Charles A. Huttar ed. *Imagination and the Spirit* Grand Rapids, Mich: Eerdmans 1971, 215-227.

Sadler, Glenn Edward 'George MacDonald' in Jane Bingham ed. *Writers for Children* New York: Charles Scriber's and Sons, 1988. 373-380.

Saintsbury, Elizabeth. *George MacDonald: A Short Life*. Edinburgh, Canongate, 1987. *Twentieth-Century Children's Writers* London, St James, 1978.

Selby, T.G. *The Theology of Modern Fiction* London, C.H. Kelly, 1896.

Spina, Giorgio. *Il Vittoriano Dimenticato* The Forgotten Victorian. Genoa, Genoa University, 1979.

Spina, Giorgio. *Il Realismo di George MacDonald*. Genoa, Genoa University, 1980.

Stott, Jon C. 'George MacDonald' in Jon C. Stott *Children's Literature from A to Z*. New York: McGraw-Hill, 190-192.

Sutter, Julie. *Letters from Hell* given in English by Julie Sutter with a preface by George MacDonald.

Swiatecka, M. Jadwiga. 'Dean Inge, George Tyrrell and George MacDonald' in M. Jadwiga Swiatecka *The Idea of the Symbol* Cambridge, Cambridge University Press, 1980. 151-168.

Triggs, Kathy. *George MacDonald: The Seeking Heart*. London, Pickering and Inglis, 1984.

Triggs, Kathy. *The Stars and the Stillness*. Cambridge, Lutterworth, 1986.

Tuke, Margaret J. *A History of Bedford College for Women 1849-1937* Oxford, Oxford University Press, 1939.

Walker, Jeanne Murray. 'The Demoness and the Grail: Deciphering MacDonald's Lilith', 179-190 in *Collins, Robert A* ed., *Pearce, Howard D. III* ed. *The Scope of the Fantastic: Culture, Biography, Themes, Children's Literature* Westport CT, USA: Greenwood. 1985.

Webb William *George MacDonald: A Study of Two Novels* Salzburg, Salzburg Studies in English Literature, 1973.

Willard, Nancy. 'The Nonsense of Angels: George MacDonald at the Back of the North Wind' in Jill P. May ed. *Children and Their Literature: A*

Readings Book. West Lafayette. IN: ChLA Publications 1983. 34-40.

Wilson, Samuel Law. *The Theology of Modern Literature.* Edinburgh, T&T Clarke, 1899.

Wolff, Robert Lee. *The Golden Key: A Study of the Fiction of George Mac-Donald.* New Haven, Yale University Press, 1961.

Articles Relating to MacDonald

Aberdeen Press and Journal. 'A Piece of Huntly in Hammersmith', CCXLX. 25 March 1966.

Aberdeen Press and Journal. Report of Edward Troup's Lecture on Mac-Donald's use of Scots Speech. 11 February 1925. Reprinted in *North Wind* 2. Journal of the George MacDonald Society, 1983, 24-32.

Alma Mater. Aberdeen University Magazine. 'George MacDonald at Aberdeen'. 18 October 1905.

Athenaeum. Review of *Phantastes* 6 November 1858, 580.

Review of *At the Back of the North Wind* 11 March 1871, 303.

Review of *The Princess and the Goblin* 23 December 1871, 835.

Bergmann, Frank. 'The Roots of Tolkien's Trees: The Influence of George MacDonald and German Romanticism upon Tolkien's Essay "On Fairy Stories".' *Mossaic*, 10 (1977), 5-14.

Boaden, Ann 'Falcons and Falconers: Vision in the Novels of George Mac-Donald'.

'Christianity and Literature (1981, Fall); 31 (1): 7-17.

British Quarterly Review. Review of *Phantastes.* 29 (1859), 296-297.

Works by George MacDonald'. 47 (1868), 1-34.

'George MacDonald at Bordighera', *Sunday Magazine*, XXXIV (April 1905), 401-405.

Bruce, Sylvia. 'Entering the Vision: A Novelist's View of *Phantastes'*.

Bulloch, J.M. 'The Elginbrod Epitaph', *The Aberdeen University Review*, XII (1924-25), 41.

Burnside, William H. 'Abridgement: Profit and Loss in Modernizing George MacDonald'. *Seven*, 9 (1988), 117-28.

Seven 9 (1988), 19-28.

Cecil, Robert 'A Tale of Two Families', *North Wind* 7 (Journal of the George MacDonald Society), 1988, 15-21.

Chesterton, G.K. Obituary of George MacDonald, *Daily News* (23 September 1905).

Child, Harold. *Times Literary Supplement* (29 May 1924), 329.

Contemporary Review 'Scottish Influence upon English Theological Thought', Vol 32 (1878), 457.

Crago, H. 'Charles Dickens and George MacDonald: A Notes. *Dickens Studies* Vol 5 (1969), 90-96.

The Critic. *'Lilith'*, 25 (1896), 58.

The Critic 'George MacDonald at Bordighera', V (2 February 1884), 54-55.

Donoghue, Denis 'The Other Country', *The New York Review of Books* (21 December 1967), 34-37.

Douglas, Alison 'The Scottish Contribution to Children's Literature', *Library Review* 20 (1965), 241-246.

Douglass, Jane 'Dealing with the Fairies', *The Horn Book Magazine* 37 (1961), 327-335.

Docherty, John 'A Note on the Structure and Conclusion of *Phantastes'*. North Wind 7 (Journal of the George MacDonald Society), 1988, 25-30.

Edinburgh Review 'Recent Scotch Novels' (April 1876).

Edwards, Bruce L. Jr. 'Towards a Rhetoric of Fantasy Criticism: C.S. Lewis's Readings of MacDonald and Morris', *Literature and Belief* (1983); 3: 63-73.

Geddes, W.D. 'George MacDonald as a Poet', *Blackwoods Magazine* (March 1891).

The Globe–Review of *Phantastes* (30 December 1858).

Gray, Mary 'A Brief Sketch of the Life of George MacDonald', *The Bookman* (Novenber 1905).

Griffin, William 'Eternity's Book of the Year', *Publishers Weekly* (December 18 1987), 40ff.

Hein, Rolland 'George MacDonald: A Child's View of the World', *The Banner* (November 14 1988), 20-22.

Hein, Rolland 'George MacDonald: A Portrait from His Letters', *Seven* 7 (1986), 5-20.

Hein, Rolland 'If You Would But Write Novels, Mr MacDonald', *Seven* 1 (1980), 11-27.

Hein, Rolland '*Lilith:* Theology through Mythopoeia', *Christian Scholar's Review* 3, (1974), 215-231.

Hein, Rolland 'Whence Came the Fantasia? The Good Dream in George MacDonald's *Lilith*', *North Wind* 3 (Journal of the George MacDonald Society), 1984, 27-40.

Hetzler, Leo A. 'George MacDonald and G.K. Chesterton', *Durham University Review* 58 (n.s. 37, 1976), 176-182.

Hines, Joyce 'George MacDonald as a Mythopoeist', *North Wind* 5 (Journal of the George MacDonald Society), 1986, 26-36.

Holbrook, David 'George MacDonald and Dreams of the Other World', *Seven* 4 (1983), 27-37.

Holbrook, David 'Postscript: A Reply', *Seven* 5 (1984), 34.

Horder, W. Garret 'George MacDonald: A Nineteenth Century Seer', *Review of Reviews* 32 (October 1905).

Horsman, Gail 'C.S. Lewis and George MacDonald: A Comparison of Styles', *C.S. Lewis Bulletin* (1981, Dec.).

Hutton, Muriel 'Sour Grapeshot: Fault-finding in A *Centennial Bibliography of George MacDonald*', *The Aberdeen University Review* Vol XL1 (1965-66), 85-89.

Hutton Muriel (on the MS Collection at the Brander Library, Huntly), *The School Librarian* Vol 12, No. 3 (December 1964).

Hutton Muriel (Description of the MacDonald Collection at Yale), *The Yale University Library Gazette* Vol 51 No. 2 (October 1976).

Hutton, R.H. '*David Elginbrod*', *The Spectator* (3 January 1963), supplement 20-21.

Johnson, Rachel E. 'The Tennyson Connection: Fragments from MacDonald's Correspondence on Particular Occasions', *North Wind* 3 (Journal of the George MacDonald Society), 1984, 21-25.

Kirkpatrick, Mary 'An Introduction to the *Curdie* Book of George MacDonald, *Bulletin of the New York C.S. Lewis Society* 5, v (1974), 1-6.

Kirkpatrick, Mary 'Lewis and MacDonald', *Bulletin of the New York C.S. Lewis Society* 5, (1974), 2-4.

The Leader–Review of *Phantastes* (13 November 1858), 1222.

Lewis, Naomi 'Children's Books: George MacDonald', *New Statesman* (10 November 1961), 693-694.

Lochhead, Marion 'George MacDonald and the World of Faery', *Seven* 3 (1982), 63-71.

London Quarterly Review 'George MacDonald as a Teacher of Religion' 31

January 1869).

Lormant, Georgette 'George MacDonald–A Novelist for all Times', *North Wind* 4 (Journal of the George MacDonald Society), 1985, 3-17.

MacDonald, A. 'The Dialect of *Sir Gibbie*', *Alma Mater* (17 February 1915), 182-183.

McEldowney, Mary M. 'The Fairy Tales of George MacDonald' (unpublished thesis, Oxford, 1934).

McGillis, Roderick F. 'The Abyss of His Mother-Tongue: Scotch Dialect in the Novels by George MacDonald', *Seven* 2 (1981), 44ff.

McGillis, Roderick F. 'The Beauty of Holiness', *Mythlore* 36 (1983), 39-41.

McGillis, Roderick F. 'Fantasy as Adventure: Nineteenth Century Children's Fiction', *Children's Literature Association Quarterly* 8 (1983), 18-22.

McGillis, Roderick F. 'If You Call Me Grandmother, That Will Do', *Mythlore* 21 (1979), 27-28.

McGillis, Roderick F. 'Letter and Spirit', *Scottish Literary Journal* Suppl. n.13. (Autumn 1980), 1-10.

McGillis, Roderick F. 'George MacDonald: The *Lilith* Manuscripts', *Scottish Literary Journal* Vol 4, No.2 (December 1970), 40ff.

McGillis, Roderick F. 'MacDonald and the Lilith Legend in XIXth Century', *Mythlore* 19 (Winter 1979), 3-11.

McGillis Roderick F. 'The Logic of Dreams', *Fantasiae* 2 (1974), 10-11.

Macleod, Helen. 'The Children's Books of George MacDonald', *Book Collector* (November 1987), 28-36.

Manlove, Colin 'The Circle of the Imagination: George MacDonald's *Phantastes* and *Lilith*', *Studies in Scottish Literature* (1982); 17: 55-80.

Manlove, C.N. 'George MacDonald's Fairy Tales: Their Roots in MacDonald's Thought', *Studies in Scottish Literature* 8 (1970), 97-108.

Massingham, H.J.–Review of Lilith and *Fairy Tales, Nation and Athenaeum* (2 August 1924), 569.

Mendelson, Michael 'George MacDonald's *Lilith* and the Conventions of Ascent', *Studies in Scottish Literature* 20 (1985), 197-218.

Milne, J.B. 'George MacDonald: Reminiscences by one of his schoolfellows', *Aberdeen Press and Journal* (13 December 1924).

Moynihan, Martin 'Note on George MacDonald and Novalis', *North Wind* 4 (Journal of the George MacDonald Society), 1985, 35-36.

Myers, Kenneth 'Untitled', *Eternity* (March 1986), 62.

Nicoll, William Robertson 'Dr George MacDonald', *Bookman* 18 (1900), 116-118.

Nicoll, William Robertson 'George MacDonald' *The British Weekly* (21 September 1905).

Nicoll, William Robertson (Claudius Clear) 'Dr Parker's New Novel–and Others', *British Weekly* (10 October 1895), 395.

The North British Review (Review of MacDonald's novels to that date), September 1866).

Page, H.A. 'Children and Children's Books' *Contemporary Review* II (1869), 23-24.

Pall Mall Gazette '*Lilith*' (18 October 1895), 9.

Parsons, C.O. 'George MacDonald and Henry More', *Notes and Queries* 9 (5 May 1945), 188.

Patterson, Nancy-Lou 'Archetypes of the Mother in the Fantasies of George MacDonald', *Mythcon 1 Proceedings* (Los Angeles: The Mythopoeic Society 1971), 14-20.

Percival, Alicia C. 'George MacDonald at Bordighera', *English* (Oxford), X1 (Fall 1957), 246-247.

Prickett, Stephen 'The Two Worlds of George MacDonald', *North Wind* 2 (Journal of the George MacDonald Society), 1983, 14-23.

Raeper, William 'George MacDonald's Missing Year', *North Wind* 6 (Journal of the George MacDonald Society), 1987, 3-13.

Ragg, Laura M. 'George Macdonald and His Household', *English* 11 (Summer 1956), 59-63.

Rands, B.W. (Henry Holbeach) 'George MacDonald', *The Contemporary Review* (19 December 1872).

Rigbee, Sally Adair 'Fantasy Places and Imaginative Belief: *The Lion, the Witch, and the Wardrobe* and *The Princess and the Goblin*', *Children's Literature Association Quarterly* (1983, spring); 8 (1): 10-11.

Robb, David S. 'The Fiction of George MacDonald', *Seven* 6 (1985), 35-44.

Robb, David S. 'George MacDonald and Animal Magnetism', *Seven* 8 (1987), 9-24.

Robb, David S. George MacDonald at Blackfriars Chapel', *North Wind* 5 (Journal of the George MacDonald Society), 1986, 3-20.

Robb, David S. George MacDonald's Scottish Novels: Three Notes', *Notes and Queries* (June 1986).

Robertson, E.S. 'A Literary Causerie: *Phantastes*', *Academy* 70 (1906), 308-309.

Sadler, Glenn Edward 'At the Back of the North Wind: George MacDonald: A Centennial Appreciation', *Tolkien Journal* 4 (1970), 20-21.

Sadler, Glenn Edward 'Defining Death as More Life: Unpublished Letters by George MacDonald', *North Wind* 3 (Journal of the George MacDonald Society), 1984, 4-18.

Sadler, Glen Edward 'The Little Girl That Had No Tongue': An Unpublished Short Story by George MacDonald', *Children's Literature* 2 (1973), 18-34.

Saintsbury, George '*Lilith*', *Academy* (12 October 1895), 291.

Salmon, Edward 'Literature for the Little Ones', *Nineteenth Century* 22 (1887), 563-580.

Schaafsma, Karen 'The Demon Lover: Lilith and the Hero in Modern Fantasy', *Extrapolation* (1987, Spring); 28 (1): 52-61.

Scribners Monthly, A Description of MacDonald Preaching (August 1871), 434-435.

Shaberman, R.B. 'George MacDonald and E.T.A. Hoffman', *North Wind* 7 (Journal of the George MacDonald Society), 1988, 31-37.

Shaberman, R.B. 'George MacDonald and Lewis Carroll', *Jabberwocky* 5 (1976), 67-87. Reprinted in *North Wind* 1 (Journal of the George MacDonald Society), 1982, 10-30.

Shaberman, R.B. 'Gustav Holst and George MacDonald', *North Wind* 3 (Journal of the George MacDonald Society), 1984, 18-20.

Sherman, Cordelia 'The Princess and the Wizard: The Fantasy Worlds of Ursula K. Le Guin and George MacDonald', *Children's Literature Association Quarterly* (1987, Spring); 12 (1): 24-28.

Sigman, Joseph 'Death's Ecstasies: Transformation and Rebirth in George MacDonald's *Phantastes*', *English Studies in Canada* 2 (1976), 203-226.

Spectator, The 'MacDonald and Scottish Writing' (16 March 1901).

Spectator, The–Review of *Phantastes* (4 December 1858), 1286.

Spina Giorgio 'George MacDonald in Liguria', *North Wind* 4 (Journal of the George MacDonald Society), 1985, 19-32.

Steig, Michael 'Reading *Outside Over There*', *Child Literature* (1985); 13: 139-153.

Sutherland, D. 'The Founder of the New Scottish School', *The Critis* 27

(1897), 339.

Sutton, Max Keith 'The Psychology of the Self in MacDonald's *Phantastes Seven* 5 (1984), 9-25.

Tanner, Tony 'Mountains and Depths–An Approach to Nineteenth Century Dualism', *A Review of English Literature* 3 m(1962), 51-61.

Triggs, Kathy 'Images of Creation', *North Wind* 6 (Journal of the George MacDonald Society), 1987, 22-2-38.

Triggs, Kathy 'The Poverty of Riches', *North Wind* 1 (Journal of the George MacDonald Society), 1982, 31-39.

Triggs, Kathy 'Worlds Apart: The Importance of the Double Vision for MacDonald Criticism', *Seven* 5 (1984): 26-33.

Troup, Edward 'Notes on the Boyhood of George MacDonald', *The Deeside Field Club* (Aberdeen 1925). Reprinted in *North Wind* 1 (Journal of the George MacDonald Society), 1982, 4-9.

Walls, Kathryn 'George MacDonald's *Lilith* and the Later Poetry of T.S. Eliot', *English Language Notes* (16, 1978 pp 47-51).

Walsh, Susan A. Darling Mothers, Devilish Queens: The Divided Woman in Victorian Fantasy', *Victorian Newsletter* (1987, Fall); 72: 32-36.

Watkins, Gwen 'A Theologian's Dealings with the Fairies', *North Wind* 7 (Journal of the George MacDonald Society), 1988, 5-14.

Weekly Journal, The (On *Hymns and Sacred Songs for Sunday Schools and Social Worship*) (13 December 1951).

Westminster Review–Review of *The Portent* and *Adela Cathcart*, 2 (1864), 258-259. Review of *The Princess and the Goblin* 41 (1872), 581.

Willis, Lesley 'Born Again: The Metamorphisis of Irene in George Mac-Donald's '*The Princess and the Goblin*', Scottish Literary Journal 12 (1985), 24-39.

Wilson, Keith 'The Quest for "The Truth": A Reading of George Mac-Donald's *Phantastes*', *Etudes Anglaises* 34 (1981), 140-152.

Wolfe, Gregory 'C.S. Lewis's Debt to George MacDonald', *CLS: The Bulletin of the New York C.S. Lewis Society* 15 (1983), 1-7.

Wolff, Robert Lee 'An 1862 Alice: "Cross Purposes" or *Which Dreamed It?*', *Harvard Library Bulletin* 23 (1975), 199-202.

Wolff, Robert Lee 'The Preacher in FairyLand', *Times Literary Supplement* (15 November 1974).

Woods, Katherine Pearson 'A Little Glory', *The Bookman* (New York, October 1895), 133-135.

Index